ST. MARY'S
COLLEGE OF EDUCATION
D0120159

FACING THE MUSIC

Facing the Music

AN AUTOBIOGRAPHY

Joseph Cooper

Weidenfeld and Nicolson
London

To Joan and Garrett

Copyright illustrations have been reproduced by courtesy of the following: Bristol *Evening Post*, 9; Society Wedding Press, 12, 13; Universal Pictorial Press and Agency, 11; Kurt Heinze, 15; Southern Press Agency, 19; John Heddon, 20; Simon Eadon, 29; Ian Howell, 30; Roger Holmes, 34, Christina Burton, 36, 37, 38, 39, 40, 41, 42; Behram Kapadia, 43; Barry Swaebe, 44; Lauri Tjurin, 45, 46, 49; Charles Chilton, 47.

First published in Great Britain by
George Weidenfeld and Nicolson Ltd
91 Clapham High Street, London SW4 7TA
1979

ISBN 0 297 77718 1

Printed in Great Britain by
Butler & Tanner Ltd, Frome and London

Contents

Illustrations

Preface

That this book ever got off the ground can largely be attributed to the weather of January 1979 – I do not mean the awful winter weather we had in England, but the weather in the Canary Islands. A friend of ours, Mrs Kathleen Yates, had very kindly lent us her apartment in Tenerife; our idea was to go off and get two weeks' sunshine preparatory to sitting down and writing the book. We took the precaution of packing a miniature dictating machine and a typewriter just in case a flash of inspiration was sparked off by the heat.

As it turned out, it never stopped raining for ten days; so in desperation I got out the dictating machine and started talking to it, going right back to the beginning of my life. My wife typed away like mad. We left Tenerife as pale and as tired as when we arrived, but we had at least written the first hundred pages of the book. Although the rain forced us indoors, the peace and quiet and absence of domestic worries enabled me to find the right mood for letting early recollections float to the surface.

While we were in the Canaries, my wife's parents were staying in our house here – quietly and patiently sorting all my publicity and programme material and making order out of chaos. In particular I want to thank my mother-in-law, Olive Borg, for personally *ironing* a thousand press notices.

My thanks are due to Lord Weidenfeld for inviting me to write my memoirs in the first place, and also to his colleagues, Christopher Falkus and Alex MacCormick, for much help and encouragement. However, I take responsibility for every word written in this book and, for better or for worse, I have not used a ghost.

I want to thank my neighbour and friend, Owen Russell, and my brother-in-law, Colin Borg, for help with research; also an old Bristol friend, Josephine Flint Taylor, for lending me an early photograph of David Willcocks and myself.

I am especially grateful to my old schoolfriend Keith Woolley for jogging my memory about life at Clifton College.

I thank my brother, Bill (three years my senior), for filling in some details of my very early life. Bill decided to make Bristol his headquarters and, blessed by a wonderfully happy marriage to Joyce Steadman, he has made a great success in many fields of business.

Many acknowledgments of help throughout my career have been made in the course of the book, but this is a good place to remember the unseen, largely forgotten, but highly important man – the piano tuner. So, in conclusion, I want to say to piano tuners everywhere, 'All my thanks.'

Joseph Cooper

Trocks Mill Cottage, May 1979

1

Memories of Childhood

The village of Westbury-on-Trym, near Bristol, lies at the bottom of a fairly steep hill. It used to be the terminus of the trams that went right into the heart of Bristol; in fact Westbury is separated from Bristol by the famous and lovely downs. Just before you reach the hill that goes down into Westbury is a road called Southfield Road and at the top of it is Southey House, where the poet Robert Southey once lived. Southfield Road is itself quite a big hill; about half-way down on the right is Southdene, the house where I was born on 7 October 1912. I was the youngest of three children: my brother Bill was the eldest by three years, and my sister Mollie was one year older.

With the passage of time more and more buildings have gone up and Westbury-on-Trym has been rather swallowed up by Bristol, but it still preserves a village atmosphere.

At the time I was born my mother's father (Grandpapa Elliott) lived just a few houses further down the same road at Denehurst, and my father's parents also lived in Westbury, in a lovely old farmhouse. At the bottom of our road was a gate, because the lower half of Southfield Road was private. Once a year, always on Good Friday, there was a ritual closing of the gate all day, which by law had to be done in order to claim the right to keep it as a private road. This custom was observed for many years until time swept it away and the road was taken over by the corporation.

I remember the gate very vividly. I also remember three glorious elm trees and a sweep of fields almost immediately opposite our house, where my father had an allotment. At right angles to the end of the road was Stoke Lane, and if you turned right, you came to a tiny little shop called Pepworths. That was where you could buy the most delicious sweets and chocolates; I often found myself just happening to go for a little walk to take the dog, and just happening to pop into Pepworths to get a packet of sweets. If you went straight on (crossing Stoke Lane) you could walk along a small, narrow path for about a hundred yards and then you came to another road called Canford Lane. Cross it, climb a stile into a field and you were in the domain of Westbury Court, where my father's parents lived. They had a farm – I don't know how many acres, but the fields stretched for miles – and you could clamber your way to the farmyard and reach the house via this field. It was my favourite way of arriving at Westbury Court, although of course there was a front entrance which you could reach through the village.

I specially liked to go to see my grandmother via the famous stile, because on the way I always met some of the farmhands and I liked to stop and chat with them, pat the horses, examine the corn and smell the hay. One of my favourite jobs was to feed the chickens and collect the eggs for my grandmother. In fact I was brought up very much as a country boy, not a town boy.

Anyone visiting Westbury-on-Trym today would find all this rather hard to believe, because there is not a trace of Westbury Court, and Westbury-on-Trym itself is very much a suburb of Bristol. All signs of the farm have now been swept away and built over, but up to ten years ago I could still find signs of barns and farm buildings, which I showed people proudly, and I could trace the layout of the whole place. Its vanishing is a pity, because not only was it very picturesque, but Westbury Court was one of the oldest houses in the village, dating back to 1300, with some walls three feet thick; how there wasn't a preservation order on it I don't know. But when my grandmother died in the late 1920s the road planners could hardly wait to take down the whole house and farm because they wanted the land to build a new road (Falcondale Road) to bypass the village of Westbury.

My father was bank manager of the National Provincial Bank in Westbury village, only just a few minutes' walk from our house, and also only a few minutes' walk from his parents' house at Westbury Court. So, with my mother's father living only a few doors from us down the hill, both sides of the family were well represented. My mother had been born and brought up in Guernsey, where one of her two brothers remained and ran the family tobacco, wine and spirits company of Bucktrout.

Two years before I was born, the Edwardian era had been swept away and the much more stable and authoritative figure of George V ascended the throne. But two years later, of course, in 1914, the Great War broke out.

I remember none of this; I haven't a single memory of the beginning of the war – in fact my first memory was of the sound of music in the house, because my mother played the piano incessantly. She had a Steinway grand and was an excellent pianist; she had a very good finger technique and had been well trained, was an excellent sight-reader and, in addition, had a very sweet singing voice. From the age of one or two I used to sit on a cushion under the piano and listen as my mother played – in fact my mother used to say that she was playing a duet with me just about an hour before I was born – and she said, 'You rather got in the way!'

I used not only to love the roar that came from the piano – because the piano sounds much louder when you sit underneath it – but I liked to watch my mother's feet operating the pedals; her right foot sometimes moving very fast indeed. I was to discover later that my mother's tastes in music were not above reproach, but at the time I believed everything that she said and I loved all the pieces she played, which were all arrayed on the piano desk or in the Canterbury beside the piano. She played her repertoire frequently – she knew most of it by heart. It contained all the old favourites, from 'The Rustle of Spring' to 'Pale hands I love beside the Shalimar'. Also *Hiawatha's Wedding Feast* which my mother knew very well – she had sung in it at school.

My father was very nearly tone deaf and he was an embarrassment at concerts, as he invariably went to sleep and snored loudly. But his mother was musical; in fact she not only possessed a piano (a Victorian instrument, with a clangy sound) but she had a small but well-made pipe organ at Westbury Court.

Grandpapa Elliott died in 1919 and the Cooper family in due course sold Southdene and moved down to Denehurst, inheriting the house complete with some Louis XV furniture (authenticity unproven) and some nice pictures. As I have no memory of the move, it is possible that we children went to stay with my Aunt Kathleen and Uncle Charlie (my mother's other brother who retired early from Bucktrouts). Exactly when and how the move happened is unimportant.

One thing I do remember is that Uncle Charlie was a frequent visitor to Southfield Road. He had a natural ear for music and encouraged me to copy his 'ad libs' at the piano. My uncle would perch me on his knee, and show me which finger to place on what note to produce pleasing sounds. He restricted me to three-note chords on white notes at first. But between his visits I would experiment on my own, gradually discovering the geography of the keyboard. When Uncle Charlie next came I had invented a tiny piece using his chords in various octaves, up and down the piano. I fished out a few left-hand notes that 'mated' with the right hand. 'More chords, please,' I asked him. So he showed me the difference between major (smiling) chords and minor (sad) chords. This opened up a new world of sound for me, and revealed – I say it without a blush – that I had an instinctive 'feel' for the piano and a natural grasp of harmony. Uncle Charlie had started me off. My mother now showed me the rudiments of time. I couldn't have had two better early tutors.

These elementary lessons started when I was about four. The first indication that I had any natural gift for music had been, at the age of two, when I apparently sang the notes of 'God save the King' while being taken out in my pram on the downs. By the age of three I was always pestering my mother to play the piano. When I was alone I would go to the piano and pick out with one finger the tunes of certain often repeated favourites, such as Beethoven's Minuet in G and MacDowell's 'To a Wild Rose'. My mother would listen outside the room.

I have no memory of any of these musical activities, but heard about them (many times) in later years. It was my mother's idea to enlist the help of Uncle Charlie, when it became obvious that I had an unusual gift for music: and I have total recall of all he did and said.

By the time I was able to walk on my own, one of my favourite pastimes was busying around Westbury village. I used to potter down the hill, through the gate at the bottom, which of course was always open (except on Good Fridays), past Pepworths and round the village. I used to have a chat with the newsagent, the fishmonger and the ironmonger – there were two ironmongers – but perhaps my closest acquaintance was Mr Cleaves the grocer. Quite apart from having a first-rate grocer's shop (I loved watching him cutting the hams and bacon in the slicer) he was intensely musical. He played the organ and his daughters played the violin and cello. Mr Cleaves seemed to be Assistant Emergency Sub-Organist at Bristol Cathedral – anyway he was a great friend of Dr Hubert Hunt, the Organist of Bristol Cathedral.

One day Mr Cleaves thought it would be a great treat for me if he took me over to meet Dr Hunt and sit in the cathedral organ loft for a service. Up until then I had been to Westbury Church, but never to a cathedral. I was enormously excited at the prospect of going in Mr Cleaves' car (very few people had cars in those days). We arrived at Bristol Cathedral and he took me up some steps to the organ loft and introduced me to Dr Hunt, a benign little man with owl-like eyes: we shook hands and Dr Hunt said, 'I hear you are a budding musician. Is this your first visit to our great cathedral?' I cannot remember what I replied, because my attention was entirely absorbed by a smell – a horrible kind of fishy, burning-rubber smell coming from the organ. Dr Hunt said, 'I'm sorry about the smell, but the electricity is overheating. Let's hope the whole thing doesn't go up in smoke!' At those words, alarm struck me – we might go up in smoke and here am I, miles from home! 'I must get out of here at once,' I said to Mr Cleaves, and I rushed down the organ loft steps, trembling and in floods of tears.

Mr Cleaves came after me and said, 'Dr Hunt was only joking, you know.' But I was not to be comforted. 'With that awful smell of burning fish he must have meant it.' Mr Cleaves could see I was very frightened, so he said, 'Very well, you sit in the aisle, but I must go up and rejoin Dr Hunt, because I turn the pages for him.' So I sat in the aisle, very ashamed of myself. But I enjoyed the service and I sang away. In the middle of one of the lessons I saw Mr Cleaves coming down to me again. He asked if I felt happier now, because he said Dr Hunt would love to see me in the organ loft: I started crying again, so he told me not to worry and that he'd pick me up at the end of the service and take me home.

Driving home across the downs I said to Mr Cleaves how sorry I was that I had behaved so stupidly, but I had felt terrified at the thought we might be burned alive in the organ loft. He reassured me, 'Don't worry,' he said. 'We all have these fears; forget about it. But I shouldn't say too much to the family when you get home – just say you've had a very nice time.'

When we were very young children the three of us were used to being taken by our nursemaids in pushchairs or perambulators up the hill and onto the downs, passing Southey House at the top of the hill and then turning right. We used to pass some imposing gates with a lodge and drive, and in the distance could see a house which looked like some rich mansion; in fact it was a girls' school called Badminton House – it was rather like a small replica of the Duke of Beaufort's own Badminton House in Gloucestershire, after which I think it was named. It is now called Badminton School; in those days it had a kindergarten for very young children of both sexes.

My mother decided that Mollie and I should start at Badminton House – my mother always made all arrangements to do with the children, because my father was so busy with his clients, both during office hours at the bank and also after hours when he used to see them in the evening. I think in those days bank managers had a great deal more to do personally than they do now. For example bank managers today don't normally entrust themselves to deal with wills; but my father not only spent many an evening helping people make out their wills, but also advised them on stocks and shares and all manner of private matters. So he really didn't have time to look after us.

Quite apart from that, my mother's personality was so strong and outward-going that I think she was better at handling family situations than my father. She was quite prepared to stand up to anybody, although she was only five feet tall. She was a very determined, dynamic little lady, with a lot of sturdy Scottish blood in her. She had thick black hair, dark eyes and a long, very straight nose – a good-looking person, who looked you straight between the eyes.

She went to see Miss B.M. Baker, headmistress of Badminton House, and it was arranged that Mollie and I should join the school, five-year-old Joey (as I was always called as a child) to be in the kindergarten.

Each morning we set off from home, taking with us a snack for elevenses – usually sandwiches made with demerara sugar, because it was delicious and much in fashion at the time. We used to ask our various friends if *they* had demerara and if they didn't we would say 'Oh you poor things', in a rather condescending, snobby kind of way.

If we *were* at all snobby that was soon going to be changed by the arrival of a man on the scene to assist Miss B.M. Baker. His name was Mr Lynn Harris and he had what my mother would call socialist ideas about how children should be brought up. Our lifestyle changed. At lunch-time we were expected to fetch our food from the kitchen; when we had finished it we were told to wash up the plates, knives and forks and dry them, and clean the tables.

When my mother heard about this she was furious and went to see Miss Baker, who said she welcomed new ideas, but that my mother could put her point to the new master. She did, but Mr Harris stood firm; he did not agree with class distinction, he felt all children should be treated alike and taught to be useful. This horrified my mother and she said, 'Well, I will let you know in writing what we decide to do; we may take the children away.' Mr Harris was very courteous and said he would await her letter.

My mother got home and discussed it all with my father, but he wasn't really concentrating – he was probably thinking about somebody's will, or whether the chickens were doing well at Westbury Court. I don't think he ever really listened to my mother, who used to prattle on by the hour. However, she insisted on explaining the position, said she thought it was disgraceful, that the place was turning communist and we should be taken away.

My father said extremely little, merely that to him it did seem a good school and he thought we should give it a trial. My mother reluctantly agreed because she, too, felt the teaching was good there; also she liked the house and thought the playing fields were lovely; it was nice and near and it was essentially a school for well-bred children and she liked that. But, she added, 'As for that Mr Lynn Harris, they'll have to get rid of him, or I'll write to the *Daily Mail*' – my mother was always going to write to the *Daily Mail*, but she never actually got round to it!

Every morning at school we had prayers for the whole school, followed by a little voluntary on the piano, played by one of the mistresses on the music staff, while the children marched out to their classrooms. One day Miss Baker announced that all the music mistresses were ill and we would have to do without the final music at prayers, unless there was anyone who could play a march or some similar piece. I, having no problem over improvisation, got up and said: 'Yes, Miss Baker, I'll play a march.' 'You, Joey, at your age! Are you sure you can play a march?' 'Yes, Miss Baker, I'm quite certain I can play a march.'

So when the service was over I sat down at the piano – I could hardly reach the pedals – and I improvised a splendid march (at least it seemed to me splendid) and the children went out, swinging their arms and marching to my music. When everyone had gone Miss Baker called me back and said, 'That was a nice little piece – who composed it, Joey?' I said, 'I made it up as I went along, Miss Baker.' She said, 'Joey, you little fibber, you must tell the truth.' I was terribly upset, because I was telling the truth. To be fair to Miss Baker, she might genuinely have thought it was a piece of music, because I had by then started to take piano lessons and had learnt to read music fairly fluently.

One of my problems was that although I had learnt to read, I was rather apt to put in what I called 'improvements' to the composer's original notes. It wasn't that I was reading them wrongly by mistake, it was that I thought I was improving the piece by altering a chord here or a chord there; I was the despair of the poor lady teacher who was entrusted with my tuition. So much so, that she felt she couldn't handle me and I was sent to another teacher (they were both resident in the school). I think in all I had three different teachers and they all said the same thing, that here was an obvious, very unusual talent, but talent could only be put to full use if I stuck to the composer's copy and observed his intentions in every detail. This I did not wish to do.

My mother, always ready with practical advice, decided to make contact with Dr Hunt, whom I had already met on my disastrous first visit to Bristol Cathedral. She invited Dr Hunt to come to our house and asked if I could play to him and if he would give me a few tests and tell my mother what she should do next, because the situation at Badminton House was becoming very unhappy, to say the least. Dr Hunt was only too willing to help; he came over and I played to him.

He also gave me little sight-reading tests. He gave me one particular piece that had a chord I didn't like, so I altered it. When I had finished playing Dr Hunt pointed to the chord I had altered and said very gently: 'You played that chord wrong.' I replied: 'Yes,

Dr Hunt, I know, but I didn't like the one that was written. I thought mine was better.' 'Joey,' he said, 'one thing you must always remember, the composer knows best. When you write your own compositions you have every right to alter what you've written, but you must not alter what another composer has written.'

Dr Hunt was so charming and gentle, with his funny, blinking eyes, that I happily took all this in. My mother was present and he turned to talk to her. His advice was that I should leave Badminton House forthwith; it was time for me to go to a boys' preparatory school and take some specialist lessons, in order to prepare for taking a music scholarship to a public school in a few years' time. My mother had already put my name down for Clifton College, in Bristol, so choice of public school was no problem. The immediate problem was to find a preparatory school that would teach me on the right lines, in both music and general subjects.

My mother had very good contacts and I think these were helped by her fondness for games – she was a member of the Westbury Badminton Club and played two or three nights a week at the village hall. She was also a member of Westbury Tennis Club, and she played a lot of bridge. In any case, my mother had enterprise, optimism and a keen ear for all that was going on.

Quite near, in the opposite direction to Badminton House, there was a new school starting called The Manor House. It sounded promising. Again, it was a big, old house, with a large garden and an open-air swimming pool. The headmaster was Mr H.S. Holman and his idea for this new school was to have very small numbers, not more than ten or a dozen boys at the most, and to give them special, individual attention. An excellent matron was engaged, Miss Brewster, and an assistant master, Mr Gibson.

When my mother visited The Manor House to have a good look round and see if she approved, she came back home entranced by young Mr Holman, who in addition to being good academically, was a keen and tough sportsman (he was a good boxer and a member of Clifton Rugby Club). She also liked the large kitchen garden and the fact the milk came from their own dairy herd – the whole country atmosphere that we were used to and which she liked so much.

My mother also felt that this idea of a small school would be specially good for me; I wouldn't be intimidated by a lot of bullying older boys – we were all roughly the same age. Another point that struck her was the comprehensiveness of the syllabus; where Mr Holman and Mr Gibson couldn't supply the tuition there were imports. We had an excellent French teacher – she was English but spoke very good French. Most important of all, there was a good piano teacher, Miss Bernhardt. My mother felt it was a good German name for a start; she met Miss Bernhardt and I think probably told her about one or two of my little weaknesses, such as the liberties I took with the composer's music.

In any case it was decided I should go to The Manor House. Getting there was quite simple; it was only half-an-hour's walk, but I quickly learnt to ride a bicycle and, apart from having to walk up Southfield Road (it was too steep to ride), it was all plain sailing and I could get there in ten or twelve minutes.

The Manor House was almost entirely likeable. The balance of activities was so beautifully arranged: not too much work, not too much play, plenty of both and plenty to keep one occupied. The standard of work expected was high and if any boy misbehaved or indulged in any stupid pranks he was promptly given a gymshoe on his bottom. I was a recipient of that, but I took care that I only had it once because it was very painful. Incidentally, it made me a believer in mild corporal punishment, because it hurt so much that I wasn't going to get found out again and I was much more careful not to commit crimes – they were not very serious ones, but silly things like throwing paper darts across the room in the middle of a class.

Apart from the school work, we played a lot of games; there was a tennis court and the open-air, rather primitive swimming pool. This was my only bugbear – I was frightened of the water. I couldn't swim and envied those who could. Matters were made worse by the headmaster's method of giving us swimming lessons. He used to put a belt round our middles and attach the belt to a string; he then stood on shore at the deep end, holding the end of the string, and we had to go through the motions of swimming while he kept us afloat. I was all right so long as I was in the shallow end and in my depth, but as I gradually went out of my depth I panicked – and, of course, as I panicked I choked, swallowed water and usually had to be lifted out.

These lessons became a matter of mighty dread for me. I confided in Matron, Miss Brewster, that I didn't know if I could stand them any longer (I hadn't said anything at home). I think Miss Brewster must have had a word with the headmaster, because in my case he changed the method and encouraged me to practise by holding onto the side and kicking my legs about. But of course I didn't learn to swim there – I think once you are put off by real fear, you don't easily come round and probably need a change of venue if you are really going to succeed.

Lunch was always a very enjoyable affair. We had a long table in the bow window of the large dining-room and the cook, whose name was Mary Jarratt, was superlative. I have used that word with complete conviction: it's getting on for sixty years ago, but I have never since tasted rissoles or fishcakes the way Mary made them. From a very early age I loved my food and I have loved it ever since (especially good old English cooking). Unfortunately, as time has gone on, more and more things come out of packets or have been ruined by insecticides and I have become increasingly nostalgic over my memories of what that early food tasted like.

I hadn't been at The Manor House very long before it was decided, both by my mother and the headmaster, that I needed toughening up. I think they felt that I was being rather spoiled by going home every day; for example, as soon as I got home there were crumpets (or pikelets as we called them in the West Country) in front of a hot fire, the dog and the cat and the general home life that one associates with the child. This was fine for the holidays, but it was felt that to be at school the entire time during the term, cheek by jowl with the other boys with the rough and tumble of boarding-school life, would do me a lot of good.

I remember a slightly teary scene, on both sides, as my mother kissed me goodbye for the beginning of the new term when I was to be a boarder. There was one boy who was more frightened than I was: he ran away from school, but was eventually brought back. I stuck it out, but for the first two or three days I was very nervous; after that I loved it. I soon got into the rhythm of the life and I greatly enjoyed the evenings that we had at school, which I had previously missed by going home before tea. We had a light supper, after which Mr Holman would sit and read to us; this was marvellous because he had such a very expressive voice, and he gave us a varied recital of stories. He always gripped one by getting to an exciting situation and then saying that was all for tonight and he would continue the next evening.

As well as the readings we had interludes of music. The gramophone, of course, was very primitive, but there was an interesting selection of records, including some Gilbert and Sullivan and some piano recordings. The chief pianist on record was Mark Hambourg. I remember being absolutely stunned by the way he played the cadenzas in Liszt's *Liebestraum* – nowadays it is not considered done to play them at that speed, as they are meant to be part of the music; but for sheer dazzle and display they were really quite astonishing and they showed me just how slowly my fingers moved by comparison.

The bathtime arrangements were carefully looked after by Miss Brewster, who made sure our backs were scrubbed and that we washed behind our ears. There was always a big cake of Wright's coal tar soap and nice white towels; bath night was very enjoyable, especially as there was plenty of hot water.

There was a floor above our dormitories in which the assistant staff had their rooms. One night there was tremendous drama: we could hear great activity going on – people rushing about. But we didn't know what the trouble was until the next morning. We then discovered Mr Gibson had been taken ill with an appendicitis and the ambulance had had to be called. He was rushed off to hospital and operated on immediately. Fortunately the operation was successful and it wasn't too long before Mr Gibson was back with us. We were all very fond of Mr Gibson, so were shocked at his sudden illness and very glad to see him back again.

To offset this drama we had a very exciting piece of news, and that was that the headmaster had become engaged to the beautiful young French teacher.

Every Sunday morning we were spruced up and marched down to Westbury-on-Trym Parish Church, where we had seats allocated in one of the side aisles. It used to amuse me to see my own family in their accustomed pews across the way, and also I watched the arrival of Sir Sidney and Lady Humphries, the local dignitaries.

In the distance I watched Mr Haydn Cox going up to his position at the organ. Just about that time he retired and a much younger man, Mr Geoffrey Mendham, took over the job. After one of the services I stayed behind and introduced myself to Mr Mendham, telling him I was a budding musician. I also met the Assistant Organist, who used to play for the children's service in the afternoon; he was a young man called Ken Filer. While I was at The Manor House he had a very bad motor-cycle accident and was in hospital for some time. This meant there was no one to play the organ for the afternoon children's service, so I said to Mr Mendham, 'I wonder if I could oblige, sir?' 'Can you play the organ?' he replied. 'I think I can, I can play the piano and I have watched organists.' He said I wouldn't be able to reach the pedals, but I said I thought I could manage and would he please audition me. He agreed and so I got the headmaster's permission to play to Mr Mendham. He gave me a couple of hymns to sight-read and asked me to improvise, then said, 'Good! Will you please be my sub-organist?' So at the age of nine I was the Sub-Organist of Westbury-on-Trym Parish Church (unpaid).

On the academic front all was going well. My bent for classics was quite obvious; in fact my Latin was progressing very fast. I had a bitter but friendly rival in a boy called John Athelstan Richards, who was clearly a very brilliant scholar. I was determined to beat him and I worked awfully hard at my Latin, because there was going to be a prize in about a year's time and I coveted that prize.

My piano lessons with Miss Bernhardt were proceeding well and my playing became more accurate and disciplined. But Miss Bernhardt didn't teach the theory of music and there was nobody else in the vicinity. So arrangements were made with Clifton College for me to go over there on my bicycle for private lessons with the teacher of musical theory, Mr W.E. Smith. It was a journey of about three miles, but I bicycled off and used to enjoy the ride.

But the fact of the matter is that those theory lessons did not go well; after two terms Mr Smith, who was not very pleased with me, wrote on a piece of paper the following words: 'Joe's homework on Theory is not up to standard.' It was put in an envelope and I had to give it to Mr Holman when I got back. Mr Holman was very displeased with me and asked for an explanation. I confessed that I found the theoretical side of music very dull and uninteresting, but he said that if I were going to be a fully fledged musician the paperwork was as important as the playing. How could I compose if I hadn't learnt how to put the notes down on paper?

The remainder of The Manor House story can be told in a few words. I did win that prize for Latin and I was very proud of it. Also, I did my theory homework, as set by Mr Smith; he in turn seemed quite pleased with my progress.

But quite suddenly, at the end of the Easter holidays 1926, as I was about to get my books ready for the new term, my father told me there would be no new term – The Manor House School had been closed down. I was absolutely dumbfounded – especially as my father didn't give me any reason. I think the sudden closure might have been due to some financial problems; perhaps with so few pupils Mr Holman had been unable to make the school a paying concern.

Sorry as I was that The Manor House had closed, this was no time to mope; I had two events ahead of me on which my whole future career depended. One was the music scholarship to Clifton College, and the other was the entrance examination to get me into the college once I'd got the scholarship.

So without any delay at all we found a coach who was known to be very reliable: he was an ex-army type and his name was Matthews. He very much expected you to call him 'sir' when you entered the room. He was coach to a number of boys wanting to get into Clifton and he lived very near the school, just off College Road. It was explained to him that my school had closed down unexpectedly and he said he was quite happy to take me on in any subjects I needed to prepare for my examination. I felt no great affection for him, but in the circumstances there was no time to be wasted – this was a crash course and it needed someone who was a real disciplinarian. His initial severity thawed when I brought him well-prepared work.

On the musical front I continued to have my theory lessons with Mr Smith. I 'retired' from the post of Sub-Organist of Westbury Parish Church, because Mr Filer had recovered sufficiently to take on the post again, but I badly needed an organ to practise on. Until then I had never really played the pedals of the organ. A lot of people don't realize that the pedals of the organ are quite different from the pedals of the piano. On the organ, the pedals actually play notes and you have to learn the scale with your feet (in some of the great Bach organ works your feet are playing a page or more, entirely solo). I think one of the reasons why there are curtains round most organ lofts is that it looks rather bizarre to see an organist holding onto the stool (which is always very wide) with his hands and playing the pedals like mad with his feet. It looks comical and, if you are not used to it, it can raise a smile. But to do it really well is an act of almost Fred Astaire-like skill. A good pedal technique is very important for the organ.

There was an organ at the village hall in Westbury-on-Trym, where my mother played badminton. Underneath the stage there was the pump handle, which someone had to work up and down to blow the wind into the bellows. And guess who the victim was – my mother! She was perfectly happy to come along and blow for two hours at a time if necessary. I couldn't get anybody else to do it. Later on, of course, those pumps were done away with everywhere and electric machinery installed. But at that time it was quite the regular thing to have someone to pump the wind, and a tiring job it was.

Fortunately there was a thing called a mouse, which came up and down on a piece of string as the pumper pumped away (it was really a piece of lead attached to a strong piece of string); when the mouse was right down at the bottom it meant that the bellows were full of air. If the player suddenly pulled out all the stops and played loudly it used up an awful lot of wind and the mouse would start going up, so the person doing the blowing had to be very careful to keep enough air in the bellows. If you played softly you made the ration of air last much longer, so for my mother's sake I used to practise softly, because volume didn't matter; I just wanted to get used to playing the organ. I made very rapid progress, because I enjoyed it; but I felt so sorry for my mother in what we used to call 'The Black Hole of Calcutta'. I used to say, 'Never mind, in two hours' time you'll be on that court playing badminton.' And she was – her energy seemed inexhaustible.

In addition to the organ I put in about four hours a day on the piano, doing scales and exercises, and learning the pieces I was to play for the scholarship itself. I was allowed to play anything I liked: I chose, among other things, two Chopin preludes.

In my spare time I started taking up tennis in a rather serious way; it helped me to keep fit and certainly didn't do my organ or piano playing any harm. Just at the bottom of our hill was Canford Park, with excellent hard courts; I used to go there every day for an hour and practise, either with my sister, brother, or perhaps somebody else. We used to play hard and I got very keen on tennis. I was terribly disappointed when I arrived at Clifton and found the tennis courts were planned, but had not yet been built. But I did work away at it, always in the holidays, and became quite a good player – if a trifle erratic. I also had coaching lessons at the Bristol Lawn Tennis Club.

The tennis club lay next door to the Chapel of Ease of Westbury-on-Trym Parish Church – I've never really understood to this day why Westbury had to have what was called a Chapel of Ease at Redland, which is two miles away. It was a charming Wren-type church with a very good organ; I was allowed by the vicar (who was vicar of both Westbury-on-Trym and the Chapel of Ease) to use the organ whenever I liked. That organ did have a motor, so I was independent; I didn't need anyone to blow. So I was able to have my coaching on the tennis courts for one hour, and then I would go over to the organ and practise the organ for two hours – a very satisfactory arrangement.

By this time the Cooper family had a motor car, a 11.9-horse-power, four-seater, Bullnose Morris Cowley, of which I was extremely proud. I used to polish that Bullnose every day until it shone and I bought all sorts of special creams to keep the bodywork looking immaculate. I loved that car.

When the fateful day of the Clifton scholarship came in July, my mother, who was the only driver in the family at that time (my father never drove and, of course, we were all too young), motored me across the downs to Percival Road, to the house of Dr Beachcroft, the Director of Music at Clifton, who was going to examine me for my scholarship.

It all seemed to go quite well, apart from one disputed note in a Chopin prelude, where Dr Beachcroft thought it should be E flat and I, backed by my mother, thought it should be E natural. Apart from that (and it's always been an open question) he seemed rather happy, but he didn't say anything. He gave me sight-reading tests, ear tests, improvising tests. Luckily I never found ear tests any problem; not only did I have perfect pitch, but an infallible ear as well – if someone put down five notes on the piano, without looking I could say immediately exactly what notes they were.

Dr Beachcroft also asked questions about composers and who my favourite composers were. I said I thought Chopin, Beethoven and Rachmaninoff. I had the good sense not to mention any of the Victoriana that lay on my mother's music desk, because I had an instinct it would not have gone down well with Dr Beachcroft. He was a fierce-looking man with very shaggy eyebrows, but behind a rather rugged face he had a kindly smile.

This was to be my last close encounter with Dr Beachcroft, because he was the outgoing Director of Music at Clifton College and the newcomer to the directorship was a man from Australia, who had recently come from Radley College where he was a music master; before that he had been Organist at Melbourne Town Hall. He was Mr William McKie, later to become famous as Sir William McKie, Organist of Westminster Abbey.

Very few of us have not experienced that awful aching feeling when you are waiting to hear the result of an examination. Days seem to go by and nothing comes. In my case a feeling of failure overcame me; I thought, I haven't got it. Suddenly the telegraph boy arrived and my mother opened the telegram. It said, 'SON AWARDED MUSIC SCHOLARSHIP CLIFTON COLLEGE'. We hugged each other and danced and jumped around the room, thoroughly excited.

The scholarship was in the bag. Now it remained to continue working with my coach, so that I would pass the entrance examination which was a few months later. I kept working hard; I didn't let the success of the scholarship go to my head – it would have been fatal. I took the examination and this time I heard quite quickly – I was in. After the holidays (and I was ready for them) I was to enter Clifton College as a music scholar in the autumn term of 1926.

As a family in those days we shared our joys and sorrows. If things went right, as on the occasion when I got the scholarship, everybody was very happy. Even my father, who was certainly not prone to wearing his heart on his sleeve, used to appear very appreciative and warm if one of us had done well at school, or if my mother had done extra well at badminton or tennis. When my father was happy, his face relaxed and those blue eyes of his, which were two of his most remarkable features, seemed to look even bluer than usual.

Soon we were starting to pack up and get ready for the summer holiday. We usually went either to Devon or Cornwall and this year we chose St Ives. We were booked in at a boarding house and it was just a question of getting the car prepared and packed. Each of us had our own little packages and my mother had endless suitcases and parcels – she was not the world's most tidy packer. My father never seemed to have very much, but very often he didn't come with us on that journey; he would follow down later by train. He liked to stay behind for a few days, tend the garden and make sure everything was all right with his parents at Westbury Court.

Fortunately none of us was prone to car sickness. What we were prone to was arguing. We left the house at 5 a.m., because a Morris Cowley, 11·9-horsepower, would take a long time to do the Bristol to St Ives journey – nearly 200 miles. We hadn't been going for more than an hour before somebody would criticize the way my mother had negotiated a gear change. Although none of us children officially drove, we used to practise taking the car up and down the drive and we knew all about gear changing and noticed when my mother sometimes muffed her gears, with the resultant awful grinding noise. Or she might take a bend too sharply, or brake suddenly if a cat crossed the road, jolting all the luggage out of position. Her driving frequently came under criticism and she didn't like it and used to argue back. There would be a scene, very often with one of us taking my mother's side; sometimes we stopped altogether and argued it out. Fortunately we all had a sense of humour, none more than my mother, and she usually saw the funny side of all this, saying: 'Look, here we are on holiday and we've had our first row. Now let's have a good laugh and be on our way.' And off we went until something else happened.

The chances were this would be what my mother called 'looking for a friendly hedge', which was a polite way of saying nature had to be attended to on the journey. Unfortunately we didn't all coincide, so a number of stops had to be made. Then my mother would get fed up and say: 'We've had to stop four times. I wish you could all perform at the same time, children, because it really is a frightful nuisance to keep on stopping. We shall never get there.' So that would cause a minor row.

But the major build-up of tension was caused by the proposed stop for lunch – *where* to pull in at a beauty spot with a nice view. Scorn and derision would be poured on any stopping place where instead of a pretty view all you could see was, for instance, a very ugly house, or a factory. About half a dozen false stops would usually provoke a row, but when my mother felt there had been enough of it she would quickly pull in somewhere and we would get on with our lunch. We were all so hungry by then that without further argument we tucked into my mother's beautifully prepared picnic lunch.

I always dreaded our having a puncture, because this meant a terrible turn-out, but fortunately my brother Bill was mechanically minded and he knew exactly what to do; he got the jack and tools out and changed a tyre very easily and efficiently. Occasionally we used to run out of petrol, but in those days you carried a spare can on the running board, with two gallons in it, so you always had that to rely on – as long as you remembered to fill it up once you had used the precious reserve! As one of the 'drills of vital action' we made a point of filling it before we started on our long trip to Cornwall.

If my mother was not exactly a virtuoso of the gearbox, she was a driver of enormous panache and self-confidence; she felt it quite within her rights to call out criticisms if she thought other drivers had not done well. For example, she would shout out, 'Why do you pass if you don't want the road?' and comments such as, 'Silly man, going far too fast round that corner!' 'Why did you cut in like that? Take his number, Bill.' However, even if we were in the open (the hood was put down if the weather was fine) her silvery voice only just carried above the engine and certainly couldn't be heard by the driver in the other car.

We arrived at St Ives in the late afternoon, found our way to the boarding house and very soon got to our rooms, unpacked, and lay exhausted on our beds, really feeling tired. However, we knew we were going to have supper later – we weren't going straight to bed, not us! My mother seemed quite fresh, she didn't even lie down – her usual dynamism was to the fore until the time when she saw us all into bed after supper. The great day ended. We had arrived at St Ives and we all slept better than we had for months.

In the early Twenties there were no vast crowds at St Ives even in the height of the season. The tourist industry had not yet started and motor cars were few and far between. One didn't have to bother about parking lines or traffic wardens; apart from one or two narrow streets where a car simply couldn't get up or down, there was no problem at all and you could leave the car anywhere. Even in mid-August the beaches were only just pleasantly full.

If the mornings were fine (and this particular summer they usually were) I used to like to get up very early, called by the cry of the gulls above, and thread my way through the narrow streets down to the harbour to watch the fishermen bringing in their fish from the night's haul. The air seemed so much cleaner than stuffy old Westbury-on-Trym and one felt brimful of energy all the day long. Back to an enormous breakfast at the boarding house and then we would plan our day.

On the beach at St Ives you could hire a tent complete with deck-chairs; this we did and made it our daily headquarters. The sand was golden and lovely and the sea, although I can't pretend it was warm, was inviting; one could get into the deep part quite quickly, or if you were still a slight water funk (as I was at the beginning of that season) you could stay in the shallows. My brother was already an excellent swimmer and he had a very enviable American crawl, which I used to watch and admire. With a little help from him, I was soon floating and then swimming; by the end of that summer I had lost all fear of the water. Of course, the extra buoyancy of the sea helps to keep one up, and diving into the waves, once you've overcome the initial fear of doing so, is not only fun but a good way of keeping warm.

But I never went out of my depth; that was the fatal mistake that had been made in my initial swimming lessons. I kept well within my depth the whole of that summer, so that if I wanted to put a foot down I was safe and not going to get myself into trouble. Over the years along those Cornish beaches there have been too many tragic accidents; idiotic people, who are not sure of themselves, swim out and suddenly either get cramp or get tired, or panic, and too often it leads to tragedy. So I built up my confidence slowly and I couldn't have had a better tutor than my brother, who really was quite superb in the water.

One morning my mother was very excited because there was a letter from my father. In it he said he was coming down in two days' time and named the train and would we meet it. It was lovely to see how overjoyed my mother was and her whole day seemed lit up by the thought of the arrival of my father. If his arrival was indeed a slight anticlimax I think it was because he couldn't conceal the fact that a seaside holiday was really not for him, that he would have been so much happier with his grapes and his garden and his visits to Westbury Court. But he did his best and I must say that all the things that he could do, like walking and fishing and eating and drinking, he did with suitable enthusiasm. He didn't get a lot of pleasure out of the sea itself: apart from the occasional paddle, he didn't swim, but he was quite happy to sit on the rocks with a fishing line, or even just to sit in a deck chair, usually smoking, half asleep or reading the paper.

My mother had brought all her tennis gear, because she had been told there was a good tennis tournament at St Ives. She entered and, of course, this caused enormous excitement in the family and we watched her progress with great interest. This tended to take us away from the beach for some of the time and our priorities were somewhat divided – we loved to stay on the beach, but on the other hand we were terribly anxious to see how mother was progressing, so we did a kind of shuttle service. It wasn't very far to the courts and she did extremely well. I remember my sister coming down one day and saying: 'Mummy's got into the semi-final! Quick – we must all go and watch.' And we all tore up to the courts and watched. But I confess with shame, I cannot remember whether she got through the semi-finals or not! I know she didn't actually win the tournament, but she played well and she enjoyed herself. She looked immaculate in her white dress and we were very proud of her on the court.

Another vivid memory of St Ives was the dancing. Ballroom dancing had become the rage, the great fashion of the early Twenties and it was in St Ives that my brother, sister and I learnt the Charleston. Bill and I also bought hideous Oxford Bags. We swished around with these wide-bottomed trousers and Charlestoned madly at the local Palais de Danse.

At that same hall there was a music competition. As I had a rather nice soprano voice I decided to put in as a singer. I sang a bowdlerized version of Beethoven's beautiful little Minuet in G; it was called 'Mignonette' – I have an idea it was by Horatio Nicholls. Anyway I won the competition and my prize was a clock. It wasn't a very grand clock, but I was extremely pleased with it and it lived in my bedroom at home for about ten years, until its days were done.

We had already made many friends on the beach and they came to support my effort at the local hall. When the holiday finally ended we all agreed to meet again next year, which is exactly what we did.

The journey home from St Ives was uneventful. My father had not stayed the full course of the holiday; so we travelled four up, as on the journey down. This was perhaps just as well, because during the holiday we had bought extra summer clothes and swimming wear, so that the Morris Cowley was very cramped for space.

We started off about 9.30 a.m. after a big breakfast and bought our lunch, consisting of four large, succulent, hot Cornish pasties, at Launceston – the last town before crossing the River Tamar into Devon. This time not one of us queried the need for a beauty spot for a lunch stop, because the smell of those pasties made us all ravenous. However, my mother very sensibly insisted on driving for another hour, remaining quite immune to our incessant pleas to pull in. 'You will only complain of hunger long before tea-time if I give in now,' she shouted over the roar of the engine. She was forced to go down into second gear more often with the extra weight of luggage, so conversation became impossible for long stretches of hilly Devon. This was perhaps fortunate because, apart from my mother's usual advice to fellow motorists, there really seemed nothing to say.

Lunch always put us into a very good humour, and those last Cornish pasties of the year never tasted better.

We usually planned to get well into Somerset before we stopped for tea, so that we could give the car a rest, find a garage and fill up with petrol, and generally prepare ourselves for the one hazard of the journey – the long, steep Red Hill. Nowadays, of course, it is hardly noticed as a hill, but then the road hadn't been made up, and for a car with not much horsepower it was a long and tiring ascent. In fact, nearly always about three-quarters of the way up the hill, the engine boiled and steam and water started pouring out of the radiator. One could go slowly on, but it might be really dangerous for the engine. So it usually meant a stop – on the steepest part of the hill – and then there was a nasty feeling that the brakes wouldn't hold and we might go backwards. But they did hold and after about five minutes, when the radiator had stopped boiling, we crawled up to the top where there was a godsent garage. We opened up the bonnet, let the engine cool until it was safe to remove the radiator-cap, and filled up with more water. In the meanwhile my mother had what she called 'a quiet cigarette'.

One great luxury in those very early days of motoring was the performance of the AA, the Automobile Association, which worked in rivalry with the RAC, Royal Automobile Club. We were staunch members of the AA and we had a badge on the front of the Morris which I polished with as much enthusiasm and care as I did the Bullnose itself. When you met an AA patrolman he saluted, almost like an army soldier saluting an officer. In the AA handbook it said in large letters, 'If an AA man fails to salute, always stop and ask the reason.' It meant there might be some danger lurking ahead, or some emergency. Occasionally the AA man noticeably didn't salute and then we were tremendously excited. We stopped, but nearly always it was something rather undramatic like a road under repair ahead, or some flooding somewhere. Just occasionally we were told there was a speed trap and our speed was being watched.

After we made Red Hill the rest of the journey home was easy and we used to arrive and find a welcome from my father. There was always supper to look forward to after we'd unpacked and taken a walk round the garden. We admired my father's grapes, let him show us how things were growing, heard how everything was at Westbury Court, *and* of course welcomed our dog and cat, whom we couldn't take with us when we stayed at boarding houses. Normally they were seasoned travellers, and often used to sit in the car patiently awaiting a drive.

Half an hour on the beloved Steinway and off to bed.

2
Clifton College

After that memorable holiday we still had a few weeks to go before schools went back. One important decision had to be taken before I started at Clifton and that was whether to be a boarder or a day-boy. I had no strong feelings either way. One great advantage with sleeping at home was that I would be able to put in many practising hours in my spare time on a decent Steinway grand piano, whereas at school the available pianos were all worn-out uprights in claustrophobic 'cells'. What decided me firmly and finally was a ruling written up in large letters 'No two boys may share a cell'. So one of the most valuable forms of musical training, i.e. playing piano duets, was forbidden for a start. At home I had, apart from my mother, boys and girls of roughly my age only too eager to sit down and read through duet arrangements of Beethoven symphonies and Schubert's many original works for piano duet.

On my first day I, along with the other new boys, was introduced to Mr H. Norton-Matthews, the housemaster of North Town (Westbury lying to the north of Bristol). There was another house, South Town, for southerners and there was an inevitable but entirely wholesome rivalry to beat each other at various house competitions, especially games.

Mr Norton-Matthews was middle-aged, tall and slim, and with his finely carved features, silky white hair, upright carriage and resonant but expressive speaking voice, impressed me. In fact after a few weeks, in which I had come to know all the masters by sight, he stood out as my choice, if I had had to make one, for a housemaster. I knew that any little troubles or fears that must assail the heart of the boldest spirits on entering an enormous public school could be safely confided in H.N.M. I had cause on more than one occasion to seek his advice. How lucky I was, because the time had come to end maternal cosseting. That last soprano solo at St Ives was my childhood swan song. At the end of the first term, my voice broke quite suddenly and I was speaking like a man. So now I had to learn to become one.

I was also very lucky in the choice of my first form master, a man called Horace Merrick. Merrick had been wounded in the war, he had a very brave war record and had won the Military Cross. Due to the shape of his figure he was universally called 'Tubby' Merrick. He had his own, very special, brand of humour, comparable to that of Sir Thomas Beecham. A remark would be made, Tubby Merrick would reply with a spontaneous quip and he would have the form in stitches. Such situations came up quite often. He wasn't playing for laughs, any more than Beecham appeared to. I wonder if anybody has ever kept a list of 'Merrickisms'; but unless you actually heard the man himself deliver them, with the extraordinary voice which he had, almost impossible to describe – deep and drawling – perhaps some of the effect would be lost.

He called me back after my first lesson with him and said: 'I wonder if you know my brother, Frank Merrick?' I replied: 'At my age I can't say I have had the honour of meeting your brother, but I have heard him play – what a fine pianist.' 'Well, he certainly plays an astonishing number of right notes,' he replied. As Frank Merrick had been a conscientious objector in the war, and was even imprisoned for a time, I felt the conversation had better terminate at that point.

Tubby Merrick was so easy-going and kind, underneath this pretended glum exterior, that it really would take a very lazy person to fall out with him. I must confess, however, I did have one small brush, not so much due to laziness as perhaps the fact I had practised the piano rather more one evening when I should have translated my piece of Latin prose rather better. Anyway, he looked it over and said quite suddenly: 'I have had enough of your messes, Master Cooper. Now take this home tonight and bring me back a decent translation tomorrow.' There was no hint of a smile on his face, but neither did he look revengeful. I just knew that I had better do what he said.

It should be stated here that I was endowed with a sense of the ridiculous, a sense of humour and tendency to giggle, and also a capacity to mimic people – with, I'm told, astonishing accuracy. It's as well to admit all this now, because sometimes it went down very well, especially with masters who had a great sense of humour like Tubby Merrick, who never minded any amount of burlesquing out of school. But you had to know your master, and one master who did not like any form of tomfoolery from students was the new Director of Music, William McKie. This could be because he was Australian and had a different sense of humour – there is a difference, I've noticed it time and time again. Or it could have been simply that he was, in a sense, a new boy too, and was feeling as lost and as nervous as his pupils, especially the music scholars.

The giving of the music scholarships was so arranged that music scholars overlapped and there were always at least two there at the same time; there could be three or even four, if someone stayed on an extra year. When I arrived at Clifton there were certainly three senior scholars; also another boy, nearer my own age and a brilliant pianist, Christopher Wood.

We all studied piano and organ with McKie and for our theory of music we went to my old acquaintance, W.E. Smith, with whom I had studied privately when I was at my preparatory school. We were the music specialists and because of this we were allowed an hour or two off each day from the normal curriculum, in order to put in either extra music lessons or extra music practice. This wasn't enough, but in those days I don't think it was fully realized just how much work a music student had to do to be in the running for the top rank.

There were three or four other music masters to deal with, if I may call it, the rank and file of music students – boys who didn't want to take up music professionally, but wanted to learn to play the piano. There was also a violin teacher, cello teacher, and if you wanted to learn a wind instrument that could be arranged. All the wind instruments were taught by the bandmaster of the corps; this might have accounted for the rather strident tones of some of the brass.

The music school was across the road from the main part of the college; it was only a short distance, and it backed directly on to Clifton Zoo, which although small was considered one of the best zoos in the country. Many an awkward situation was averted when I played more than my usual succession of wrong notes – a sudden squawk from a parrot or roar from a lion could bring humour into the music room. Humour was badly needed in the music school, because William McKie didn't see the funny side of life. I don't think he was at all well; he told me years later – we have always remained friends – that he suffered from gallstones at one period of his time at Clifton.

My relationship with Mr Smith had improved greatly, but I'm afraid it was not as cordial as it should have been. I think in a way we were fond of each other, but my early disgraces at theory had not been entirely overlooked.

Light relief was brought by the presence of another aquaintance of mine, Geoffrey Mendham, who had been Organist of Westbury-on-Trym, but who now had a position at a nearer church and was one of the assistant music masters. He had a quiet and delightful sense of humour and although he never said anything, I think he used to look at me sympathetically when he knew McKie had been in an unusually bad mood.

There was also Dr C.S. Lang, nicknamed 'Beaker' Lang as he had an extremely long nose. He supplied what might be called character more than humour. At the end of a morning's work Dr Lang would come to the gate of the music school, pull out a cigarette and stick it in a long holder; what with the nose and the holder and the cigarette, there was a great deal of Dr Lang that would be seen coming round a corner, before Dr Lang himself appeared. He was very proud of his even and pearly scales on the piano, which he was prepared to demonstrate to all and sundry. But he never played an actual piece; and his piano accompaniment to Parry's 'Jerusalem' in a sing-song in Big School was noticeable for its virtual inaudibility. This was due perhaps to physical weakness, because on the organ (where the volume is not man-made) no one made more noise than Beaker Lang. He wrote a magnificent Tuba Tune which rang round the college chapel whenever he played it (which was when McKie was off duty). It was number one in the organ voluntary charts, and the 'school', instead of trooping out leaving a handful of listeners, used to sit it out, and would have cheered if applause had not been strictly forbidden. Once Lang looked through his mirror and saw that no one had moved. Pulling out even more stops he gave himself an encore until the marshal strode up the nave and pointed to the exit with violent gestures. He wanted to lock up. The chapel quickly emptied.

A great boost to my morale on the original first day at Clifton back in September 1926 had been the issue to each boy of a small, slim blue soft-covered diary. It would slip easily into the pocket. Apart from giving the names of the headmaster, housemasters, form masters and boy heads of house, it contained a complete list of boys (scholars in italics – how I revelled in those italics) plus much other relevant information about each boy. The Blue Book also contained a calendar of fixtures. For instance, on 7 October (my fourteenth birthday) after the preliminary round of rugger house matches, there was to be a lecture on acting by Sir John Martin Harvey (it was very dull by the way).

The Blue Book of the following summer term (1927) had a red letter day – Thursday, 2 June, 'Opening of Science School by HRH The Prince of Wales.'

I was on excellent terms with McKie, having just won the Harry Bonas Music Prize – five beautifully bound music books, including the miniature scores of Beethoven's nine symphonies. So McKie turned a blind eye to my poor practice output, while I turned a totally engrossed eye on the arrival of wooden planks, awnings, tent-poles, canvas by the mile, and crates full of goodies no doubt, but what? I noted in my Blue Book (which also contained a day-to-day personal diary) 28 May: 'Keep daily watch on the two sites, namely School House garden, and just outside Science School.' By 1 June a mammoth marquee had gone up in School House garden. There was a heat wave on, so everything was laid out ready bar the food. One hundred and fifty yards away, in front of the science school, was the dais, red carpeted with a festive awning over the top.

On the great day itself excitement among the boys was intense. From the moment the thirty-two-year-old Prince appeared with Earl Haig (the distinguished soldier and an old Cliftonian) a roar from the school (such as only a lion-trained Clifton can give) visibly shook His Royal Highness. Then he removed his bowler hat and waved back at the boys, who waved their straw hats at him; and the royal smile turned into a broad grin. He mounted the dais in front of the new science buildings and – an instinctively human touch – suggested that the boys put their hats on, as a protection from the scorching sun. As an almost comic gesture he kept his bowler hat on, although entirely shaded by the awning above. He then suggested an extra holiday to celebrate the opening of the new science school.

During his visit the Prince of Wales found time to challenge the school's champion squash-rackets player to a game in the recently opened courts. Shorts and sweater were found for him. Nobody was interested in the result. The Prince of Wales won the day and all our hearts – game, set and match.

Other highlights of my days at Clifton College were regular visits to Colston Hall, in the centre of Bristol, to hear all the greatest pianists of the day: Cortot, Solomon, Myra Hess and, above all, Rachmaninoff. When Rachmaninoff came to Colston Hall our excitement knew no bounds and I think we all agreed that he made a sound that we'd never heard before. I remember Geoffrey Mendham remarking to me, 'That's a sound you'll probably never hear from any other pianist, it's unique.' And McKie was equally wildly enthusiastic.

We learnt a tremendous amount from those visits. It did us good to get away from the music school, for one thing, and to hear people of world class was a very great privilege. I couldn't believe that Rachmaninoff was actually playing on an ordinary piano, the sound was so superb, and when the first recital was over I stayed behind. As we had seats at the back of the piano, we were on stage and I just touched a few notes of his piano, until the officious organizer of the concert came and told me I was very impertinent and to remove myself post-haste. But I found it was just a beautiful Steinway concert grand, nothing different about it – it was the magic that Rachmaninoff himself was putting into it. The other thing about Rachmaninoff was, whereas when I went to hear Cortot I felt a kind of despair – I felt whatever I did I could never get the kind of magic that Cortot had – when I heard Rachmaninoff, I can't tell you why but I found a lot of people agreed with me, I immediately wanted to go home and practise. I felt that he gave one hope. He seemed to do things that were possible, if only you worked at them the right way. I can't enlarge on this because it's really totally irrational – in fact I don't suppose there has been a greater piano technicians this century, except possibly Horowitz. Horowitz didn't come to Bristol during my time at Clifton, but I heard later from Charles Lockier, the agent down there, that his concert had to be cancelled from lack of support from the Bristolians!

In addition to solo pianists, I heard Yehudi Menuhin for the first time when he was still in shorts, and was absolutely astounded at the beauty of his playing and his tone. John McCormack came, Paul Robeson, and there were many visits from symphony orchestras. There was one concert when Moiseiwitsch came and played with Malcolm Sargent; the concerto was the Schumann. In the last movement, which is a very treacherous one, Moiseiwitsch took a wrong turning and played a chord which meant that in fact he was jumping about six pages. As soon as Moiseiwitsch had played the chord, Malcolm Sargent, the conductor, hummed quite loudly the top note of the chord Moiseiwitsch should have played, which would bring him back on track. Moiseiwitsch took his cue; he just lifted his hands from the wrong chord, onto the right chord, and without even looking up or smiling they went on as though nothing had happened. Apart from the music staff and the music scholars, I don't think too many people in the audience knew that Malcolm Sargent had saved Moiseiwitsch from an awkward moment.

It gave me a great shock. I had never had any trouble with memorizing – I used to memorize music very quickly and played at the school concerts by heart. It had never occurred to me that one would forget. But I remember suddenly thinking: how awful, I wonder if other people ever forget?

Another highlight was of a quite different order. There was in the school a young master called Martin Hardcastle, whose father was at the time Archdeacon of Canterbury. Martin was an extraordinarily tough man, who used to climb the treacherous cliffs of the gorge that ran up from the River Avon to the downs; he was also a born actor, with a tremendous sense of humour and he organized a troupe of like-minded, humour-loving people, and formed a sort of concert party. Among the other names was Yngve Lidell (brother of the famous announcer, Alvar Lidell), and a brilliant student who was to make his name in the world, especially in the BBC, Felix Felton (remember the Mayor of Toytown?).

We performed at both Clifton and Canterbury, but we started with a trial run at Clifton; it was at the first of these concerts that the whole idea of the Dummy Keyboard was born. Martin Hardcastle called himself 'Pader' and another master called himself 'Rewski' (Paderewski) and we had in the school two ancient dummy keyboards. The two men wore evening dress and put on enormously long wings. While Felix Felton and I (backstage) played frantically to give the effect of two pianos, Hardcastle and his partner synchronized to our music.

At rehearsal I went round to the front of the house in Big School, where the entertainment took place, leaving Felix Felton to play alone, so that I could watch the performance; one simply couldn't tell that the two 'pianists' weren't actually playing – they mimed to the music so well. It made a most amusing act.

As well as that, there were extracts from Gilbert and Sullivan, and old Victorian chestnuts – and because Martin Hardcastle came from Canterbury, the group was called 'The Canterbury Chestnuts'.

McKie's attitude to the Chestnuts was interesting; for one thing he was very nervous about performing in it, but agreed to play a piano solo. Reluctantly, but effectively bewhiskered, he played 'To a Water Lily' by Edward MacDowell and played it beautifully. He also wrote a brilliant skit in the style of Handel to the words of 'Jack and Jill'. I wish that I'd kept that skit, because it was quite the equal of the Victor Hely-Hutchinson Handel parodies that Owen Brannigan and others used to sing later on. But McKie pooh-poohed the idea that the skit was clever and when the concert was over he tore the manuscript into a hundred pieces and put it in the wastepaper basket. This was a pity, because it was clever by any standards; but this was rather typical of McKie's unsureness of himself, of his curiously nervous, highly strung temperament, and perhaps a reflection of the over-earnest and humourless atmosphere of the Royal College of Music from which he had lately emerged (the RCM is very different today).

I had an opportunity of savouring this atmosphere when McKie very kindly arranged for Christopher Wood and myself to visit the Royal College of Music with him during term-time, with the full approval of Mr Norman Whatley, the headmaster of Clifton. On the train to Paddington, and on the brisk walk across Hyde Park, McKie was jaunty and even quite talkative. Just as we arrived at the Royal Albert Hall, before going down the steps to the Royal College, McKie stopped us and said (gently) to Christopher: 'One thing, Wood, about your little mannerism, don't keep saying "Yes, that's right" every time Sir Hugh Allen addresses you. If Sir Hugh says anything, of course it's right. Got it?'

Once let into the sanctum sanctorum – the director's office – both Christopher and I were quite overawed by the great man's supercharged and (apparently) aggressive manner. Wood said 'Yes, that's right' about ten times a minute. The door burst open and a shaggy, untidy figure came in. It was Dr Vaughan Williams. Sir Hugh introduced us. But R.V.W. said 'How d'you do, how d'you do', and vanished.

On the way home we thanked McKie for all the trouble he had taken, and sitting eating an enormous Great Western Railway tea (alas, quite different today), Christopher and I agreed it had been an experience we would never forget.

My mind was now on a collision course. I could not see why 'serious' musicians had to take themselves and their music so seriously. My natural inclinations were towards the enjoyment of all kinds of music – even the newly imported jazz from America. However, the musical establishment took a different view. When it became known that I sometimes played jazz with the school's jazz band, my housemaster dropped a broad hint that I was asking for trouble and that I could even risk losing my music scholarship.

After that warning I kept my own performances of jazz or dance music to the holidays and the subject wasn't referred to again. The wireless was now coming in in a big way and I was able to tune in to late-night broadcasts from the Savoy Hotel, where I could listen to either the Savoy Havana Band or the Savoy Orpheans. This, of course, was dance music, which was different from jazz, but had its roots in jazz. I loved listening to dance music over the air – to me it created a glamorous world that was quite beyond my dreams.

As young children we, in common with many other children in Bristol, had been regularly to Mrs Hay's Dancing Studio, 20 West Park, Clifton, quite near the Bristol BBC. Despite the fact the lady pianist hadn't the slightest idea of the feel of modern dance music, Mrs Hay and her sister had such enthusiasm that I think many Bristol children developed a real passion for ballroom dancing. We three certainly did, so in addition to listening on the wireless to these various dance bands, we took every opportunity we could of going to dances.

When you were invited to a dance you were given a dance-partner card, so that you could pick your partners for the evening. A bonus was the Paul Jones, where you had a chance to change partners. When the music started the girls moved round in a circle one way, while the boys circled in the other direction. When the music stopped you grasped the nearest partner, say for a waltz. If you saw a fat, ugly one coming you pretended you didn't see! The whole process happened several times.

This whole world of dancing was very satisfying, because it was so completely different from being at a boys' school, where you never saw any women, apart from the matron. It was a change to be able to hold a girl in one's arms – a novel sensation and one that I think should be encouraged.

Apart from the summer holidays, which were always kept for Devon or Cornwall, we used to go a good deal during school holidays to stay with my cousins and their parents (my Uncle Charlie) at Bournemouth. My cousins, Doris and John, were roughly our ages and were as keen on dancing as we were. We all used to go to the King's Hall, which adjoined the Royal Bath Hotel, where we danced under the tutelage of Mr and Mrs Oakenfold. Occasionally I was allowed to dance with Mrs Oakenfold herself; I realized then what 'following' meant, because most women didn't 'follow' on the dance floor – they were like old cab horses and you had to drive them round the room! But Mrs Oakenfold suggested to you by her movements what you should do, and when you did it, she followed. It was a sensation I shall never forget.

In addition, my cousins had an excellent hard tennis court and we played a great deal of tennis. The matches were fast and furious. There were great battles between cousin Doris (a left-hander) and sister Mollie; they were fairly evenly matched and they both hit like blazes. My mother had instilled in us all an acute awareness of sportsmanship. If she saw a sign of anybody pouting if they lost in any sport, she would remind us that games are to be enjoyed and help you to learn in life to be a good loser. We all took in this very good advice.

Back at school there was a boy called Colin Rankin who was a very keen tennis player. He and I formed a partnership and used to play a lot of tennis in our spare time. We got ourselves invited to tennis parties, because the school's lack of tennis courts was compensated for by many splendid courts attached to private houses around Clifton. One day Colin asked me if I would like to join him for the doubles in Junior Wimbledon. I laughed and said: 'Surely we're not up to that standard!' He explained we would have first to enter some tournaments and qualify, by either winning them or getting into the semi-finals, but then we would be eligible. This we did and we got into Junior Wimbledon 1929.

Colin Rankin's family lived in Arthur Road, Wimbledon, only a short walk from the actual courts; I stayed with the Rankins and found them such a charming family and the atmosphere so pleasant, that everything seemed to be propitious for a successful tournament. However, I have to confess that things didn't go quite as planned – my nervous system wasn't equal to the occasion in spite of a good start. We got through three rounds, but I then started over-compensating for my nerves by hitting the ball very hard; at one point I hit up a lob that landed right over the stop-netting into the next court. This was just 'not done' at Wimbledon and caused some commotion. Colin was putting up a manful display, covering for me and running about the court, but he could do nothing to stem the tide of our attackers.

Nevertheless I really enjoyed that visit to Wimbledon and it's rather fun to say: 'I played in Junior Wimbledon' – even though I have to be honest and add, 'And I played like a boot!'

At the end of one term Mr Norton-Matthews, who was shortly to retire, asked me round to tea as he wanted to have a chat with me. He told me he was rather worried about me and he went on to elaborate by saying he had watched my school career with great interest. Although I'd dropped some bricks (I hadn't always excelled by any means) Norton-Matthews said he thought my rollicking sense of humour and my mimicry had been much appreciated, because I'd helped to improve the morale of the school and make everybody cheerful. But he said I was in danger of trying to take on too many things, that there I was, going off and playing at Junior Wimbledon, playing rugger, and rushing off to dances, wasting a lot of time and not really giving enough time to my piano practice or appearing to enjoy my organ playing. 'In short, Cooper, what do you intend to do when you leave school?'

I remember this tea party so vividly, as funnily enough I'd never thought about my future very seriously. As my family had insisted they were going to keep right out of school affairs and let me grow up my own way, as best I could, this episode rather jolted me. When I got home I thought it was a good idea to open up the discussion in front of both my mother and father. Rather surprisingly, it was my father who came up trumps this time. He said: 'Norton-Matthews has got a very good point. I have privately been worrying about you for some time, though of course I never say anything. But what I suggest is this: I have a pianist contact in Bournemouth, a lady who was a gold medallist at the Royal Academy of Music, and I can write to her and see if she will hear you play and give a verdict on your chances of becoming a solo pianist.'

I thought this was a good idea and I wrote to my Aunt Kathleen and Uncle Charlie in Bournemouth, telling them the plan and how I was to be auditioned by a Mrs Brodie Carpenter. I asked if I could stay with them and practise very hard on their piano. A sweet letter came back: 'Come when you like, stay as long as you like.'

The big day came. I chose to play two pieces by Chopin. The first I knew I played very well – the Scherzo in B flat minor. The other I played with great panache but not all that accurately – it was the G minor Ballade. Mrs Carpenter was a large lady with henna-coloured hair and enormous hands, hands very like a man. I thought she looked rather fierce, but I wasn't nervous – when you are in the presence of professionals who have been through the mill, you know that they know what they are talking about, and to get a first-class objective opinion was very valuable to me at that moment.

I played the Scherzo. Mrs Carpenter said: 'Fine – do you want a break before your next piece?' I opted to go straight on with the G minor Ballade. When it was over Mrs Carpenter commented: 'I'm just wondering why you played the Scherzo so much better than the G minor Ballade? It was like two different pianists playing.' I had to admit straight away that I had practised the Scherzo with far more loving care, at a time when my love for the piano was totally and completely undivided – other attentions hadn't claimed me. Whereas the Ballade had been learnt amid the clamour of tennis and dancing and all the other enjoyments I took part in.

Mrs Carpenter rightly said: 'This won't do. If you are going to be a pianist you must give everything you've got to it. And are you prepared to do that? Because if you're not, you'll get nowhere. There are plenty of good young pianists who can play nearly as well as you, although I think you have the divine spark; but even the divine spark can easily be extinguished by laziness or inattention. So you had better go away and think about it – whether you have the devotion and the dedication to become a solo pianist. If you haven't, you must think of an alternative plan, which is not for me to suggest.' A formidable lady, but she gave it me straight from the shoulder.

Mrs Carpenter wrote to my father, saying very much the same as she had said to me. After a lot of discussion, during which Mr McKie was consulted, it was agreed that the career of a solo pianist was not the right one for me, because I was too erratic and hadn't got the concentration and the dedication. It would be much safer to follow the paths of so many of my predecessors and try to get an organ scholarship at either Oxford or Cambridge. I could then become either a cathedral organist, if I were good enough, or perhaps become a schoolmaster.

To this I reluctantly agreed; but in my bones I felt indignant, I knew that I had let myself down. What a fool I was to indulge in so many different activities. For McKie's last term at Clifton (Christmas 1930) I would give him my very best; I would give him my very all on the piano, and just see what happened.

McKie asked me if I would like to play the first movement of Rachmaninoff's Second Piano Concerto in C minor at the school concert. I jumped at the suggestion and McKie told me to go off and learn it. I fell in love with the music straight away and it came to me quickly and easily. I practised it with tremendous dedication; each hand separately, checking my fingering, listening to the tone that I was making and watching any technical difficulties.

A fortnight later I went to the music school: 'Sir, I've memorized the Rachmaninoff No. 2 first movement.' 'Nonsense, you couldn't have done!' McKie said. 'May I play it through to you?' I asked. 'All right. Play it now,' he replied.

I sat down and played. Mr McKie commented: 'It just shows what you can do when you try. I wish you could always give me that standard.' So the Rachmaninoff was put on ice, ready for the concert, which wasn't to take place for another six weeks. In the meantime I feverishly got on with my organ practice, to prepare for an organ scholarship, which was the next thing that I was going to have to do. Not only was McKie's time at Clifton coming to an end, but I was only going to outstay him by two terms, under the new Director of Music.

After four years at Clifton, with McKie at the musical helm, his recurrent bouts of sudden ill-health about two days before conducting an important school concert, with headmaster and parents present, suggested to both the music staff and the scholars that acute nervousness could be partly the cause. However, he always managed to be well enough for the concert itself, but looked very pale.

Before McKie's final concert at the end of Christmas term 1930 (he was returning to Melbourne), he was present at all the final rehearsals and appeared to enjoy them. The main work in the programme was to be the Rachmaninoff Second Piano Concerto (first movement), but for the other items the forces under his command included the choral society (buttressed by the buoyant spirits of the Canterbury Chestnuts) and an enthusiastic but accident-prone school orchestra, needing every lead to be given clearly by the conductor.

The final hazard (in the gallery at the extreme back of the huge hall) was the school, ready (on cue from McKie) to throw in its vast weight in, for instance, the chorus parts of Stanford's 'Sea Songs'. School singing, both in chapel and Big School, was a tradition at Clifton: all the stalwarts from the rugger field, the boxers, cricketers and oarsmen, as well as the more timid scholars, made a sound at once magnificent and melodious. 'Round the world if need be, and round the world again' echoed to the rafters. 'Captain' McKie was safe with his crew up astern.

The rehearsal for my performance of the Rachmaninoff had gone smoothly. At the concert itself, when the moment came I stepped down from my place in the choral society (behind the orchestra) and threaded my way to the Steinway concert grand. After I had given an 'A' for the orchestra to check their tuning, McKie waited for a complete silence from the hall, and we started.

I remembered my mother's phrase, 'Play with your whole heart and soul.' I did. What is more I never lost concentration for a second. Suddenly, at a syncopated passage before the big build-up to the dramatic crisis of the movement, I realized McKie had lost his place. He looked at me desperately for help. I quickly responded by playing the orchestra's part, which he picked up in a flash; and with the extra adrenalin available, the music surged forward to the great climax and we finished in fine style. The audience liked it and the gallery roared their approval. McKie whispered to me, 'Thank you for saving me. Play an encore.' I obliged with a Scarlatti sonata.

The next morning Douglas Fox, the incoming Director of Music, was with McKie in the music school. He said he had enjoyed the Rachmaninoff and would like me to play a concerto with him at the Easter term orchestral concert. César Franck's Symphonic Variations were agreed upon. I said a brief farewell to W.N.M. For the first time in four years he was visibly moved. 'You saved me last night; let us keep in touch. Maybe I can help. I will write to you from Melbourne.'

The two men walked away and I noticed for the first time that Douglas Fox had no right arm.

I said nothing of the somewhat bizarre meeting in the music school, when I got home. For one thing the family were still full of the Rachmaninoff, and were specially happy that McKie and I had parted friends. My mother had planned a concert celebration dinner for the following evening – just the family, but something rather extra special to eat and drink. I broke the news that a school friend, John Tilly, had invited me to drive over to Sandhurst where he had an interview at the Royal Military Academy, which, all being well, he was about to enter. (Most of my friends were tough, outdoor types; I avoided musicians because they always wanted to talk shop.) My mother said there was no problem. They would eat as usual at 8 p.m. because we couldn't ask Mrs Collins, the cook, to stay late. But what time could my mother expect us – 9.30 p.m.? 10 p.m.? She would personally ensure that nothing would be spoilt, or cold when it was meant to be hot, and vice versa.

John and I set off early for Sandhurst, going through the Savernake Forest and along a road with toll-gates, which I have never found since and suspect is now part of the M3. When we arrived at the gates of Sandhurst, we could see a full-dress parade in progress. I had only seen our own homespun OTC parades at Clifton and was stunned by the precision, the spit and polish, the rhythm in the marching, the ensemble. While John went off for his interview, I stayed just inside the gate, transfixed by this example of perfection, as deep in concentration as I had been during the performance of the Rachmaninoff two nights before. One day I was to learn that the top orchestras of the world had a similar sense of togetherness. At that moment music could not have been further from my thoughts.

We arrived back in Westbury-on-Trym at about 10 o'clock, ravenously hungry and having enjoyed our day (John's Sandhurst interview had gone well). To our delight my mother had kept her promise: to greet us was a bottle of champagne and then followed roast pheasant with all the etceteras, and Christmas pudding. The miracle of it all was that everything tasted completely fresh, as though it had just come out of the oven for the first time. Knowing my mother's extraordinary generosity of heart, I had a suspicion that she had suggested to the rest of the family that as I had done so well with my Rachmaninoff I was to have first priority with the food. In fact, we were probably having it for the first time – and they may have had bread and cheese. I felt it improper to ask; it seemed much nicer just to accept it all with joy and leave it at that.

The Sandhurst interlude had completely put out of my head the shock of my first meeting with Douglas Fox and the revulsion I felt at noticing the missing right arm. But I had not forgotten the Symphonic Variations by César Franck; the next morning I went to Bristol, to Duck, Son & Pinker's music shop – a name, by the way, I'd never recommend to stutterers and those prone to Spoonerisms, as it can land one in complications. The shop was usually crowded and busy, largely due, I think, to the enterprise and personality of the man behind behind the counter, Mr Denny. He was short, bespectacled, full of energy and a storehouse of gossip and general knowledge of all matters musical.

I did just mention Douglas Fox and Mr Denny said in a very quiet voice: 'Lost his right arm in 1917 in the war, but it's never talked about; when you next meet him at the beginning of term, offer your left hand. He will give you his left hand in return, and will know that you have been briefed. In a few days, if you get on well with him, he will probably make some light-hearted reference to it. In the meanwhile, count yourself lucky – he is a superb musician.'

I got onto the subject of César Franck's Symphonic Variations. He had got a copy of the piano part and an arrangement of the orchestral part for a second piano. I immediately bought both, as I thought it would be a very good idea to start learning it straight away. I asked if there was a recording of it and he said there was one by Cortot, which he would order for me and he should have it in soon after Christmas. As we had so many parties and dances and were going away for a few days anyway, this was a convenient arrangement, as I didn't think I would have had time to start listening to it before Christmas – and the records could have got broken.

Mr Denny loved talking and would find any excuse for a gossip. The mention of a name like Cortot would bring forth a crop of stories. He trotted out one on the spot, which I know to be true. When Cortot came to give a recital in Bristol he came into Duck, Son & Pinker's and asked for a piano to practise on, just before the concert. Mr Denny said he had a very fine instrument upstairs that he could use, but Cortot protested that he did not want a good piano – what he wanted was the worst piano in the shop! Mr Denny was amazed, until Cortot explained that why he wanted the worst piano now was because the good piano at Colston Hall would sound so much better later on. It was not difficult to find a really bad piano at Duck, Son & Pinker, so Mr Cortot was left on his own to do his best or his worst.

In my euphoric post-Rachmaninoff mood, it was perhaps wholly understandable to want to rush off and buy the Symphonic Variations and learn them as an unscheduled holiday task. After what Mr Denny had said about Douglas Fox's brilliance as a musician, nothing but good could come from my arriving at the first lesson next term with the Franck all polished and ready for the platform. Perhaps another work for solo piano and orchestra would be given me to learn as a reward. Such triumphal thoughts gave an extra zest to all the Christmas activities.

Soon the Christmas activities banished the triumphal thoughts – a typical Cooper mental somersault. I addressed myself with relish to the dozens of parties and would even do comic turns and my imitations (mostly of college masters) when required. The generation gap was much less in evidence in those days. Children (even up to and including the awkward age) were quite happy to mix with parents. My own mother's sense of fun and capacity for turning on the charm-act would defrost a refrigerated atmosphere in ten minutes or so. My father hated parties and stayed at home, snoozing (with dog and cat), waking now and then to pop a log on the fire. Even if we were out until 2 or 3 a.m. he was always fully dressed and never cross. He liked to see all safely in, then he locked up.

There was always the greatest excitement about the number of Christmas cards we used to receive. They were carefully counted when taking-down day arrived on 6 January. A batch covered the whole of the piano, with the lid right down (the music desk was not required as I knew all the standard carols and popular songs by ear).

On about 10 January 1931, there was a ring on the front-door bell. It was a parcel marked 'Fragile – with care'. In a box, most carefully wrapped up, was the precious Cortot recording of the Franck Variations. Amid all the frivolities I had forgotten not only about ordering the record, but also about practising the music itself. I put on the record, following the music at the same time. Cortot's playing was ravishing. So was the music.

Realizing I had about a week before term started, I began working feverishly. As soon as I could play the notes (after a fashion) I put on the record and tried to keep in time with Cortot. After several attempts there were signs of improvement, though I resigned myself to leaving the left-hand detail in one or two very difficult passages to Cortot. By repeating the process over and over again, I could give a sketchy account of the piano part by heart. The 'impossible' left-hand bits were carefully filleted by me, so that only a professional would know that some notes had been omitted and that I was 'cooking' (a term musicians use for such cheating).

Well, term started and when I went to have my first piano lesson with Mr Fox I didn't feel unduly guilty, because after all I was under no compulsion to learn the César Franck Variations: I did it really because I wanted to impress Fox. If he criticized it and pulled it to pieces, I wasn't going to mind very much; what interested me was to see what kind of a man he was and what he was prepared to say about how I had worked – above all, I wanted to see if he would be prepared to talk, because one of the slight problems I'd had with his predecessor was his reluctance to discuss or chat – but one would see.

Anyway the fateful lesson came and Fox asked me what I was going to play. When I said I'd already had a shot at learning by heart the Symphonic Variations he said, 'Good gracious, already, in the holidays! You industrious chap. Would you like to play them to me?' I gave him the copy and began. The first two or three pages are fairly easy and they went all right; then came the first really nasty part, where the left hand gets awkward, and of course I put in my bit of 'cooking'. Fox didn't say anything, although I was sure he must have noticed. Eventually one comes to a natural break in the music, where the piano stops and the orchestra takes over, so I paused and asked him if he had had enough. He said, 'You might as well go on to the very end.'

So I proceeded, playing rather worse than usual, because the last pages are technically demanding and my muscles were beginning to tire. I struggled on ingloriously to the finish, rather out of breath. But at least I hadn't broken down. Fox said, 'I don't think it's too bad to have learnt it by heart in the holidays.' Then he started to ask me questions about how I had studied it; I thought I had better not give away that I had learnt it from the record, because I did feel this was a form of cheating that I ought to keep to myself (I would certainly never recommend anyone else to do it). But I did say I'd left it very much to the last moment, having intended originally to spend the holidays working on it; but of course with all the Christmas parties I'd left myself barely a week.

Mr Fox was very interesting on the whole subject of practising and I think what he said to me then was so important that it helped me more than anything so far. It went something like this: 'When you get a new work you must think in terms of analysis; you must take the thing to pieces, play each hand separately, get sensible fingering, and only work in small sections which you can mark in the copy. But above all work at a very slow tempo. If necessary get the metronome out and, having set it to a slow speed, play a few bars actually with the metronome ticking. When you can stay with it, take it off again. Then you can try it again later. When you feel you've got the passage absolutely secure and you've got the right colour, the right sound, the right phrasing, the right kind of mood for the music and all the expression marks, every dot and dash, at the slow speed, then just notch the metronome up a fraction and see if you can take it a bit faster. If your mind starts to wander, take a break. Five minutes' good work is better than fifty minutes' bad.' The advice went on along those lines and Mr Fox finished up by saying, 'Take the Franck away, operate on it according to prescription, and bring it again in about three weeks' time.'

I felt very relieved; and I was sure his advice was going to prove to be very sensible and useful. He then changed the subject and reminded me that I soon had to sit for my Keble organ scholarship; he himself had been Organ Scholar at Keble College, Oxford, so he was the ideal man to coach me. In his opinion the Clifton organ was not ideal to practise on, because it had four manuals or keyboards, whereas Keble had three. But there were two church organs near with three manuals, where we could get permission for lessons and for me to practise.

The essential point was to get used to playing on a three-manual, so that I wouldn't get in a muddle on the day. He also pointed out that Keble College used plainsong, instead of the ordinary chants we usually sing in church. Plainsong, with its modal characteristics, was entirely new territory for me, but Fox knew it inside out and made it so interesting that I really enjoyed it. He chose for me to play on the organ Bach's 'Dorian' Toccata and Fugue in D minor (not the famous D minor). The same rules applied to organ practice as to piano, namely doing everything slowly and carefully. With regard to the pedalling, to look down at your feet was the hallmark of the amateur! I found that, inspired by Fox, I started very soon to play the organ much better than I dreamt I ever would, and the 'Dorian' Toccata and Fugue was progressing extremely well.

One day after the lesson at one of the churches, Fox said he had to go down into Bristol to buy some music from Duck, Son & Pinker, and asked if I would like to go with him. I accepted and asked if we were going by taxi, but he replied that he would be driving his car. I felt very uncertain about this, because I didn't see how he could drive with one arm, but he told me to jump in and we tore off, taking corners at hair-raising speed. I was terrified. We arrived at the shop, picked up the music and went back to the music school. I commented that he drove very fast, but he said he was very fond of driving and he hoped I wasn't nervous. 'Not a bit,' I said (I thought if there was ever a time to tell a white lie it was then). I heard afterwards that Fox diced with death every time he drove! But he had excellent road sense and a first-class safety record; however, many people hated going out with him.

Douglas Fox never ceased to surprise me. One day I came into the music school and could see him sitting at the grand piano in his room, facing me so I could not see his fingers; but I could hear, coming from the piano, the music of the César Franck symphony. The orchestra-like sound appeared to be covering the entire lower half of the keyboard, as if played by two hands. The synchronization was so extraordinary between the bass and the middle that I just didn't understand how he did it. Later on I happened to see him practising and watched how he would dive down with lightning speed and pick up a note in the left hand, then dive back again to a chord in the centre; like a conjuring trick really. He did it so quickly that the chord was almost together. He hardly ever played a wrong note; just occasionally a dive would misfire, but nine times out of ten he was accurate.

At home I explained what Fox had said about the César Franck Symphonic Variations and warned people in the house they might hear sounds of the metronome and some very slow playing going on for a bit, but I'd got to put the work right back to square one and start playing it accurately. This method actually started to produce results; in three weeks' time I took the reformed Symphonic Variations back to Fox and asked if I might play them through to him. So I went through them and waited for his comment at the end. I remember it exactly: 'My word, Cooper, you've done wonders to that.'

As the Keble organ scholarship approached I became more and more nervous; the Symphonic Variations were perfectly happy – they could by then take care of themselves with occasional stoking up; but the scholarship was getting rather too close for comfort and I wasn't sure whether my nerves would be steady because I was never as happy on the organ as I was on the piano. But I can only say again that, thanks to Mr Fox, when I actually left for Oxford I had a curious feeling that all might be well.

My examiner was John Dykes Bower (now 'Sir'), who was then Organist of New College, Oxford, and who later became Organist of St Paul's Cathedral. I played my 'Dorian' Toccata and Fugue, I did some improvising, I did sight-reading tests, transposition tests, and all the business I had expected on plainsong. Keble College organ loft, by the way, is very high up. I think it's the highest college chapel in Oxford and it rises to something like ninety feet. I've never liked heights very much, but on this occasion I was so intent on what I had to do that I wasn't unduly frightened by it. I gave of my best that afternoon. But was it good enough?

At Oxford I knew nothing at all about how I had done; the only thing I had been told was that the field of entries was musically the strongest they had had for years. Not a nice thing to be told.

I went back to Bristol and Westbury-on-Trym, and then a reaction set in. I stayed away from school for two or three days, feeling really rather ill; nothing seriously wrong, but a sort of nervous apprehension. The days ticked by and I felt I had better go back to school; my mother had a word with the housemaster and he said I should stay home if I wasn't right, as I wouldn't do any good work until I knew the result.

One morning I was looking through the paper – I always kept my eye on the results of scholarships. Looking down the list I came to Keble College, Oxford: Organ Scholarship awarded to J.E.N. Cooper (Clifton College). I read it, looked again, couldn't believe it!

I called out to my mother who was upstairs and asked her to come down quickly. 'Come and see this.' I pointed to it and she said, 'It's extraordinary, we've had no telegram; I wonder if there's some awful mistake.' We didn't feel too happy about it, in case it was a misprint, but about half an hour later the bell rang and there was the telegraph boy with a telegram. We tore open the envelope and it read 'SON AWARDED ORGAN SCHOLARSHIP KEBLE COLLEGE OXFORD'.

If my mother performed a dance of enthusiasm last time for the Clifton scholarship, I can't describe our feelings of joy this time. It isn't a question so much of the fact you are going to get some payment, it is the honour that a scholarship at Oxford carries and it is something that nobody can take away from you (except possibly the college if in some way you badly misbehave yourself).

The next day I went back to school and, having received congratulations from the headmaster and housemaster, I went across to the music school to see Douglas Fox, who in his quiet way expressed delight at my success. He asked me some questions about the examiner and if I liked the Keble organ, and I told him I did, but I didn't like the height of the organ loft; he said I'd soon get used to that. Then he changed the subject and said he thought I ought to have a spell of piano practice and he wanted me to play the A major K.488 Concerto by Mozart. He said it wouldn't be done at school, but with a small chamber orchestra at the Bristol Music Club.

I realized Douglas Fox was setting me a very big task: Mozart is one of my favourite composers, but I am not naturally a Mozart player. I lack the meticulous kind of fingerwork required for Mozart (Clifford Curzon is matchless as a Mozart player). However, I got the copy and worked at it until a few days before the big concert with the Symphonic Variations was due. There was never a dull moment. The Franck went very well. Fox conducting with his one arm could do prodigious things. His movements could be extremely wild sometimes. But he was really very inspiring and as he knew the music so deeply himself, he communicated almost by the force of his own mind when he failed with his stick.

Some of my friends complained that I went around looking awfully pleased with myself these days, but I said, 'Wouldn't you be – I've won a scholarship to Keble, I'm the first schoolboy pianist to have played at one of the professional orchestral concerts.' They said I'd better watch it: 'We don't want you conceited, we like our old Joe, no new smug Joe, thank you very much.' There was really no time to be smug, because I was faced with another dread and that was School Certificate. Most of the subjects I felt fairly confident about, but I had one appalling weakness and that was my mathematics; I had never been any good at them, and although I was taking extra tuition in maths, I felt sure that I would fail them and that meant that I wouldn't get my School Certificate. The arrangement used to be that as long as you got your School Certificate you didn't have to take the official entry exam into Oxford, which was known colloquially as 'Smalls' but called officially Responsions – it's since been abolished. If I failed School Certificate I'd have to sit for this other exam, which, although not a very extensive affair, was a nuisance and something else to be reckoned with. I didn't get my Certificate and I did have to sit for my Smalls, but fortunately I got through and so I was safely into Oxford with no more barriers in my way.

The final task (extracurricular) of the term was the performance of the Mozart A major Piano Concerto K.488 at the Bristol Music Club. Fox conducted a local chamber orchestra. I simply had not had time to give it the Fox 'prescription', and the concerto, not having been injected with this health-giving medicine, tended to suffer from rushes of blood to the head – specially the exciting finale.

Besides, I had had enough public exposure for a bit, and was more than ready for some holiday relaxation.

With only one more term to run – the summer term – I was starting to have regrets about leaving Clifton. For the first few weeks, however, I was living only for the present. I had been made a praeposter (prefect) and was in the sixth, the top form of the school. Much of the time in class was spent in reading aloud Greek plays – the various characters being allotted to different boys in rotation. You were encouraged to speak the words as if you meant them (of course you understood them or you would not have been in the sixth).

Curiously, a very young new master was put in charge of us, Mr Leslie Styler. He had had a brilliant academic career, with a double first at Oxford. But he did have some mannerisms which the rest of the class encouraged me to study. He also lacked any experience in how to cope with a class of boys – specially this class of boys, most of whom had come up through the various forms *en bloc* and knew in a flash which masters had developed defensive weapons for mickey-taking.

We saw at once that this Mr Styler was trusting that innate good manners would prevail, and if 'sabotage' started he would be helpless. For example we all (at an agreed time by the clock on the wall) sucked a bull's-eye. Then on a signal from me, everyone was to take a deep breath in, and exhale very slowly with mouths half open. 'Do I smell a bull's-eye?' said Styler. Silence from the class. Then I, who had 'palmed' my bull's-eye with my left hand, remarked, 'Now you come to mention it, sir, there is a strong smell of peppermint.' Mr Styler decided (wisely) to leave the matter and press on with the play reading.

The play was *Antigone* by the tragedian Sophocles. Antigone has been condemned to death by King Creon, but manages to kill herself first. I thought I would add dramatic emphasis to her final words by breaking into high falsetto. The rest of the class, taken by surprise, burst out laughing. The master himself, though I suspect secretly amused, called for order. Turning to me, he shouted: 'Cooper, I have had enough. Go and report to the headmaster.' I held my ground. So he ran to the door and gave the handle a violent pull; it promptly snapped off, leaving us prisoners in the classroom.

We were stranded on the top floor of the building, overlooking the zoo, some way from the main school. Mr Styler, highly embarrassed, forgot about me and said, 'How are we going to get out?' He accepted a bull's-eye and asked weakly for suggestions. I had had my own lucky escape, and left it to the rest of the class. Mass shouting from the window failed – it only caused the parrots to shriek and the lions to roar, which in turn started up endless other animal noises. Finally, four of the toughest boys decided, on a count of three, to hurl themselves against the door. It broke off at the hinges and crashed onto the floor outside the classroom. Applause all round; even the master was laughing. He gave us the rest of the morning off, and went to consult the school carpenter.

By the next morning the classroom was all 'ship-shape and Bristol fashion'. But tragedian Sophocles was dropped in favour of comedian Aristophanes, where the laughs are built into the story. We read *The Frogs*, which is a skit about tragedian Euripides and tragedian Aeschylus contending for the tragic prize among the dead. This time the Frogs' 'croak' was allotted to the entire class: 'Brekekekex koax koax' repeated several times seemed like an initiation ceremony for the young master. His apt, if ironical, choice of play, 'acted' with relish by the sixth, brought the whole form round to his side. Mr Styler was soon to be liked and respected; the next few weeks saw the sixth form working hard and enjoying it.

When McKie was at Clifton College, one or other of the scholars was usually in attendance in the organ loft during the services, but this was really as much to help the music scholar as to help McKie. By watching McKie in action and seeing how he prepared all the music in advance, how he managed to coax along a sluggish school, which it sometimes was, and generally to see his whole control of the musical side of the service from the organ loft, some distance away, was a lesson in itself. If you are preparing to become a cathedral organist you have to get used to being able to control a choir a long way away from you; in some cathedrals the distance is very great. Your only visual contact as a rule is a mirror, which you can adjust to get a good view of the choir and the clergy.

With Douglas Fox, the situation of course was different. He had to have help in the organ loft; with only one arm it was impossible to do all the things required of an organist. The Organ Scholar used to pull out stops, turn over pages and have the music ready for him.

When I wasn't actually on duty helping Fox, I used to invite myself into the organ loft as a spectator. There was plenty of space in the Clifton organ loft and one could watch without getting in anybody's way. I used to be amazed at Fox's dexterity and ingenuity. For one thing he had a very large hand with a long thumb, and he could play a trumpet tune by putting the trumpet stop on one manual and thumbing the tune, while playing the accompaniment with the other four fingers on the keyboard above. Just very occasionally an accident would happen and that fantastically mobile and usually accurate thumb would slip off a note. That would cause consternation below, because the trumpet is a piercing stop and everybody noticed. On such occasions I always stood up and peered over the organ loft, just in case anyone thought it was me playing. But this happened only very rarely and Fox's reliability with that one hand of his was quite out of this world. What he couldn't manage with his one hand he used somehow to transfer to his right foot and his pedalling was quite extraordinary to watch.

The time had now come for me to play a whole service at the organ. Before I had just supplied, say, a voluntary, or been allowed to play a hymn. In my last term I was literally given the freedom of the organ loft and told that I was in charge. Fox discreetly disappeared from the scene altogether; whether he was present downstairs I don't know. He never said anything and I had the organ loft to myself – or if I wanted, a junior scholar would always come and give me a hand. At first I did want company, because it was pretty nerve-racking having that large school below, and keeping up the remarkably high standard McKie and Fox had set in the college chapel. But later I went 'solo' to prove that I could.

One morning in about the fourth week of term I woke up feeling very unwell. I got up and went to school, but all day my head ached and I felt I had a temperature. As the weather was warm and sunny I couldn't think that I had 'flu and I didn't like making a fuss about health; but when I got home my cheeks were so flushed my mother asked if I'd been running. I confessed that I was feeling rather poorly, so my mother suggested I went to bed and supper would be brought up. In fact she herself brought my supper and noticed round the top of my chest some red spots – I had got measles. This was really a disaster, because I wanted to enjoy every minute of my last term at Clifton. It's a horrible disease; not only are you infectious, and therefore nobody can come and see you except people who are specially immunized by already having had measles, but the after effects are very unpleasant. I felt helplessly weak and really had no interest in life at all.

My mother decided that as soon as I was no longer infectious the best thing would be to take me to Weston-super-Mare (our nearest seaside resort), where the air was supposed to be full of ozone and frightfully good. She booked the two of us into a small hotel, making sure there was a piano; the big music competition was only a few weeks away and the hotly contested Kadoorie Cup was at stake. I was determined to win it.

The piece Fox had agreed I should learn was a very difficult one, *Jeux d'Eau* by Ravel. I had bought the copy, but had not had time to start learning the notes before I was struck down by measles. So, partly by learning it in my head and fingering it out on the table, and partly by playing it on the upright piano in the hotel lounge, I got the notes memorized. The hotel residents couldn't make head or tail of what I was doing, because I was faithfully obeying all Fox's rules about slow practice. I also kept the soft pedal on, to make it as innocuous as possible. When I'd spent a session working on the Ravel, I would then play a piece which would give pleasure all round, such as a Chopin polonaise or a waltz.

Within a few days I felt much better and after a week I had not only mastered *Jeux d'Eau*, but although a bit run down I was ready to come back and 'face the music' at Clifton. I played *Jeux d'Eau* through to Douglas Fox. He was delighted with it and had very little to say in criticism – just a point here and there, chiefly concerning the pedalling.

Fox said he would like me to play the organ for the last service but one, and that he would like me to trot out one of my best voluntaries, because then, with the Kadoorie Cup coming just a few days afterwards, the school would have a chance to hear me at my best on the organ, and on the piano. Fox had an uncanny way of noticing things (all his suffering had made him terribly sensitive and aware of other people) and whether he had noticed I was a bit depressed I don't know. But his suggestion acted like an immediate tonic. I started thinking what I would play for my organ voluntary and decided on the famous D minor Toccata and Fugue by J.S. Bach. This I played and it went well. A few days later came the music competition and I'm happy to say that I won the Kadoorie Cup. The adjudicator on this occasion was none other than Dr Beachcroft, who had been the examiner for my original music scholarship. He referred to this in his little speech, in which he said, 'I was here to welcome Cooper into Clifton, and I am very glad to be here now to give him all my best wishes for his career.' Dr Beachcroft then wrote some remarks on the report about me; he said *Jeux d'Eau* was very well played and he was delighted to see how much I had come on, but equally he knew, and I knew, how much there was still to do.

For the last service of all in July 1931, I was down in the chapel and I remember being completely overcome with feelings of grief that this was to be my last ever service as a schoolboy. Clifton chapel had come to mean a great deal to me. I found it very easy to believe in a benevolent God, who watched our affairs, and I had had the great privilege of hearing great organ playing from McKie and Douglas Fox, and had had an excellent musical grooming. None the less, the feeling that it was all coming to an end was more than I could stand, and I confess, with perhaps a touch of shame, I quietly wept my way through the entire service.

3

University Challenge

It was impossible for me to remain depressed for long about leaving Clifton, as there was all the excitement and anticipation of my going up to Keble in October and many arrangements had to be made.

We knew in advance that the rooms at Keble College were very sparsely furnished, so it was decided that a comfortable armchair was necessary; also a table or two, and some pictures to put on the walls. Most vital of all was a piano. Luckily we had an upright piano in a basement room at Denehurst. It was made by the local music firm, Duck, Son & Pinker, and was an extraordinarily good little instrument. It had a very nice tone and could stand up to the roughest of treatment (by pianists or removers).

Then there was the question of clothes – my mother didn't know if I had stopped growing; I was already about 5 feet 11 inches, and thin as a rake; so she decided to buy me only a few extra clothes and see if I expanded or stayed the same. People who are familiar with my rather ample figure nowadays might be amazed that I was so very thin when I left school, but there are some photographs in this book which testify to the truth of this statement!

The local remover, Mr Palmer, a friend of mine, took all the furniture, including the piano, to my room at Keble College just before term began. On my arrival at Keble my first job was to call at the Porters' Lodge, on the left just inside the main gate. There were three porters, and as I struck up an immediate friendship with them, which remained throughout my three years at Oxford, I feel I must include their names. They were known as Baker, the head porter, who was an army sergeant-major type; Jack, who often liked to break into a song and tap-dance routine; and Day, who was wizened and gentle. They were never known by any other names. All three had a sense of humour and responded to mine.

The Porters' Lodge also had the college telephone exchange in it and I don't think it would be an exaggeration to call the Lodge the nerve centre of the college. If the Warden or a don wanted to speak to one of the undergraduates, he would immediately contact the Porters' Lodge by telephone; the porters had a very simple way of getting hold of people – they would stand outside the Lodge facing the main quadrangle and would shout the name wanted. They didn't have to shout very loudly because the acoustics of the quadrangle were as clear as a Greek open-air theatre – as I was presently to discover when I started playing the piano in my room.

My mother, who had brought me up to Oxford in the car (a new car, the old Bullnose Morris had had its day), helped me put all my trunks onto the pavement and with the remark, 'Write to me and tell me all the things I've forgotten and I'll come back in a week or two's time,' quickly left, smiling as usual.

I went to find my scout and asked if he would give me a hand to get my trunks across to my room; he was immediately friendly. I enjoyed his company. He liked to gossip about old times, including the fact that when Douglas Fox had been an undergraduate he had been a scout then. He told me all about the buttery, which was rather the equivalent of the Clifton tuckshop; you could get almost anything you wanted, from personal items such as soap or toothpaste, to fattening things like buns and bars of chocolate. Mrs Butler ran the buttery, a charming lady with a very friendly smile, and everybody loved her. Then there was the lady who cleaned the steps and the landing outside the rooms in my particular block, who rejoiced in the name of Mrs Luckett. She loved undergraduates who joked with her and she didn't mind a bit if you made up limericks about her name.

So far I hadn't met any undergraduates or any dons, but I was soon summoned by my moral tutor, Mr W.H.V. Reade: he looked rather like a squat, slightly fatter edition of my father, but his cheeks suggested a great love of port. I sensed immediately that here was one of the college's real characters. He said rather drily: 'I'm your moral tutor, but I don't look after your morals. In any case I imagine you would understand that anybody coming to a place as spiritual as Keble would have to have impeccable morals.' I didn't fail to see a twinkle in his eyes, but in case I had taken him wrong he then quickly added: 'Now to be serious for a moment, I take a deep interest in music, not only the music of the college, but the music of the university as a whole. My sister, by the way, plays the viola and is always available to play in any orchestral concert you may have to organize, including the Keble Eights Week Concert, which is your most important function. You will be responsible for training the choir and conducting the concert on the night itself. If it's any interest to you, every year Leon Goossens comes up and plays the oboe for us – he's a personal friend of mine.' Billy Reade paused for a second or two and we were both quite relaxed. 'Have you met The Crab?' he asked. 'Crab, sir?' 'Yes, The Crab,' he repeated. 'No, sir.' 'You will, you will. That's all for now, my dear Cooper.'

I thought I had had about enough for one day, so I went to dinner in hall and then retired to bed. Next morning I was called by my scout, with a very hearty 'Wakey, wakey' – he had served in the Great War and this was the standard phrase. I asked him quickly about The Crab, because I wanted to be prepared. He told me The Crab and Billy Reade were both classical dons and The Crab lived on the floor below Billy Reade; they were not enemies, but certainly not friends, and they tended to have little verbal sparring matches which sounded rather ill-humoured. The Crab was also interested in the college music and university music as a whole – whether he knew more than Billy Reade I was never sure, but he did compose a little and used to write chants which the Organ Scholar was expected to perform.

I got up, dressed, and went immediately over to play the organ for my first service in chapel. I went up those well-remembered spiral stairs until I reached the high organ loft. The service proceeded without difficulty or incident. The plainsong went splendidly, so did my first voluntary.

After the service I came down from the organ loft, went out of the chapel and there was a figure, waiting, in an MA gown, through which I could see a suit which appeared to be covered in cigarette ash. I asked a friend: 'Who is that ramshackle figure?' 'That's The Crab,' he whispered. 'Look, he is beckoning you.' I went over and the figure said: 'I am A.S. Owen. I like to identify the voluntary each morning. The one I think you played this morning was 'Rhosymedre' by Vaughan Williams?' He was right. I was amazed as each morning The Crab seldom made a mistake. Only once did I get the better of The Crab and that was when I played a popular

1 ABOVE Joe feeding chickens at Westbury Court.

2 BELOW LEFT In pixie costume age six and a half, at Badminton.

3 BELOW RIGHT Joe, Bill and Mollie playing croquet at Westbury Court.

4 Uncle Charlie.

5 Having just left school – with Laddie at Brean Down, Somerset.

6 Joe and David Willcocks bracing themselves for the St Merryn visitors' concert.

7 Group at Harlyn Bay with Dorothy Sayers centre back.

8 Joe, Mollie, and Primrose and Lydia Yarde-Buller at Harlyn Bay.

9 Joe playing to the troops, 1939.

10 ABOVE LEFT The sound locator on Mendips searchlight site.

11 ABOVE RIGHT Joe and Jean's engagement photograph, Thatched House Lodge.

12 BELOW Bride and groom, 15 November 1947.

13 After the wedding: (*left to right*) Lady Greig, Joe's father and mother, and Sir Louis Greig.
14 Jean and Joe riding in Scotland.

15 Skiing at Lenzerheide.

16 Joe, Jean and André Navarra in Poona, 1953.

17 Wearing mock Indian headdress for a party.

18 Jean, with nephew Simon Cox on her lap, and Joe in June 1958.

tune called 'Today I feel so happy' in the style of a Bach fugue, which I improvised and then waited to see what he said. He beckoned me as usual and remarked: 'If I am not mistaken that was a very good example of early Bach'!

Incidentally, after you had been at Keble for a short while, especially if you were the Organ Scholar and got on well with The Crab, there would come a time when he would say 'Call me Crab' and you knew that you were 'in'.

Each morning after breakfast I went across to the Porters' Lodge to see if there was any post. One day Baker said, 'You've saved me having to shout for you – I've just had a call from the Warden. Will you go and see him immediately.' I looked apprehensive: 'Do you think it is anything serious?' 'Oh yes, I expect you're in trouble already.' But there was a smile on his face and I didn't think it would be anything to worry about. He showed me the way through the porch and sharp left, and told me to knock on the door when I arrived.

I went in, met the Warden – white-haired, tall, with gold-rimmed spectacles – and he told me that he urgently wanted to talk about the choir. Keble had an all-male choir, of course, all undergraduates; but several had gone down the previous term and we were rather short in numbers. The Warden arranged to put a notice on the Junior Common Room noticeboard, saying that anyone who would like to join the choir should come and see me and I would audition them. It seemed the Warden took a personal interest in the choir, because although he was not in the least musical himself, the names of the choir members were always in his handwriting. He gave me the list as it stood and said we could do with at least three more.

Luckily the volunteers were not slow in coming; I auditioned them and quickly found three excellent voices. I asked the choir if they would mind doing a little extra rehearsing, because I was new to them and they were new to me, but they were full of enthusiasm and I think we really enjoyed those choir practices.

I next had a message to call on the Bursar, which I promptly did: he was Colonel Milman, a regimental type with a crisp voice. 'I wanted two things – first of all to meet the new Organ Scholar, and secondly to tell you that my wife has a lot to do with the Keble Eights Week Concert and if you write her a letter she will arrange to meet you and will, I'm sure, be very useful to you and help you all she can.' I thanked him, called him 'sir', which he liked, and promptly went back to my room and wrote a letter to Mrs Milman. Here I made a rather bad mistake: I should have been formal in my wording. Unfortunately I wasn't and instead of saying, 'I would very much like to come along and have the benefit of your advice,' I said, 'I would very much like to come along and we could have a chin-wag.' Such an expression was not to be found in the *Concise Oxford Dictionary* of those days (although it is in all the dictionaries now). But it is, for all that, 'slang' and not the kind of thing to put in a letter to a stranger, even today.

I heard on the grapevine that Mrs Milman was not best pleased with my letter and she took a very long time to answer. When a reply eventually came it was in frigid terms, but she arranged to meet me. She soon thawed and could not have been more helpful. Mrs Milman had the addresses of all the members of the choral society (nothing to do with the Keble chapel choir), to whom she very kindly wrote and arranged a first rehearsal in a small room at Keble. Later on, in collecting the orchestra together, she was equally helpful.

We had to prepare well ahead for this concert, because although it wasn't until the summer term, it was really one of the biggest musical events of the university year (it has since been disbanded, I believe). The choral society were all amateurs and people who could only be available in the evening. I was left to choose, with Mrs Milman's help, the kind of things they were able to sing. I played for safety for my first concert and opted for three groups of madrigals or part-songs, which didn't require the orchestra. I felt that as the orchestra wouldn't gather until the actual morning of the concert, and as I had never conducted an orchestra before (or for that matter ever trained a choral society), I wanted to make it as easy as possible for myself. It turned out that I got on very well with the choral society and the weekly practice sessions were enormously successful from all sides.

At the end of my second term I was moved to what was the Organ Scholar's proper room; apparently it had been under repair when I first arrived. I was very relieved to be leaving my present room, because it was impossible to practise without being heard in every corner of the quadrangle. As I was shortly to give a recital in the

Holywell music room (where much university music-making took place) I decided I should put all my old pieces through the 'Douglas Fox' method of slow practising. You can imagine the insults poured upon my head: 'Oh, we didn't know we had a beginner in our midst,' and similar kindly remarks.

When I moved to the new quarters, not only did I find a room twice the size that could house two pianos, but also it was much more comfortable and more like a don's quarters. Above all, the room was almost soundproof; and being very near the chapel I could go straight there without having to go into the open air.

With a larger room, of course, more furniture was required: I hired an extra upright piano, because I thought it would be useful to have two pianos, and I borrowed some furniture from a friend in North Oxford. My sister very kindly came up with me, just before term started, as she had made me some nice curtains. I borrowed a step-ladder and Mollie was busy hanging the curtains, when who should appear at the door but The Crab. Incredulously The Crab gazed at Mollie for several seconds – then he looked at me and said, 'What is that?' 'That, Crab, is my sister Mollie,' I said 'Mollie, come down and meet Mr Owen.' My sister came down – she had been told about The Crab and what to expect – but I could see she was about to have hysterics, so I said I was sure she wanted to get on with the curtains while it was still light. I hadn't realized at the time that not only was it not customary to have a young lady in your room, it was positively discouraged. Keble was a monastic society. When I explained to The Crab that it was my sister, all was forgiven – but the look of total surprise on The Crab's face indicated he thought he had been going to catch me red-handed in a very immoral stituation!

Happily installed in my new scholar's room at Keble, attention now had to be confined very largely to the forthcoming Eights Week Concert. Plans were already well in hand; as mentioned earlier, the choral society's songs had all been planned and put into rehearsal, and we had received several suggestions from musical undergraduates and musical dons about the contents of the rest of the programme. One particular item and artist intrigued me; the work was the Grieg Piano Concerto and the artist suggested was Thomas Fielden. The name was familiar to me at the time; he was well known as a teacher and, apart from being a professor at the Royal

College of Music, he had written an interesting and rather controversial book on piano technique.

Fielden was a powerful and imposing figure. He rather gave one the impression – and I don't mean this unkindly – that the other piano pundits, such as Tobias Matthay, had really got their facts slightly wrong and Fielden had been sent by God to put Matthay and everybody else right. The fact that he was not a celebrity as a performer did not matter, because the Keble College Eights Week Concert was always a sell-out in advance, quite regardless of the artists and the programme. My only consideration was whether I, who had never conducted before, would be up to conducting Thomas Fielden. I liked him, I admired him; in addition he had a boisterous sense of humour; but I felt slightly intimidated by the way he spoke so disparagingly of other teachers. I just wondered how on earth he would treat me – a greenhorn if ever there was one.

Feeling a sense of panic at never having conducted before, I decided to consult one of the nicest and kindest people in all Oxford, Reginald Jacques, who was at the time the conductor of the Oxford Orchestral Society and a fellow of Queen's College, Oxford – a very distinguished musician and a man that one could always go up to and talk to and have no fear of being snubbed.

I went and called on Dr Jacques at his rooms, said I had a problem, and with his usual engaging manner he asked what it was. I told him all about the concert and he asked what I wanted of him. 'Dr Jacques, I would like two lessons, for which I am more than prepared to pay, in which you could just show me the elements of conducting.' He laughed heartily at the idea of two lessons for somebody who had never conducted before, but I pleaded with him. 'If you could just show me how to start an orchestra and how to stop an orchestra, that would be something.' 'All right,' he said, 'I'll give you a lesson now.'

Handing me a baton, he went to the piano: 'Here we are, here's the opening of the Grieg Piano Concerto, you're the conductor, I am the drummer and you are going to bring me in. Bring me in.' I produced a downbeat; dead silence from Dr Jacques. He laughed. 'It's no good just giving a downbeat – there must be some "upness" before your downbeat, otherwise the downbeat reaches the drummer at the back of the orchestra too late.' The baton – or stick as it is usually called – must go up first before it comes down; and that is how you start.

'As far as stopping is concerned, as long as you know where you are and don't actually lose your place, there should be no problem about the end; you can adopt what method you like if it is a long chord.' He gave me demonstrations of various ways, but said that usually the movement to stop a great chord comes instinctively.

Dr Jacques gave me all sorts of other hints and tips and showed me how to hold the stick, which he regarded as extremely vital. He told me to come back in a week's time and have another lesson; he absolutely refused any form of payment, saying, 'It is a pleasure to help a young colleague and I wish you all success.'

I went straight back to Keble and started working on all the exercises Dr Jacques had given me. I bought a record of the Grieg Concerto and did a mock conducting right through, several times, so that by the time I went for my second lesson with Dr Jacques I felt that I could conduct the Grieg Concerto in my sleep. He was amused when I told him this and said I had forgotten one thing: 'You've been listening to one particular pianist on the record – probably very good, but you don't know what Thomas Fielden is going to do. He may play entirely differently; he may make sudden changes in speeds and his overall *tempi* for each movement could easily differ from that record.' I was immediately frightened by the thought there could be another interpretation, because I felt that this record (which was about the only one available) must be standard.

However, I took Dr Jacques's advice and felt I had learnt enough to give me at least hope that I wouldn't break down and that I would justify my position as conductor of the Keble Eights Week Concert.

On the morning of the concert itself, the carpenters (disregarding late breakfasters) had moved in and were busily putting up the stage. A little later the Steinway concert grand piano arrived and a very imposing conductor's rostrum. I had only an hour-and-a-half to get together my scores and make sure that all our guests had arrived. Above all, I was very anxious to meet Leon Goossens, who had long been a hero of mine, both in the concert hall and on gramophone records; but according to my stalwarts at the Porters' Lodge neither he nor Thomas Fielden was available at that moment.

My mother and sister were coming up from Westbury-on-Trym,

and my Aunt Kathleen and cousins Doris and John were coming from Bournemouth. I had impressed on them all the importance of 'dressing up to the nines'; I had told them it was the greatest day in my year and I wanted to be proud of them. I asked them to be at the Porters' Lodge at 10 o'clock and I would meet them and show them to my rooms before I had to go and rehearse.

Both families arrived punctually at 10 o'clock and I was delighted with the sight of them: the ladies looked rather like a mobile herbaceous border, with all kinds of colours, and hats of all sizes and descriptions. I rather wanted to impress the college with my relations and had put the word round that they were arriving.

I think my cousin Doris stole the show, with an enormous hat festooned with osprey feathers. We strode across the quadrangle towards my room and undergraduates came out from all corners; but I couldn't understand why there was a crescendo of laughter as we walked forward. In fact the laughter became so loud that I thought something must be wrong; I dropped back a step or two, so that I could view the procession from behind – 'behind' was the operative word! Something had gone wrong with Doris's attire. I rushed to my sister and whispered to her to drop back and report what she thought and she whispered telegramatically: 'Dress stuck in knickers.'

This is in fact what had happened, and what was revealed to the quadrangle, from the back view, was a pair of voluminous blue silk knickers and no skirt! But I was sorry for my cousin Doris, because I knew she had spent a great deal of time and money to please me. Instinctively I thought we must get to the shelter of my room before I told her. She was naturally very upset when told, but explained through her tears that the loo on the train was just not large enough for her to make all the necessary adjustments, and her hat – a source of much trouble and irritation during the day, although admired by many – made it almost impossible for her to move in the confined space of the train's cubicle.

The pacification of Doris had taken rather a long time. I suddenly looked at my watch and realized I was very nearly late for my orchestral rehearsal, so I picked up my scores and my baton and sped for the hall. On arrival I found the orchestra seated, but that was quite in order because a conductor always expects to find the orchestra ready for him.

Simulating great confidence (which I had been told by Dr Jacques was very important, however I felt!) I mounted the rostrum and started off with a Beethoven overture. I got through it creditably.

Next the piano was moved into position and Thomas Fielden appeared. We started on the Grieg: he did play it very well, there was no question about that, but his *tempi* were quite different from those I had expected.

By this time I had located Leon Goossens and had exchanged smiles with him – he was obviously prepared to be on my side. I couldn't help noticing, by the way, quite a number of inaccuracies from Fielden in his performance of the Grieg. But I thought, after all he is a professor of the piano and probably teaches far more than he actually practises and hasn't time to put the fine edge of perfection on this very difficult piano part. I equally thought that he might not have been bothering too much because this was just the rehearsal – perhaps he was saving his best for the evening.

We ran through the choir numbers, just to test the balance in the hall, and they were in first-rate condition; I was more than happy with them. I knew that they had been thoroughly rehearsed.

After we had finished the morning's work, I lost no time in going to speak to Mr Goossens. We got on extremely well. When I told him that I was nervous about the evening because I had never conducted before, he said he might be able to be of use to me and should there be any difficulty anywhere I should keep an eye on him and he might be able to steer me back into the currents of law and order. I thanked him for this very generous suggestion and I knew exactly what he meant.

Happily when the concert came all went well – nearly all! There was one awkward moment in the last movement of the Grieg. I think perhaps I had been a little bit too pleased with myself because it had gone so well, but suddenly I felt that things were not as they should be and I was in danger of being 'out' with the orchestra. I looked across desperately to Mr Goossens. By a series of wagglings of the oboe up and down, somehow he got the orchestra back safely under my beat, and I don't honestly think the few bars' untidiness was noticed by most of the audience. Just for the record, during the actual concert, Mr Fielden added considerably to his earlier score of wrong notes.

One of my family had had the kindness and presence of mind

to bring me a bottle of whisky, and my scout produced a syphon of soda water and some glasses. At the reception following the concert I went to thank Leon Goossens and asked if he would care to come and have a nightcap in my room.

We went over, and as soon as he saw the two pianos Leon Goossens sat down at one and started to play one of the latest dance numbers of the day. I joined him at the other piano and for over half an hour we played our own kind of jazz, which was not really jazz at all, but a passable imitation of it. I was surprised that Leon Goossens, apart from being an outstandingly brilliant oboist, was such a good pianist. It was so delightful to find a musician of Leon Goossens's eminence in the classical world sitting down and enjoying dance music and revelling in it. It made me feel less guilty about my passion for lighter forms of music.

In addition to playing all the popular dance tunes of the day I occasionally composed one or two myself, making up rather awful words. One of these was 'Sleepy' – about which there is a story. I was taking part in one of the OUDS 'Smokers'. We had a very strong line-up that particular term: Angus Wilson, Terence Rattigan, Paul Dehn and Ronnie Waldman. My contribution was to play one or two dance tunes at the piano, and then play and sing, in my dreadful voice, 'Sleepy'.

We were having a run-through in the morning and I was just in the middle of 'Sleepy'; the stage hadn't been lit, the front curtains were down, so I was more or less in the dark. Suddenly Paul Dehn came up to me: 'Stop playing a minute, I've got something to tell you. You'll never believe this, but in the front row at this moment are Fay Compton and Ivor Novello. Fay Compton is in a new play of Novello's at the theatre across the road and they've popped in to our rehearsal. Now do you dare go on?' 'Not me!' I said, and I stopped immediately and shut the piano lid.

But then I had a message that Miss Compton wanted to see me; so, rather frightened, I went up to this most lovely lady. 'Was that you singing?' she asked. 'Well, croaking,' I replied. 'It doesn't matter about that,' she said, 'it was a very pretty song. I am looking for a song to put in a new play called *Indoor Fireworks* at the Aldwych Theatre, London. Do you think I can have that song? I like it?' I was absolutely astounded: 'Yes, of course, I would be very honoured, but I don't think it is even written down.' Fay Compton replied, 'You would not only have to write it down, but it would have to be published; you might even make a little money on the royalties of the sheet music.'

So the song was duly written down, published, and Fay Compton sang it in London. I was at the first performance and I was thrilled when she got to 'Sleepy'. Not only was she a very accomplished actress, but she had a very charming singing voice. I went round to see her afterwards and she said, 'I hope I did you justice.' I didn't know what to say, but I felt terribly honoured.

Not long after that, the sheet music of 'Sleepy' by 'Joe Cooper' (not Joseph Cooper), with a glorious picture of Fay Compton on the cover, was available at both Acotts and Taphouses, the two music shops in Oxford, who displayed them prominently in the window. Nobody in the academic world seemed to be at all disturbed by my little foray into the light world of music, or if they did feel anything, no complaints ever reached me.

I was asked to compose another song for Fay Compton, which was to go into a film, and I produced a song called 'Wandering to Paradise', but I couldn't manage the words, so I asked Paul Dehn if he would do them; so this was a collaborative affair, music by Joe Cooper, words by Paul Dehn. I went down to the studios with Fay Compton, whom I had got to know quite well by then, and listened to her singing the song. But when we finally saw the film the song was absolutely butchered – only a few lines were left in it. We were all rather disappointed.

In the meanwhile we had our annual visit to Cornwall for the family holiday. A year or two earlier we had found a new bit of the North Coast of Cornwall – Harlyn Bay, with a spacious guest house called Tresillian run by two energetic ladies – Mrs Thelwell and her daughter (not related to *the* Thelwell, although the mother looked like one of his cartoons). The food, acceptable in all respects, was notable for a home-made Aberdeen sausage of unmatched succulence. The vocal exchanges between mother and daughter emanating from the kitchen during the sausage's manufacture suggested that no effort had been spared to perfect its appearance and taste.

We stayed at Tresillian during two summers, but began to tire of the necessary regulations about meal times. We longed for a small bungalow, hut or caravan that would belong to us. It wasn't very long before two adjacent bungalows were on the market, both remarkably cheap. My brother bought one and my father bought the other. There was a well at the bottom of the garden (on neutral ground) which supplied both houses with water. If you forgot to turn a little switch, you might fill the wrong tank, causing screams of mirth from all except the exhausted pumper (it *was* hard work and ladies were exempt unless they insisted).

The bungalows lay in an ideal position at the end of a quiet cul-de-sac. Sloping gardens at the back of the house led to a shared path (near the well) that took you down to the sea. Ours was made enturely of wood and called, appropriately, The Cabin. My brother's, a more solid structure in stone, was called The Haven – entirely appropriate retrospectively, as he and his wife have used it as a veritable haven from the hurly-burly of city life for over forty years.

My brother used to lend The Haven to friends when he couldn't get down himself. Among a bevy of interesting visitors, my favourite was Dorothy Sayers, who came twice with Muriel St Clare Byrne, with whom she collaborated on *Busman's Honeymoon*, a play which they had just finished on their first visit. I had read *Murder Must Advertise*, *The Nine Tailors* and *Hangman's Holiday* and was a complete fan. We started an over-the-fence friendship and when I spotted the Sayers bubbly, eccentric sense of humour, I volunteered, 'I hope Lord Peter doesn't find the pump too heavy.' Her reply was instantaneous: 'He does, he does; come and have a drink and discuss it.' It turned out that Lord Peter Wimsey was very much part of her life. The dictionary describes 'whim' as 'a fantastic creation of brain or hand'. Lord Peter was just that. Which is why he lives so vividly when she commits him to paper.

Apart from the owners of the few bungalows, the regular summer holiday visitors consisted of a few delightful families who set up camp (widely spaced) in two privately owned fields. The owner's fear that the temporary population might increase into invasion proportions, as camping and caravanning was catching on, made him a martinet about any new arrivals, who were promptly turned away (the present incumbents were friends). There were no class distinctions, and no age distinctions: just one strict regulation – you left your camp-site as clean and litter-free at the end of the holiday as you found it on arrival.

Harlyn Bay has one of the most glorious beaches in England – or probably anywhere – nearly a mile of flat golden sand, and days when large rolling breakers would give you magnificent surfing. A regular visitor was Dr Harold Darke, the famous organist from St Michael's Cornhill (I could never make out whether he was wearing very long shorts or very short longs!). Another visitor was the then unknown Clifton music scholar David Willcocks, who found Harlyn more restful than his native Newquay twelve miles down the coast. Who would have guessed that David (a pupil also of Fox at Clifton) would one day become Sir David Willcocks, Director of the Royal College of Music and top of the English musical tree.

Nearby St Merryn had a visitors' concert every year, organized by the dauntless district nurse. David Willcocks and I were both roped in for it one year. The piano was worse than anything Cortot could ever have dreamed of, but the concert was wildly popular. This was largely because of the enthusiasm of the amateur performers, who never minded being prompted by the audience if they broke down. One hardy annual always recited John Masefield's poem 'Sea Fever': 'I must go down to the sea again.' The 'again' was drowned by a chorus of spectators screaming 'seas – seas – seas'. 'Seize what?' stammered the performer. She then stumbled her way to the end, forgetting lines and having them corrected. Next year there she was again, and unconsciously became the star – the whole of Harlyn Beach came to hear. And she always, wrongly, kept her sea singular!

Back at Oxford, on one occasion I was asked if I would help the great Dr Albert Schweitzer, who was coming to give an organ recital at New College, Oxford. He needed two people to help him with the stops; his wife would take care of the right-hand side and I was asked to take care of the left-hand side. John Dykes Bower was the Organist of New College at that time. As a matter of fact he was to leave shortly, but I was delighted to have a chance of meeting the man who had given me my Keble scholarship and who was soon to become Organist of St Paul's Cathedral.

Anyway, Dr Schweitzer explained to us that everything marked in red in the copy was to do with the stops on my side of the organ, while everything marked in blue was Mrs Schweitzer's responsibility. We had to wait for the German word *jetzt* (pronounced 'yetzt' and meaning 'now'). As he said the word, either Mrs Schweitzer or I, according to the colour on the copy, had to pull the necessary stops out. It was a fascinating exercise, but demanded very great attention and very clear eyes.

Mrs Schweitzer had some difficulty and unfortunately she made a mistake at the rehearsal and mistook the colour. Dr Schweitzer lost his temper and ordered her out of the organ loft; she went, weeping. Fortunately Miss Margaret Deneke, who was one of the great musical pillars of North Oxford, was on hand. A great friend of the Schweitzers and a natural diplomat, she calmed Mrs Schweitzer down, talked to them both for some moments and persuaded Dr Schweitzer to forgive and forget. Then the rehearsal went on.

A few minutes later, Dr Schweitzer, now all smiles, asked John Dykes Bower if he would be kind enough to play part of one of the fugues that Schweitzer had been playing, while he went down to the body of the chapel and listened to the effect. Dykes Bower, who was a most accomplished organist, said of course he would; but one problem arose and that was that Schweitzer played everything half as slowly as any other organist. Dykes Bower felt that he must imitate Schweitzer's speed, otherwise there might be ructions – and yet suddenly to play something half speed when you are used to playing it at your own *tempo* is very difficult. I give John Dykes Bower full marks for reducing the speed and yet playing accurately and convincingly – the only thing was, it was so much better than Dr Schweitzer's own playing, but nobody commented on that.

Miss Margaret Deneke, by the way, was a very versatile lady: it is said she once gave a double lecture to the Women's Institute – the first part was called 'Brahms, man and composer' and the second was a demonstration on how to skin a rabbit.

Another famous Oxford hostess, and I think a friendly rival to Miss Deneke, was Mrs Maitland who lived up Headington Hill, a long way from North Oxford. On one occasion the Organ Scholars and various musical luminaries of the university were invited to a recital to take place at the Maitlands' house (Mr Maitland was librarian of the Holywell Music Room) to hear a new young pianist from France, Vlado Perlemuter. The crowd assembled in the large drawing-room and waited expectantly for Perlemuter to appear. During the pause before he arrived, an elderly spaniel walked in and, without any apology or delay, made a most unfortunate solo performance under the piano. None of us knew what to do or say and in the end we decided to let the matter rest. Mrs Maitland was quite unaware of what was going on inside and finally announced Vlado Perlemuter. Just as he was going to sit down at the piano she said, 'I'm awfully sorry, but there is a very funny smell in here.' Someone pointed to the source of the trouble. Mrs Maitland gasped and called for her husband.

One of the main difficulties was trying to explain to Vlado Perlemuter, who then spoke hardly any English at all, the crisis that had taken place. In halting French Mrs Maitland explained how the dog had, '*fait quelque chose méchante*' under the piano and we would all have to '*quitter la chambre*' while she cleaned up. Fortunately it was a nice afternoon and Mr Maitland volunteered to take us round his very lovely garden to occupy the time. The majority of us were most amused about the whole astonishing situation. Perlemuter wasn't in the least upset by the delay or the reason for it (after all, *merde* means 'Good luck' in French!). When we eventually returned he didn't seem to object to the strong smell of disinfectant coming from under the piano. He gave us a glorious hour of piano playing.

Vlado Perlemuter, who was then about twenty-eight, made a very deep impression on me and revived my longings to improve my piano playing. I went straight back to Keble and practised for about three hours on end.

This was in 1932. I had been at Oxford a year and already my cool relationship with the organ was beginning to turn rather towards hate. I couldn't express myself on the organ like I could on the piano. The total lack of interest in the piano at Oxford helped me in making an important decision and that was to have a few lessons in London with a good piano teacher and take my ARCM the following year. I chose Arthur Alexander (then a well-known professor at the Royal College of Music) and I am happy to say I did get my ARCM. I have still got the certificate, signed by the president of the RCM at that time – none other than Edward Prince of Wales (hero of my school years at Clifton).

I was very pleased to have got through and I wrote down 'Joseph Cooper, ARCM' – I thought whatever degrees I get or don't get, I've got that! It was for solo piano, I was told that I got a very high mark, and Arthur Alexander himself was quite pleased with me – he was not a man for bestowing praise lightly, so I took that as a great compliment.

In the same year I gave a joint recital at Watford with Elsie Suddaby, a well-known soprano of the time. I accompanied her and played two groups of solos. Apart from the very enthusiastic press, the public – and it was a rather discerning audience used to the finest string quartets and highly serious in its approach to music – applauded warmly.

I also gave the first performance of *The Rio Grande* by Constant Lambert in Oxford, a work for choir, orchestra, and alto solo, and with a very brilliant solo piano part. The conductor was Trevor Harvey, Organ Scholar of Brasenose College, Oxford. Douglas Fox invited me back to play the same work at one of the Clifton orchestral concerts and I remember the difficulty the orchestra had playing the initial rumba rhythm before the piano comes in. Mr Smith (my old harmony teacher) played the viola in the orchestra; he said to me afterwards, 'We simply can't manage these new-fangled rhythms.' At the time, of course, *The Rio Grande* did cause quite a sensation: it is now a period piece, but one still finds it very engaging to hear now and again. It certainly caused a mild stir among the academic circles of Brahms-sodden Oxford.

The weekly concerts given in the Holywell Music Room by professionals were very popular. Organ Scholars took turns at being secretary of the Oxford University Music Club, which sponsored the concerts. The secretary used to go to Ibbs & Tillett in Wigmore Street, London, W1, to select artists for the following term. When my turn came to be secretary, I remember Miss Bass, whose office was a disused conservatory at the top of the first flight of stairs. She greeted me with a really friendly smile, and was so helpful over the choice of soloists. She eventually became Mrs Emmie Tillett, the Managing Director of Ibbs & Tillett, in those days very much the leading concert agents.

So far I haven't mentioned the subjects of harmony and counterpoint, the theoretical side of music which had already given me trouble some years before. Briefly, harmony is the art of 'clothing' a melody – compare playing 'God Save the Queen' with one finger, and then with nice rich chords or harmonies. Counterpoint is the art of combining melodies, rather like several voices having a musical conversation. When you first study counterpoint you have to learn, and stick to, laid-down rules that date from the 16th century.

My difficulty with counterpoint persisted, but somehow the kindness of my tutor, Dr Ernest Walker, was such that I could get away with fairly incompetent and even ill-prepared work. Dr Walker was a great character; he had a long beard, a very high-pitched voice and an extremely loud laugh. I managed to develop a very satisfactory imitation of Dr Walker and would spend most of my tutorials watching for detail and trying to make him laugh, so that I could achieve perfection! He was a great cat-lover and two very well-fed Persian, or Persian-style, cats had the freedom of the music room; this was to me, also a great cat-lover, one of the most enjoyable features of my visits and used to compensate for the monotony of the counterpoint.

The situation was to change with the arrival at Oxford of Dr Thomas Armstrong. He came from Exeter Cathedral to take over at Christ Church, Oxford, from Dr Harris who had been appointed Organist at St George's Chapel, Windsor. Dr Armstrong had been briefed to take on the counterpoint side of my paperwork, although I still continued to go to Dr Walker for harmony. I think word had got round that my counterpoint was weak and needed some fresh stimulus if I was to have any hope of getting through my final exam (I was safely through the first part). I had met Dr Armstrong once before, when I had visited Exeter and had been given a letter of introduction to him by his old friend, Douglas Fox. I liked him very much and on that occasion he asked me to improvise on the organ; when I asked him to pay me the compliment back, I always remember how beautifully he improvised.

I knew my counterpoint wasn't good enough, and after a few lessons Dr Armstrong told me quite bluntly he thought the trouble was I just wasn't putting my back into it. He got out a score of *Messiah*, pointed to one or two of the fugues of Handel and told me that was the sort of mastery he wanted to see. 'Unless you cleanse your style and purify it by mastering the strict rules of sixteenth-century counterpoint *à la* Palestrina, you haven't a hope of reaching any such standard as Handel!'

However, the strict textbook rules to achieve the pure style of Palestrina seemed to me more akin to solving an acrostic, or a crossword puzzle, than music. Three other illustrious names of the past, gentlemen who rejoiced in the names of Schütz, Schein and Scheidt, were favourites of Sir Hugh Allen, who was Professor of Music at Oxford as well as Director of the Royal College of Music. They were seventeenth-century composers – links between the sixteenth-century composer Palestrina and the eighteenth-century composers Bach and Handel. We were able to appreciate their music to a certain extent by trying to sing it and trying to play it on the piano.

Now, forty years later, these three composers have all come into their own and are well represented in the classical gramophone catalogue, especially Schütz, who has become very popular. This is, of course, all part of a return to the early centuries in musical tastes and a veering away from the Romantics.

If only just occasionally Sir Hugh had rung the changes – if only he had said one week we were going to study a work by Schoenberg, I think we would have found the contrast enormously invigorating. But Sir Hugh Allen could no more have appreciated the subtleties of Schoenberg than I could understand the subtleties of Schütz, Schein and Scheidt.

So, at loggerheads with the establishment, I quietly went my own way. I studied the Beethoven Fourth Piano Concerto and played it at one of the Saturday evening concerts in Holywell Music Room with the Oxford Chamber Orchestra, and generally followed where my tastes took me. For example, I developed an infatuation for Elgar, and wondered why his name was never mentioned by any don or by the professor himself. I fell in love with the First Symphony, the *Enigma Variations* and then I studied the Violin Concerto and had a nodding acquaintance with the Cello Concerto.

In February 1934 the OUDS were going to perform Marlowe's *Dr Faustus* and I was asked to help prepare the music. It was really a question of choosing suitable background music to be played on the organ behind the stage, at Oxford town hall where the performances were to take place. We decided to use the variation 'Nimrod' from the *Enigma Variations* to mark the arrival of Helen of Troy, and I played the opening phrase under the words 'Was this the face that launched a thousand ships, and burnt the topless towers of Ilium?' The effect was magical and it was said that the audience wept audibly.

One night, on my way to the town hall I read on a placard just two words, 'ELGAR DEAD'. It absolutely pierced my heart.

At our next merry Saturday morning meeting with Sir Hugh Allen, to our great surprise he said, 'Elgar has just died, so we might as well spend part of the period discussing his music.' He got out the symphonies and *The Dream of Gerontius* and said, 'As you know, my firm belief is that if a piece of music sounds well played as a piano duet it's a good piece.'

Two of us started playing a little bit of the Second Symphony; Allen stopped us after a short while and said, 'It doesn't sound right,' and then proceeded to demolish Elgar – not bitterly, but firmly enough for us to realize that Sir Hugh Allen was a man of very strong views. Oxford's music was clearly in a strait-jacket.

At that time, of course, I was in no position to criticize anything or anybody; in a few weeks my examination for part two of my B.Mus. was coming up and that was the only thing that mattered. If I didn't get through complications were going to arise after I had left university.

The melancholy fact is that my three-year stint at Oxford came to an end ingloriously – minus the second B.Mus. But at least I was safely through the non-musical subjects for the BA.

4
Customers and Benefactors

I wasn't too down-hearted at not getting my second B.Mus. because I could always go back to Oxford for a short time, study the subject afresh and take the examination again. This couldn't happen at once because I had no money, so somehow or other I had to get a job, even on a short-term basis.

While I was at Oxford I had come across a lot of very interesting people, some of whom had money. Several rich and musical undergraduates invited me to stay during vacations, when I met the rest of the family, which sometimes included musical sisters. Due partly to my flair for playing almost anything to order, I soon found myself being asked to help the girls with their own piano playing. From there it was only another step to their mothers asking me to give the girls professional lessons. So I hired a room at the Wigmore Hall Studios where I started to teach. The weakness in all studios, of course, is that you are surrounded by other people teaching or practising; also, the atmosphere is singularly cold and uncosy.

As some of my lady pupils were breathtakingly pretty I could see that more comfortable surroundings would give the lessons more enjoyment for all of us. Obviously I needed somewhere to live: the West End was clearly out of the question, because even in those days it was very expensive. But I did have some friends in Blackheath who helped me find a very comfortable abode. Two elderly ladies, the Misses Hainworth, Jessie and Lily, had a big Victorian house and were willing to take a paying guest. They let me have a large room which could easily house a grand piano, a bed and a ping-pong table. The rent asked was only very small, with all food found and laundry done. Very soon I was almost like a nephew to them and I formed a deep affection for them.

I needed a good small grand piano – preferably a Steinway. In those days it was possible to find second-hand reconditioned pianos at very reasonable prices. I found just what I wanted in Steinway's showrooms. By explaining to Frank Usher, the chief salesman, that my pupils were mostly daughters of the rich, to whom I would stress that a Steinway was the only piano to have, I managed to persuade him to knock some more off what was already a bargain price, due to the particular instrument's case-work being slightly worn. I had just enough in my bank account to buy it, and I proudly produced a cheque book and bought the piano there and then. Mr Usher said I could expect delivery in a few days and there would be a small extra charge for this, for which he would send an account later.

In addition I arranged with my friend Mr Palmer to collect my upright piano and other furniture from Oxford and bring it to Blackheath next time he had a load for London. Within ten days I had the Steinway and the Oxford upright safely installed in my room.

I invited a brilliant young pianist, Joan Carr, who had recently married Lord Moore and whom I'd met at a party, to come to tea. We played through several works for two pianos to 'christen' them in their new setting.

The pupils flocked down to Blackheath. They loved the visit and the two 'aunts' (as I soon called them) were thrilled to see all these delightful young people, to whom they gave a very good tea. I always made a point that I wouldn't take anybody just because they were rich: they had to be promising and have some talent. Two of my most gifted pupils were twins: they were famous in their time, the Paget twins, Mamaine and Celia. They were exactly alike. I couldn't tell one from the other – in fact I used to call one the Chopin Ballade and the other the Bach Fugue, because those were the pieces they were playing when they first came to me. Gradually as time wore on I got to know them apart, but they could imitate each other and trick you, so you were never absolutely certain! Mamaine afterwards married Arthur Koestler, with whom I have kept in touch by correspondence, although she died many years ago. Celia, with whom I keep in sporadic contact to this day, lives in Cambridge and keeps up her music, but purely for her own enjoyment.

In spite of various attempts on the part of my early mentors (both secular and religious) to persuade me to the contrary, I have always preferred the company of the opposite sex. However, a full and complete relationship, although longed for, had yet to be realized. One of the reasons was that my parents (in common with many of their generation) inherited from their parents a fear of sex as formidable as their fear of death. So that when I found myself alone with some of the most beautiful girls of the day, whose upper-class background had given them sophistication, assurance and charm, is it any wonder that my natural instincts – almost fossilized by now – should bestir themselves!

Of all the talented lady pupils that I had, by far the most bewitching was Primrose Yarde-Buller, the daughter of Lord Churston; not only did she have almost the most beautiful eyes I have ever seen, but she always wore a most exotic scent, which I found entirely intoxicating – in fact my mind was not always on the crotchets and quavers. Often, too often, I would stop Primrose playing and ask her to turn round so that I could talk to her. And with those magical eyes looking at me I would give her advice on how I thought the passage should be played, working myself up to a private frenzy as I did so – especially as it was nearly always very romantic music, which was what she preferred. I would then sit down at the piano to show her what I meant, using the piano as a safety valve to stop me making a fool of myself. After all, my first consideration was that I was making money, I was earning a living; at that moment I was doing a professional job and must keep it that way.

Another excellent pupil was Virginia Gilliat, who was introduced to me by Primrose Yarde-Buller. Virginia was more extrovert than Primrose. Her vivaciousness and sense of humour were hard to keep in check during lessons. I allowed her a fairly free rein, because her previous teacher apparently had been so solemn that Virginia felt crushed and dispirited and was about to give up the piano when Primrose said, 'Try Joe Cooper.' Letting some laughter into the lessons did the trick. Virginia even managed to play the first movement of the Rachmaninoff Concerto No. 2, taking the difficult passages slightly under *tempo*.

One of my youngest pupils was little Lord Uxbridge, who used to be brought by his governess for lessons; he was extraordinarily musical, though not I think ever likely to set the Albert Hall on fire with his talent. He is now Lord Anglesey and has kept up his tremendous enthusiasm for music and the arts generally.

There were many others on the list; when the word got round that my lessons were enjoyable and that I had something to teach, still more queued up for lessons; in fact I had to shut up shop and say that that was all I could take for the moment. It meant that I could put my fees up a bit. Quite a lot of money was coming in from my little home-made school of society performers.

I also found a job as an organist and choirmaster at a church in Blackheath, which was notable both for its vast congregations (due largely to the magnetic personality of the rector, the Reverend F.H. Gillingham) and the excellence of its choir. However, the salary was depressingly low. The hard task of keeping the choir up to standard, as well as maintaining a consistently high standard myself on the organ, was time- and energy-consuming and out of all proportion to the pittance given in return. I looked around for another local job to step up my income.

The GPO had a film unit in Bennett Park, Blackheath. I decided to call on the off-chance that they might need the services of a musician. I gave my name to an attendant on the door, telling him why I had come. He invited me in and said he would try to get hold of Mr Cavalcanti – 'He's the big noise around here.'

Alberto Cavalcanti appeared. He looked at me, smiled and in what sounded like a broad French accent said, 'Why didn't you write and make an appointment?' I said, 'I don't know, I just had the urge to call; but I had better go away again.' 'No, don't go away again,' he said. 'A young man that has such courage as you to come unannounced like this must either be foolish or talented. Stay for a week and I will tell you which.' So I walked in. He asked for my name again and I gave it. There were two young men busily working on a score and a script. Cavalcanti said to them, 'This is a new man who says he wants to work with us. His name is Cooper. This is W.H. Auden, a poet, and this is Benjamin Britten, a composer. You'd better stay and watch carefully what they do. If I find that you can contribute anything I will introduce you to John Grierson, he is the head of the whole unit.'

I stayed and watched. Britten and Auden were extremely friendly, as indeed was Cavalcanti, and I immediately felt I was going to enjoy myself. I also saw what the work was all about – you had to write music to fit films, documentary films. I didn't even know what the GPO Film Unit did until I arrived, but Britten was working on a film of coal mines and he was producing all sorts of instruments and strange noises to represent the sounds of coal mining for the soundtrack. Another film he was engaged on was *Night*

Mail, showing how the GPO gets its letters onto trains through the night. Auden was supplying words for the script that went with all this.

After a week it was declared that my face fitted and I was duly introduced to John Grierson. Cavalcanti then set me the task of writing some music for a film to be called *Spring on the Farm*. I was shown the film and then I was told exactly what to do, and to go away and do it. There was something delightfully homespun about the GPO Film Unit in those days; it was in a rather dilapidated building at the end of Bennett Park, close to the little village of Blackheath which had a very good pub where we had lunch every day. Everything was friendly and informal, but you were expected to be efficient. Cavalcanti often used to ask me how I was getting on with the film and said as soon as I was ready with the music I was to play it through to him on the piano. This I did; he approved, both of the music and the fact that I had scored it for a small orchestra. The music then had to be fitted to the actual film as it was thrown up on the screen. So not only was I the composer and conductor, but also I was told I had to book the orchestral players. At this stage I knew very few people, but by making a few enquiries from Britten I soon discovered how to do this.

When Grierson saw the finished *Spring on the Farm* he expressed pleasure and asked me if I would stay on and do some more. I said I would be very pleased to, but I had to warn him that my plans were very uncertain at the moment, because I had an unfinished degree to take at Oxford, and generally speaking life was rather at the crossroads. He told me to stay as long as I could and said they enjoyed having me. He asked me if I got on well with Mr Cavalcanti. I said, 'Yes.' 'Good, but he has his bad moments,' observed Grierson.

Cavalcanti, it turned out, was Brazilian born and had a truly Latin-American temperament; when things went wrong he could raise the roof in fury. At these times the presence of the painter William Coldstream, another member of the unit, came in very handy; he was gentle and quiet. Bill Coldstream's tact saved many an awkward situation.

The more I saw of Benjamin Britten the more I realized that my talent was quite microscopic by the side of his: for one thing, I noted the speed with which he composed his pieces, and also the unerring skill with which he found the appropriate 'noise' for the ever-changing scenes in a film. He didn't look as I would expect a genius to look: he seemed perfectly ordinary, in fact we used to play quite a lot of ping-pong in our spare time.

There was only one moment when I had a feeling that all wasn't well – I told him that the night before I had been to a Prom and heard Henry Wood conducting Brahms' First Symphony, and he didn't answer. I thought he hadn't heard and I repeated it. 'What on earth do you want to listen to Brahms for?' 'I think he is a great composer,' I replied. 'Do you!' Britten retorted, and walked away. I was completely stunned by this and couldn't make it out, but I heard afterwards that Britten couldn't stand the music of Brahms and it really upset him even to hear Brahms' name mentioned. The matter was never referred to again, nor was the name of Brahms!

After a couple of years I had made sufficient money with the GPO Film Unit, who were very generous to me, and my private pupils and my pin-money from the organ job, to give the whole lot up and return to Oxford as I had always planned, to have an intensive crash course and re-take part two of my B.Mus. The question was, who would be the best person for coach?

Dr Sydney Watson had arrived at New College when John Dykes Bower left; he was already there before I had left Oxford and I knew him to be a brilliant musician, a very delightful person, and an instant communicator. I had heard him take rehearsals and I realized that here was a man who could put things very clearly and also had enormous patience. I decided to ask Dr Watson if he would give me a course of strict counterpoint, because I was determined to get my second B.Mus. He laughed and said he would, but, 'Before we start any counterpoint I want you to write me something – write me the first movement of a violin sonata.'

A week later I took my composition to Sydney Watson – it was really rather effective, especially when he played the violin part in the higher register of the piano. He was very complimentary. He then chatted for the rest of the lesson. I told him of my three-fold campaign in Blackheath to make some money, dwelling specially on my success at writing background music for films. His whole manner abounded with confidence and enthusiasm, For the next few weeks we worked on counterpoint, from very easy to difficult. I would do a few bars and he would edit, explaining as we went.

Finally he gave me a mock question and I worked it through in silence. Verdict: no mistakes.

When the day came for the actual examination, I worked coolly and confidently. I felt almost as though Sydney Watson were guiding my hand when it came to the strict counterpoint. It 'ran' as it should, smoothly and easily. A few days after the examination I happened to meet Dr Watson in the street. I knew he would be one of the first to be told the results. I also knew in moments of tension he had a pronounced stutter. 'Well, any news?' I said. Dr Watson uttered: 'You fuf-fuf-fuf-fuf- Passed.' I nearly passed out with joy. I tried to thank him, but this time I couldn't speak for the lump in my throat.

That was a marvellous moment in my life – I'd got my second B.Mus. and I could face the world.

An added bonus on my second visit to Oxford was that by this time Edward Heath and George Malcolm were firmly installed at Balliol. We attended the same classes and I became friends with both; we have kept in touch ever since.

I immediately sent a telegram to Aunt Jessie and Aunt Lily at Blackheath, with just four simple words: 'PASSED EXAM BACK TOMORROW'. I knew that they would be anxiously awaiting news and I was quite sure something extra would be laid on for dinner to mark my success.

There were horse-drawn cabs outside Blackheath station in those days and I felt in a mood of celebration that I should take one of these and drive ceremoniously across the heath to St John's Park, where I lived. I don't know which was the oldest, the driver, the horse or the cab, and our progress was extremely slow and stately. But I was in no mood to hurry; I sat back enjoying every minute of the drive. I had prepared myself not to expect too vociferous a welcome from these two white-haired Victorian spinsters, but I must say I was surprised at the momentary loss of self-control and the hugs and kisses, instead of the usual rather formal handshakes. A bottle of sherry was opened and, as I'd expected, a sumptuous dinner had been prepared.

Quite soon after I got back, Aunt Jessie said to me, 'By the way, Mrs Gilliat, Virginia's mother, telephoned and wants you to ring her as soon as possible about something very important.' I rang Mrs Gilliat and she explained her idea, 'I have decided to have a musical party and I want you to be the principal soloist – I may have a singer, I don't know yet, but I am going to ask a lot of people. Among a crowd that will know very little will be one or two connoisseurs who really know their music. My husband, by the way, adores music and musicians. I haven't actually fixed a date, because I wanted to discuss it with you first.' I naturally felt very thrilled about this, but asked to be given a little time to practise so that I would be in good form, as I had hardly touched a piano for several weeks. The concert came and the room was full of very smart people, many of whom I was sure knew extremely little about music; however, I was a little worried about that sentence of Mrs Gilliat, 'There will be one or two connoisseurs, people who really know their music.' But I had come prepared.

The next day the *Evening Star* in its gossip column came out with a headline 'A Budding Horowitz'. Underneath it read: 'Mr and Mrs John Gilliat gave the ideal party last night ... the "pièce de résistance" Mr Joe Cooper, a young undergraduate just down from Oxford ... as certain of reaching the top of the tree as any young pianist I have heard for years.' The telephone continually rang – many people had noticed my name in the press. But I had to wait to hear what the other side had to say, the little band of connoisseurs. One was the mother of Primrose Yarde-Buller, Lady Churston as she had been, now Mrs Theodore Wessel. She was a remarkable lady; although every inch a socialite, behind a façade of glittering charm, she was a very sound and well-informed musician; she was an excellent pianist, violinist and singer. Above all she was intensely critical; her mother had been, apparently, a near-professional pianist and Jo Wessel (as she was called) certainly would have something to say about my recital; but she had the grace and kindness to say it privately.

Mrs Wessel asked me to go and have a drink at her flat as soon as possible. I did this the very next day, because I was very anxious to know what she really thought. 'It's quite clear to me you are born to be a pianist,' she said, 'but you lack technique, especially your fingerwork which needs far more brilliance and clarity. I don't know who you have been studying with, but you must change immediately and you must go to somebody who really knows how to teach technique.' I pointed out that I had no money; but Jo Wessel was firm, 'I think I can arrange something. Leave it to me. You won't hear anything for a few days, but I will see what I can do.'

It appears that Jo had got in touch with her son-in-law, Loel Guinness, who had married her eldest daughter, Joan Yarde-Buller, and she arranged for us to meet. Loel himself wasn't a musician, but he loved music and he turned out to be tremendously friendly and very anxious to help. I played to him and we chatted. 'Jo has told me the form and the answer is yes, I will help,' he said. 'I'll give you what you need for some good lessons. I expect it will be expensive, but not too expensive I hope. But this is not the moment for skimping. Jo tells me you have promise and I feel I am investing in something, so I'm sure you won't let me down.'

Nowadays grants are given to deserving students who need extra training. But in the Thirties unless you could find a sponsor who would pay for the best coaching available, a would-be solo performer was gravely handicapped. Sometimes a generous teacher would give the lessons for nothing. This could lead, however, to guilt feelings on the part of the student and/or the teacher expecting too much gratitude. I have seen several promising relationships end in disastrous rows. No, someone must pay the teacher.

In my case two wonderful acts of friendship (from Jo Wessel and Loel Guinness) should, with luck, and if I could behave responsibly, pave the way to the concert platform. Think of it, I might one day play before thousands at the Royal Abert Hall! Putting such ridiculous ideas at the back of my mind, I started to think about a coach. I even tried going to one or two celebrated 'names' for a try-out, but without success.

Then one night I went to a Prom to hear the Brahms Second Piano Concerto in B flat played by Egon Petri. By the end of the performance I had reached a decision. Somehow I must have lessons from him. He had everything. I found out through the agents Ibbs & Tillett that I would first have to be auditioned by Miss Rosamund Ley, Petri's assistant. This I quickly fixed up. She listened, but apart from explaining how Mr Petri took a house in Notting Hill Gate for a month or two every so often and liked to teach a few gifted pupils, she kept me guessing about my own chances. 'I will be in touch with you when I have spoken to Mr Petri. So much depends on his recording and concert timetable.'

A week went by. The postman always rang the bell in those days.

I rushed every day to the front door – hoping. On the seventh day there was an envelope addressed to me in Miss Ley's unmistakable handwriting. In it was the news I longed to hear: 'Mr Petri has accepted you as a pupil on my recommendation.'

The time of the first lesson was fixed for 2.30 p.m., just three days later. I hadn't the slightest idea how long it would take to get from Blackheath to Notting Hill Gate, so I left in the morning and went by train to Charing Cross. I had a snack lunch there and then caught the underground for Notting Hill Gate. I located Horbury Crescent, found the house and then had about an hour in hand. I thought the best thing was to wander round the streets, trying to relax, because I was extremely nervous about the prospect of meeting one of the world's greatest pianists.

At 2.30 punctually I rang the bell. I was shown in by the maid and directed to a large room on the first floor with a grand piano in one corner. A few moments later Egon Petri himself walked in, looking taller and larger than I had remembered him at the Queen's Hall. He was so friendly and welcoming that I dropped my guard and found myself talking quite naturally to him. I mentioned his performance of the Brahms B flat Concerto and he expressed apparent delight that I had enjoyed it and seemed to think himself that it went 'rather better than usual' as he put it.

Then Petri asked me to play something. Knowing him to be a great Bach lover and expert, I decided – perhaps unwisely – to play the E major Prelude and Fugue from Book 1 of the '48'. I got through, but my hands were absolutely shaking with nerves. When I stopped Petri looked at me and smilingly said: 'You know Mr Cooper, I do not give singing lessons.' I said I was sorry, but I didn't quite understand. 'All the way through that Prelude and Fugue you were singing away to yourself, but quite another tune and quite out of key. I thought I should warn you.' I apologized, but I had no idea I was singing. He then said very many people did it, but it was a habit that if allowed to develop could become incurable and could irritate people in the audience.

The next thing he said was, 'Very nicely played, but what does worry me is that you do not use your fing-ers.' (He said the word 'fingers' as though it rhymed with 'singers'. That was the only mispronunciation Petri ever made in the English language; he was a great linguist and could talk five different languages, almost perfectly, and apart from 'fing-ers' you would have thought he was an Englishman.) He asked why I didn't play with my fingers and why I used so much arm movement. I explained it was the system I had been taught and that in England, on the whole, fingers were neglected. 'I know all about this, but we must get it right,' he replied. 'But don't worry; I would much rather have a pupil playing musically like you did, with a poor technique, than one with a perfect technique but showing no sign of any music.'

I suddenly felt a marvellous warm feeling running right through me, because this was Encouragement with a capital E. To be told that, in spite of my nerves, my performance sounded musical was more than I had dreamed of!

Petri then set about giving me some finger exercises and showed me how to practise, working from the knuckle, but always keeping the wrist and arm free. He wanted me to exaggerate the finger movement in everything I did, for the moment, so that I became aware that I had fingers.

After we had been working for about an hour, a charming grey-haired lady came in with a tray of tea and Egon Petri said, 'May I introduce you to my wife.' She, too, was a friendly person. She remarked good-humouredly, 'Now, Egon, drink the tea before it gets cold. And, Mr Cooper, don't let my husband work you too hard.'

Petri poured out some tea for us both, but that didn't stop him talking; he was in full spate and was getting very worked up about the subject of piano technique. In a few minutes he had removed his jacket, rolled up his shirtsleeves to the top of his arm, and was demonstrating the various movements the arm would make and showing me some of the reflex movements of the upper arm, caused by the action of the fingers and hand.

He then sat down and demonstrated all the things he had been talking about. As he played I was completely bewitched, first of all by the enormous size of his hands and also the fact that the piano sounded entirely different from when I had played it; it sounded noble and clean. He showed me what a tremendous tone range there was available, from a whispering *pianissimo* to a majestic *fortissimo*. I realized how meagre was my range of tone and how feeble was my *fortissimo*. I was so totally absorbed in all he was doing and saying, that I didn't notice the time flying by until Mrs Petri came in and said, 'Egon, you really must stop, you've been three hours with Mr Cooper.' 'I'll stop in a minute, dear, I'll stop in a minute,' Egon promised and waved her out of the room.

We finished by talking about the next lesson and Petri asked me what I would bring to play then. I suggested the F minor Ballade by Chopin, because although I had a working knowledge of the notes, there were many passages that were beyond me. He agreed on this work, arranged a time, and said I must get used to the fact he liked to give long lessons, 'So have a good night's sleep before you come next time.' He himself showed me out of the front door.

It was dark when I got outside, but the shops around Notting Hill Gate were still open. I went into a newsagent's and bought a cheap exercise book, because I felt that if I didn't write down all that Petri had told me, a lot of it might get lost and the information was too valuable not to be recorded for future use. As soon as I got into the underground I started writing and very nearly forgot to get out at the right station. When I got back to Blackheath I retired to my room and went on with my exercise book and didn't stop until I had written in every detail of that lesson – my first with Egon Petri.

After a series of very successful lessons with Petri, I reported back to Mr and Mrs Gilliat that Petri considered me almost ready to give my first London recital. His plan was that I should go and stay with him at his mountain retreat at Zakopane in Poland, for a final polishing and grooming, in the early summer of 1939, and then book the Wigmore Hall. We all felt that Loel Guinness had done more than enough. But the Gilliats suggested introducing me to Lady Ravensdale – one of the great patronesses of music – in the hope that if my playing pleased her, she would sponsor that first recital. (A young artist always has to 'buy' himself into the profession with a first concert. If the critics approve with sufficient warmth, an agent may then start finding him work.)

A day or two later a letter arrived from Lady Ravensdale inviting me to lunch. Jack and Lily Gilliat (as I was now told to call them) must have used every superlative in the book, because half-way through lunch Lady Ravensdale was offering to guarantee the concert. I protested that surely she would like to hear me play. That she said was not a condition. Perhaps, she added, I didn't know that Jack Gilliat had a remarkable ear for music and was also canny, with a shrewd eye for a saleable article. His opinion was enough for her! So I booked the Wigmore Hall for a concert in October.

Suddenly I saw myself from a different perspective. I wasn't going in for music just to make music: I was going in for music to make money. What a curious impression of an artist's role the 'city of dreaming spires' had given me – art for art's sake had seemed to be Oxford's motto. Over that lunch with Irene Ravensdale I suddenly felt I had grown up and was ready to face any challenge that the future were to offer.

Early in 1939 I had a letter from Petri saying that as events on the international scene had deteriorated so swiftly, with Hitler grabbing more and more of Europe, Petri felt he must get all his belongings out of Poland while there was still time. (By March Hitler had seized the last independent remnant of Czechoslovakia, and next he demanded from Poland the port of Danzig and the Polish Corridor.)

There was one engagement Egon Petri was determined to keep – a 'live' broadcast of the Liszt B minor Sonata from the BBC studios in Maida Vale in June. Only a few hours before rehearsal time Petri had arrived in London from Baden-Baden where he had been taking a cure. His group of faithful pupils had all been invited to the studios. We were already seated when Petri came through a door at the far end and quickly sat down at the piano. He had forty minutes before transmission, so decided to play right through the Liszt Sonata to get into playing form (he hadn't touched a piano for a fortnight).

It all sounded dazzlingly brilliant. But about midway through the half-hour work, he stopped, threw up his hands and yelled, '*Mein Gott! Ich habe vergessen*' (My God, I've forgotten). Then (remembering he was in England) he said, 'Has anyone a copy of the Sonata? Mine is somewhere between here and America!' Dead silence. He tried the passage again and came to a halt. Then he called over to his pupils: 'One of you come and put me on the track, please.' Nobody moved. On an urgent signal from the studio manager Petri left out a few bars and continued to the end of the Sonata. Five minutes later he was due on the air. He sat quietly waiting. The studio manager wished him luck. Alvar Lidell, the announcer, was sitting at a table waiting for the red light which means 'transmission on'.

That huddle of pupils would have willingly dropped through the floor at this moment, rather than see their beloved master flounder. But miraculously when Petri reached the dreaded passage, he sailed flawlessly through it, and even allowed himself a smile and a nod of the head – as if to say 'Well, that was a near one!' The whole crisis was so manfully handled, and the performance itself so unruffled and masterly, that no one listening in can have had an inkling of the ordeal surrounding the transmission. Petri joined us as soon as he had finished. He made light of the drama – partly perhaps because he spotted the pallor of our cheeks. Then he shook hands with each of us and left, with no more ado than if we were all going to meet again next day. A protracted farewell might have spelt out what was in the back of everybody's mind – would we ever meet Egon Petri again?

One needed optimists around in those days as the growing gloom descended, blocking the view ahead. One such optimist was the viola player Jean Stewart, whom I first met at Oxford; we became close friends. She rang me in March 1939 to ask if I would be willing to play the piano part in a new work by Vaughan Williams called *The Bridal Day*. The first performance would be in the autumn. If I agreed she would arrange a meeting with some other string players and me, to run through the score with the composer. If he approved of my playing I was 'in'.

It was duly arranged and we read through the work. Vaughan Williams seemed pleased and afterwards offered me the engagement, which I accepted. We had an initial trial performance at Cecil Sharp House on 27 April 1939, with Vaughan Williams conducting and singing the baritone solo.*

While people walked about the streets trying to look cheerful and thinking that in the end there might be no war, events in the outside world were happening with overwhelming speed. Britain and France had assured Poland they would come to its aid, if attacked; Hitler replied by making a non-aggression pact with Stalin, which of course removed the benefit of Soviet help to the Western powers; then Hitler attacked with his *Blitzkrieg* on Poland. Britain and France kept their promise and the Second World War broke out in September 1939.

*For further details see *The Works of Vaughan Williams*, Michael Kennedy (Oxford University Press), pp. 562–3.

We were holidaying in Harlyn Bay at the time and happily Dorothy Sayers had once more taken my brother's bungalow next door – I say happily, because her cheerful presence, and optimism that life would turn out all right in the end, made the shattering news less frightening than it might have been without her.

My sister, being of a much more practical nature than I, had already joined the ATS and had been waiting for her call-up and where to report. She was immediately informed and had to report to Bristol. She asked me what I was going to do and I said I hadn't the faintest idea; I hadn't given it a thought, but I was supposed to be giving two London concerts in October. Mollie said: 'Obviously you can't do that; in any case all concerts will be cancelled, that's for certain [they were, of course]. But my advice to you is to come to Bristol with me and join up. Life will never be quite the same again for any of us and you might as well join the army. Think how ashamed you would feel if you didn't.'

5

On Learning To Be A Soldier

Of course Mollie was right. To stay behind in Harlyn while she went to Bristol to join the army was unthinkable; so together we went back to Westbury-on-Trym.

The next morning I went apprehensively to the barracks where I had to report. At an enquiry desk I said I wanted to join up. When asked what kind of unit I wanted to join I said I hadn't really thought about it. But finding the atmosphere friendly, I told my story quite truthfully – that I was a musician, that I knew nothing about the army, that I hadn't even been in the Officers' Training Corps at school, but I was willing to have a go and try my hand at anything they had to offer me. I mentioned that I had worked for the BBC, as pianist on Dr Armstrong's broadcasts to schools, and also knew the Bristol BBC staff well.

The second lieutenant in charge told me to fill in various forms, have a medical and then, if I was passed fit enough, I could go down to Wells to the 66th Searchlight Regiment (449 Battery) to train as a gunner. Much later that day, in lovely warm sunshine, about ten of us who had filled up our forms and passed our medicals were settled in the bus for Wells, one of the most beautiful cities in the world. Our destination was the recreation ground which lies behind the shops on the left side of the High Street going away from the cathedral.

There was a great deal of activity in the field – a searchlight was being put in position and other equipment got ready, tents were being put up and vast supplies of food were arriving in army lorries. I was quite used to putting up tents, because I used to help our friends at Harlyn, so I threw myself into that for a start.

Being so completely ignorant of all matters concerning the army, I realized that I would have to pick things up gradually as the days went on, but there was one mystery that needed immediate clarification – why did so many people have uniforms, some with two stripes, some with three stripes, some with stars on their shoulders – and why did we, who had just arrived, have no uniforms? It was explained to me that we had joined in with part of the Territorial Army, which was a peacetime organization preparing for an emergency such as had now happened – war. Many of them had been at it for years and had gone in, much as I had, knowing nothing; after some time a few had done well enough to be promoted to the rank of major or even colonel. Most of their work was done at the old drill hall in Bristol, after office hours, and in uniform.

Then I wanted to know when we were going to get our uniforms. We were immediately given forage caps and arm-bands, just to show that we were soldiers; otherwise we had to use our civilian clothes, because the army clothes hadn't yet arrived.

The ORS' (other ranks) mess was the back room of a baker's shop and I soon wondered when were we going to eat because, as always, I was hungry. At about 7 o'clock we were each issued with a knife, fork and spoon, a plate and mug and told to report at the ORS' mess; we had a very satisfying, if plain, meal. There was an old upright piano in the corner of the mess and I lost no time in sitting down at the piano and playing 'Roll out the Barrel'. Everybody joined in, with cries for more.

I was warned to be careful of the battery sergeant-major. I could identify him by the fact that he was a large man – you could say a fat man – middle-aged, balding with a slight cast in one eye and a very bad-tempered face. If he appeared, be doing something very very busily, it didn't matter what, but never be caught doing nothing.

There was a large tent called the quartermaster's stores where we picked up things like palliasses, blankets and Blanco. As I went in, I identified Sergeant-Major Butler. He was saying to the quartermaster, 'Don't know where this new lot come from: proper scruffy. There's a BBC man. He'll soon know who does the broadcasting around here.' I turned my back and concentrated on the Blanco and boot-polish shelf. As soon as he left I collected palliasse and blankets.

That night I slept more deeply than I had in months. Why? The simple answer is that I, like all the other chaps, was healthily tired. We'd spent a long day, a great deal of it in hot sunshine, including putting up our tents, and then I had given the troops quite a long entertainment at the piano after supper. I had also had some fun at the expense of one or two people, giving instant imitations, which enormously amused my comrades.

Here we were, all novitiates without any training at all, except for one or two who had been in the OTC at their schools. Putting it at its most basic, there were many worse places on a hot summer night, with the smell of hay in that recreation field, enjoying the open air and good honest laughter.

Quite a lot of amusement came from my imitations, because very soon I had developed an almost undetectable caricature of Lieutenant X, who used to come round to see if lights were out and people had stopped talking. He would tap on the tent with his cane and call out abuse in a high-pitched querulous tone if anyone was making a noise. Several times I went round the whole camp-site pretending to be Lieutenant X and then a few minutes later the real Lieutenant X would come along and find everyone, thinking he had gone, chatting merrily. One night I was spotted, hauled into the tent and debagged amid hoots of mirth. Suddenly we heard Lieutenant X shouting at the next tent. No mice could have matched our sudden silence, and at the next morning's parade we were singled out as the best-disciplined tent!

I had yet to meet Sergeant-Major Butler face to face. He also proved to be a number one target for imitation, but of course you had to be extremely wary of him, because he could be a very tricky customer. He wasn't unfriendly to me. His first remark was, 'I hear you've come from the BBC and you play the piano. Well, I hope you will play, but first of all get your hair cut.' I got my hair cut, as I thought short enough, because I always wore it rather long, but the second day I saw Sergeant-Major Butler he said, 'Get your hair cut.' This went on for four days until I had almost a crew-cut and I looked a most appalling sight, but that's what he seemed to want.

But what Sergeant-Major Butler wanted even more than my getting my hair cut was for me to go to a certain pub, where he used to meet his girlfriend. There was a piano and I used to play all his favourite numbers, the popular tunes of the Twenties and Thirties. Sergeant-Major Butler was responsible for our basic training on parade, teaching us how to march, how to salute, how to form fours

– and generally trying to make us look like soldiers. He was very efficient, but I was apt to turn to the right when ordered to turn to the left. However, it was all taken in good part, so long as I played at the pub.

The dreaded moment came after the uniforms turned up one evening. Their arrival was announced from the quartermaster's stores. I was simply longing to get into my battledress. I tried on many tunics before I found the right size and chose my 'anklets web', as they were called. Several friends followed my example, and eventually we held a mock parade, with me calling the orders. But I had quite forgotten while I was doing all this that Sergeant-Major Butler was waiting at the pub for me to play the piano. It became so late the pub was closed by the time I got there. The next morning I could see a very black look in his eye and at the first mistake I made he came across. There was a deathly silence from all my friends as the sergeant-major let loose a tirade of pent-up fury. We became friends again when I played the piano the next evening at the pub, and I continued to do so. It was no effort to me at all; I always enjoyed a drink in the evening and, sentry duties apart, there was nothing else to do.

By day we had intensive training in searchlights from a fine team of instructors under the inspired leadership of an expert borrowed from the Royal Engineers – Sergeant-Major McCaffrey.

On Sunday mornings we had a service at St Cuthbert's Church. Wells is lucky in having the glorious cathedral, as well as this large and splendid church. Prebendary Cook, the rector of St Cuthbert's, explained to Sergeant-Major Butler that his organist was away on active service. Could the battery commander produce one from the ranks? 'No problem,' replied the sergeant-major, and when Sunday came Prebendary Cook invited me to breakfast before the service and asked if it meant I was missing any parades. I said I would blame my absence, if noticed, on having to go and practise the organ. I had the most delicious breakfast I had eaten for some time – and I think the last, the very last real sausage that I have eaten. That was 1939, and gradually sausages have grown to taste less and less like sausages. In my opinion, today they bear no relation to pre-war sausages. A pre-war sausage would have jumped out of its skin if you'd called it a banger.

At St Cuthbert's Church I used to try playing various popular tunes in the style of (say) Bach. People reading this book who were in the army with me will remember the beaming smile of dear old Prebendary Cook, waiting at the church door as the troops filed out, saying, 'Do you recognize it? – Berkeley Square.'

We had several weeks of training, including manning drill on the 'model' searchlight sight, lectures on gas, aircraft-recognition and hygiene. We were then told that we were going to be sent in detachments (ten on site and one spare) to various searchlight sites dotted around the Mendips, ready to put into practice all we had learnt, as soon as the enemy approached. Our searchlight site was nearly 1,000 feet up on the Mendips at Higher Pitts Farm.

Apart from the swivelling chairs for the spotters and the actual projector with its giant light, there was an extraordinary machine called the sound locator, where two men listened in with earphones. When they felt they had the sound of the enemy plane exactly between their ears they called out 'on sound' to a man in the middle. He had a piece of equipment on which he took a bearing (allowing for the sound lag) and relayed it to the searchlight team, who could then beam onto the enemy aircraft. The whole thing seemed to me very Heath Robinson, but I asked if I could be on the sound locator, because I felt it was the sort of thing – anything connected with sound – which would interest me.

Although we were now familiar with the layout, the equipment, the 'drills' dreamed up by our instructors to enable us to meet any situation including a low-flying attack on the site, the isolation – without instructors at our elbow – was rather like leaving harbour for the open sea. However, Bombardier Alexander, the detachment commander, took us through our daily manning drill.

One evening Dick Alexander told me he was going to leave the site on urgent business, so would I mount the guard if he wasn't back in time. I had forgotten and was lying on my bunk, when I suddenly became aware of an extremely regimental figure standing at the door. It was Major Brooks, the battery commander (no less). He asked who I was: I told him my name and he said, 'Where's Bombardier Alexander?' 'He's absent at the moment sir,' I said. 'Yes, and so is the guard,' he replied. 'Why hasn't he mounted it?' I admitted that I was second-in-command and had been entrusted with the task, but it had slipped my mind because I was concentrating. 'What were you concentrating on?' he asked, and I replied:

'To be honest, sir, the first movement of Beethoven's "Moonlight" Sonata.' 'Report to my office tomorrow morning,' he said, and left.

The next morning I trundled down to Wells and went to Major Brooks's office, which was a room above a shop. There was a piano there and as the room was empty I eagerly seized the chance of playing the opening of the 'Moonlight' Sonata. 'What infernal cheek, sitting down and playing the piano in my office,' Major Brooks said as he came in, 'but carry on, I like it.' I went right through to the end of the first movement. 'As your commanding officer,' he said, when I had finished, 'I have to take you to task for not mounting the guard, but I can't say much after that music, because it really was out of this world. But please remember you've now got to try and learn to be a soldier and you cannot just lie on your bunk dreaming of the "Moonlight". You've got to learn that we are in a war. The sooner we win it, the sooner you get back to what you were born to do.'

Major Brooks's humane attitude did me far more good than doling out punishment. I resolved to give of my best. Before I left Wells, I picked up some training-manuals from Sergeant-Major McCaffrey, including a book containing silhouettes and names of British and German aircraft. The importance of instant recognition had, I thought, been underplayed and I decided that, just as a schoolboy I knew the name of every car on the road, I would now master aeroplanes. Armed also with an exercise book and a copy of *The Aeroplane* magazine, which I bought from Mr Pettigrew, the stationer, I returned to Higher Pitts Farm.

Many months in fact were to elapse before we were to smell Hitler's 'whiff of grapeshot'. To give us a change of scene, we were sent to different sites. In May 1940 I was detachment commander of a site near Shepton Mallet. We had heard that on 10 May German forces had smashed into the Low Countries and France was soon to fall. One night (we were on immediate stand-by now) we could see distant searchlights and hear the sound of engines. In a few seconds a low-flying German aircraft dropped bombs all round our site, peppering the searchlight with machine-gun fire as it went. I gave the order 'Dowse' (switch the beam off immediately). The Jerry went on to the next light and then disappeared. By a miracle no one was hurt.

My next appearance was after I had returned from OCTU (Officer

Cadet Training Unit) as a second lieutenant. The blitz on the major cities had started. I was posted to a site at Wembdon near Bridgwater. One night searchlights had got clearly in their beams what looked like a Ju 88. It came right overhead and our fighters went in for the kill. A copy-book exercise. The plane came roaring down, out of control, directly over us. The screeching of its engines came so near that we lay on our stomachs, waiting for the end. But suddenly, an almight crash – then silence!

It was somewhere very near. I went with my second-in-command, Sergeant Ingrams, to investigate. We were met by two Home Guard officers. They pointed to the position of the plane and warned us that unexploded bombs were scattered around. However, Ingrams and I, with torches (and revolvers), approached the wreckage. I saw the bombs, positively identified it as a Ju 88, but saw no sign of life. I telephoned this information to BHQ on our return to site. Apparently three of the crew had bailed out, but the gunner in the fuselage gun-turret had been trapped. Bits of his body were found by the bomb-disposal crew next morning. The three other Germans had given themselves up at various farms and were given a good breakfast.

Frightening though the episode had been, I was thankful to be in action. Three months at Shrivenham, learning to become 'an officer and a gentleman', had taxed the patience of even the most peace-loving and idle of the cadets. While the German bombers passed Shrivenham on their nightly visits to Coventry, Birmingham and Bristol – the red glow in the distant sky telling its appalling tale of the blitz and cities being wiped out – we irrelevantly spent hours re-learning how to march, or to put it more precisely, how to stop marching.

In future, it was decreed, the order to 'halt' was to be given earlier (i.e. as the left foot hit the ground; the right foot took one more step and then the left foot joined the right for the halt). In the drill book – the bible of every sergeants' mess throughout the land – you gave the order *after* the left foot had hit the ground (i.e. as the right foot was passing the left). The new procedure was dinned into us day in, day out, until we were brain-washed with the idea that the re-education of any reactionary sergeants or sergeant-majors was a top priority when posted to units.

On my return to the 66th Searchlights I undertook the re-training of the halt with much zeal. One day I was invited for a drink in the sergeants' mess, apparently to toast my return as an officer. All started in high spirits, when after about half-an-hour's drinking Sergeant-Major Butler banged on the table, calling for silence. After a short speech, loaded with references to my early efforts under his tuition, he held up a cartoon of me, stuck to the cover of the drill book, with the caption 'To the man who tried to re-write the drill book'. I was presented with it to the accompaniment of peals of derisive laughter. Shocked, outraged, but clearly outwitted, I quietly got up, carrying the book, and walked out of the sergeants' mess.

I made out a strong case to the battery commander, and was finally allowed to demonstrate to the second-in-command at Divisional Headquarters (not to the General himself, who was due for retirement – and anyway had difficulty in seeing what went on below his stomach). The verdict went against me. After my making several demonstrations of both methods, I was told: 'Distinction without a difference; stick to the drill book!' (A *locus classicus* of what my young nephew forty years later was to describe as Sod's Law!)

With the blitz at its height I began worrying about my family at Bristol and my adopted aunts at Blackheath. I heard from my family that my mother and father had moved down to Harlyn Bay, which gave me a great sense of relief, because Westbury-on-Trym was on the edge of Bristol and did in fact get its share of bombs.

From Blackheath I heard no news until one morning a letter came from a relative of the two old aunts, saying the house had been bombed – they were safe, but there was very little left inside the house, which had been gutted. The letter said if possible could I get emergency leave and go to London. This I did and the first remark Aunt Jessie made restored my sense of balance: she looked at me and said, 'Don't worry, my dear, they are only *things*.' That comment was to carry me through the ordeal of seeing not only their part of the house devastated, but my own room a complete and absolute wreck with everything destroyed – except, miraculously, the grand piano. The aunts had most carefully wrapped the piano up in blankets and tarpaulin, put it in a corner and it survived the water, which was really the main problem. Water had been pumped everywhere in gallons to try and stop the fire spreading throughout the house. They managed to save the outside walls and in due course it was re-built.

In the meantime the aunts moved in with their next-door neighbours. That night I slept on the floor of one side of the neighbours' drawing-room, with Aunt Jessie the other side of the room. As the sirens had gone and enemy aircraft could be heard buzzing overhead, Aunt Jessie was a little surprised that I removed my trousers before settling down under my blankets (I did keep my underpants on). 'Young man,' she said, 'I think that's very unwise. Please put your trousers on.' I told her it was quite all right and I never slept with my trousers on. But Aunt Jessie replied: 'Just supposing something happened and you were seen with your bare legs in the street; it really would look very extraordinary!' Suddenly old Victorian values were coming to the fore, which amused me. Anyway, it was a very unsettled night and there was no question of there being any sleep, so to make Aunt Jessie feel happier I put my trousers on again.

My safety valve in extreme conditions, either to offset boredom or fear, was always to clean my army equipment. I had all my 'spit and polish' material ready and I started to have a go at the toecaps of my boots; I was already very proud of them, but they had suffered slightly in the trek to London and in inspecting the house damage. I 'bulled' away, as the expression was, and it helped the long night to pass.

The next morning I am sure those dear aunts must have used up at least two days' rations making sure I had a good breakfast before setting off. I couldn't help admiring their marvellous pluck and resilience in the face of these nightly raids.

On my way back to the West Country I decided to call in at the National Gallery to hear one of Dame Myra Hess's famed lunch-time concerts. This was my first opportunity of visiting London since war had broken out and I was delighted to find that Myra Hess was giving the concert herself that day. I had a sandwich, served to me by an extremely attractive lady, whom I afterwards realized was none other than Joyce Grenfell. At the end of a very enjoyable concert I went up to the platform and re-introduced myself to Dame Myra, whom I had previously met after a concert at Colston Hall, Bristol. There was this wonderful lady who, day in, day out, gave beautiful music to anyone who liked to come into the National Gallery to listen. She was, as usual, all smiles and charm.

As soon as I got back to my regiment I immediately made arrangements with my old friend Mr Palmer, who was still in business, to move my piano from Blackheath to Wells – some friends of mine were willing to house it for the rest of the war. The aunts had particularly asked me to do this, because they themselves had nowhere to live and were making plans to go and stay in the country, away from the bombing.

Soon after my return to my unit we were visited by the colonel of the regiment, who told us in great confidence that the equipment we were using was now considered obsolete and that in future we were going to use radar. In case we didn't understand what radar was, he explained it was the use of high-powered radio pulses which were reflected and which would locate the position of flying aircraft. I put a look of intelligence on my face, but I hadn't the faintest idea what the colonel was talking about. I had a shrewd idea that he was equally in the dark! We were told we would all be sent on radar courses to be trained in the use of the new equipment.

I knew that radar was something that was quite beyond my ken – I had read enough about the complications of it to realize that it was not for me. Luckily I had my other string (it's always a good thing to have two strings to one's bow) and that was aircraft recognition. I had never stopped keeping that book up to date, right throughout the months, including Shrivenham, and by now my head was full of information. I felt that I was ready to go on an aircraft recognition course, which was also a change of course, in another sense, for me.

Permission was granted and I was sent to the AA Command School of Aircraft Recognition at Wythiam, near Tunbridge Wells. I enjoyed it from the word go. My enthusiasm and stored-up knowledge very much surprised the instructors, including the chief instructor, Major Linton (afterwards Colonel). When the course was over he sent for me and said that I had all the ingredients to be a top-grade full-time aircraft recognition instructor, if I wanted it. But he would communicate with my commanding officer and see what was to be done. I took to Major Linton immediately; he was a Scotsman with a tremendous sense of humour, which he transmitted to the rest of the staff, and the whole course was delightful.

We had to give brief talks on our own views on how lectures on aircraft recognition should be given – which in my case included quite a good deal of irreverence and banter. I was dead against the way it had been taught in my unit, which was the official army way, and started: 'Take the head on view.' That stock opening sentence had everyone yawning and most people were asleep by the end of the lecture.

Jock Linton and his team brought in all sorts of factors in order to interest people: e.g. the theory of flight, the history of the aeroplane concerned and why, operationally, it was a particular shape. Details like length of wing-span, crew number, range, armament, gave each aeroplane 'character' and helped people to 'catch the bug' of aircraft recognition, as I always called it. Most of these details were, as it happened, catalogued in my notebook. Visits to aerodromes and short air trips were included. I left the course confident that I could now bring a new look to the subject and communicate it to any audience.

Things happened quickly. Within a week I was summoned to Group Headquarters in Bristol and told by the colonel in charge of training that I was to be promoted to the rank of captain (three pips on my shoulder!) and made chief instructor of the aircraft recognition section of the newly formed 3rd AA Group School. It started there at headquarters and later moved around the area to places such as Porthcawl, St Agnes in Cornwall, and Watchet in Somerset. I was given two NCOs as assistants, and was promised another officer, should the need arise. I chose my NCOs – both first-class aeroplane model makers. Using the light tropical American balsa wood, they made and painted (in camouflage) small models of all the British, American and German aircraft in service. Also, they gave each course of students very skilled tuition in how to make models for themselves. I formed a close liaison with RAF Colerne, near Bath, and arranged for visits and 'hops' for each course.

We soon had mixed classes. The presence of ATS added greatly to my gusto as a lecturer. Their response to my sallies, quips and occasional *doubles entendres* was often ahead of the men, which in turn put the men on their mettle. These aircraft recognition courses were talked about everywhere as something not to be missed and I was not unnaturally proud of their success. Another officer joined me and the bombardiers were promoted to sergeants.

Suddenly I had a message that the General would like to see me. This was unheard of – me asked to see the general! He told me that news of my unregimental but successful methods of teaching aircraft recognition had reached the General of the 1st US Army, who would like to 'borrow' me for a period to instruct their instructors. The US Army's temporary headquarters was at Clifton College (the school had been evacuated to Bude). I reported to Clifton. The sight of GIs (American soldiers) roaming around, instead of schoolboys, seemed a little grotesque.

For about eight months, while 'my' aircraft recognition school ran under the new officer and the resident NCOs, I travelled round with the Americans, adopting the American way of life and even learning to enjoy molasses and waffles with bacon for breakfast.

The Americans wasted no time in getting me on the road. I was lent a like-minded American officer who was very keen on aircraft recognition. We were driven around in a staff car – in fact the red-carpet treatment accorded me as an Englishman was very obvious from the start and flattered my ego. The area we were to cover was roughly from Salisbury as far as south Cornwall. Of course because it was wartime all the signposts had been taken down and my American colleague was continually pulling out large-scale maps to direct us to various sites. Most of the time I was able to say 'left turn', 'right turn', etc., because it was very much home territory to me, a West Countryman born and bred.

We started rather small recognition courses and then, as the interest began to build up, something quite unusual happened. The senior staff officers decided that these courses should be given to large numbers, not just instructors. So big halls, either drill halls or maybe cinemas, were hired for the occasion, and I was often lecturing to as many as 1,500 to 2,000 American troops, with the General and the Top Brass sitting in the front row. What was more and I think couldn't possibly have happened with the English, the Top Brass didn't mind a little 'mickey-taking' – in fact they enjoyed it. I always kept half-an-eye on the General's face and at the first sign of glumness I would have piped down. But I can't remember one single lecture that I gave – or 'performance' might be a more apt word – where the General didn't roar with laughter when a few sallies were being directed at the ignorance of Top Brass about aircraft recognition.

Well, if the Americans enjoyed me, I can certainly say I enjoyed them. I only remember one real ordeal: it was at Falmouth, where I was taking my final course of very knowledgable instructors. One of them in particular took against me and managed to persuade some of his colleagues to join forces with him. They wondered if I really knew my stuff. Here was I talking about all these aeroplanes and giving them quizzes and tests, but how would I fare if I were having to, as it were, 'Face the Music'? There was no getting out of it. I had as a test to identify a number of aircraft in front of the whole class, to prove myself. I felt extremely nervous, but I also felt that I was well trained and unless they produced the most extraordinary angles, or really bad photographs, I ought to get through all right. I came in and was shown, one by one, pictures of aeroplanes and I had to write down on a piece of paper what I thought they were. At the end I read out my results, and the particularly obnoxious officer who demanded this inquisition had to admit that I had got ten out of ten. Fortunately for me, the Americans really made their pictures quite straightforward and easy – we had been used to recognizing impossibly difficult shots of aeroplanes, from any angle.

News of this incident spread like a forest fire, and my stock rose ridiculously high. After I had finished with the Americans a copy of a letter came which I kept. It was from somebody very high up, a General at Ist Army HQ, to our General and a copy was forwarded to me. The letter said roughly that they wished to thank headquarters for lending me to their Ist Army. I had not only been a continual source of information and entertainment to the men, but my whole attitude had played a substantial part in furthering good relations between America and Great Britain.

D-Day loomed nearer. It could have been a matter of weeks, or months, by the time I was back in the Third AA Group School in late 1943. Even without rumours of feverish ship and other building activity going on in ports all round Britain, or the pregnant silences in the newspapers, or the forbidden reference to the subject of invasion in officers' messes, everyone knew, and longed for the bubble to burst. When D-Day finally came on 6 June 1944, our school was at Watchet. It closed down and the instructors were given some leave. I went down to Harlyn Bay to spend a few days with my parents. My father was in unusually high spirits. It appears that some United States GIs were having regular drill-instruction in the lane outside our bungalow.

My father found these young Americans very friendly. He also was intensely amused by a parrot (an old inhabitant of Harlyn) who, just as the drill sergeant ordered silence, called out from the open window, 'Silly bugger.' The sergeant, not then knowing the source of the insult, fulminated with rage. The GIs tried to suppress their amusement, but failed, and mass hysteria set in. My father often told the story in a dry, dead-pan sort of way that a comedian would have envied. Later from overseas he often received letters from his young GI pals, which flattered my father. And yet he was so inhibited with his own children, and we with him.

So it was to my mother I confided that I intended to join the invasion of Normandy if an opportunity arose. Troops and stores would be going in for weeks and I would be sure to find a way. I promised to get a message back to her when I had landed on the beach in France. She knew that female tears would alarm me far more than a mine-infested English Channel, so she turned emotional switches to zero and said she would give my father an edited version of my plans. And I left with no fuss and returned, as arranged, to group headquarters at Bristol.

In the train Jock Linton kept coming into my thoughts. He was now a full colonel. He might have some ideas. Either by telepathy or coincidence I was 'on target'. The sentry at headquarters handed me a signal. 'Report Deepcut soonest, Linton' was the laconic order. By a little wangling I managed to get a car and a driver and suitable maps. 'Somewhere near Brookwood,' the driver said cheerfully, 'Aldershot area.' I now knew how my American colleague must have felt when we were driving in the West Country. I navigated with care. Once there, the driver was given a bumper tea, while I went to look for Colonel Linton, Officer Commanding War Office School of Aircraft Recognition, and, apparently, Tank Recognition.

I found Jock Linton, clearly relieved to see me. I was apparently supposed to be on a tank recognition course, but what with my having been with the Americans so long, plus the almost fanatical security that we were undergoing with the imminent invasion, the original instructions had never reached me. Hence his signal. I didn't enjoy the tank recognition course, despite the splendid and very capable efforts of Ken Armitage, the instructor. Compared to aircraft, tanks seemed to me so clumsy and uninteresting, but for some reason or other I was ordered to take the course, so take it I did. However, even if I didn't get very good marks in the final exams, it turned out I was in the right place at the right time.

During conversations in the mess between people on the course and the recognition of aircraft instructors, I heard rumours that a plan was being hatched to send a number of vans complete with captain, sergeant and a driver, overseas – the vans to be equipped with all the latest aircraft recognition material and to be sent forward as near the front line as possible, to give troops 'refreshers' and put them in touch with any changes of aircraft. Apparently – and I kept my ears very close to the ground on this – they needed an extra officer to co-ordinate the efforts of the captains in charge of the vans. As far as I could gather they hadn't found anyone.

One evening I definitely heard Jock Linton discussing with one of the instructors how desperate he was, as time was running out. I butted in, bold as brass: 'I know what you're talking about, sir, and I think I'm your man.' Jock Linton looked at me with surprise. 'What confounded impertinence; it's none of your business,' he said with a chuckle. I went to bed and forgot about it. The next morning I was summoned by Colonel Linton: 'I was thinking seriously about your remark last night – perhaps you are the right person. Were you serious?' 'I've never been more serious in all my life,' I replied, 'I would love to do the job. I would love to feel that I was going overseas taking all the aircraft recognition experience that I've absorbed and helping in some way to keep the knowledge of aircraft recognition in the forefront of people's minds.'

What happened after that was shrouded in secrecy, but eventually we were transported to Tilbury Docks and boarded a ship that I think I recognized – it was one of the old cross-Channel steamers (now camouflaged). I made friends with the chief engineer; he seemed to have seen me before, perhaps on a Channel crossing before the war. He kindly said that as he would be on duty all night I could use his cabin. I told him I was a musician and wasn't really quite as sure of myself as I looked, and I think he took pity on me. I gave him the address and telephone number of my parents in Harlyn Bay and he promised that when he returned he would get in touch and say I had landed safely on the beaches – he did this for several of us.

We were told two things – that we were travelling by night and we were not to ask what route we were taking. Apart from that, there was plenty of food and drink on the trip and we were to relax; those of us who weren't good at sleeping on such occasions could happily drink their way through the night. It turned out afterwards that we were following an extremely long course, which had been mineswept. We went as far as about Brighton and then made across roughly in the direction of Le Havre and from there slightly to the right, or starboard, for the Normandy beaches. Mulberry Harbour had been badly damaged in a recent gale and so we didn't enter it, but anchored just outside and landed with 'ducks' (Dukw), which were amphibious landing-craft. (Incidentally, I heard much later that Harlyn Bay had received the message of my safe arrival from the kindly chief engineer.)

My memory at this point becomes a bit hazy. We had arrived safely on the Normandy beaches and I know a sense of enormous relief overtook us all, as well as a sense of tremendous fatigue. Bundles of us were taken in lorries to various orchards only a few miles inland, where there were camps already in position. We were given breakfast and then told to return to our bunks.

The immediate area was by now completely clear of Germans, but we had to wait a bit before we could make the looked-forward-to liberation of Brussels; there was still a pocket of resistance around Falaise. It must have been about a week before we heard the news that the Germans had been trapped in the Falaise Gap and quite soon after that we were on the road making for Brussels. I won't dwell on the terrible sights of carnage we occasionally came across on our journey. I remember being very moved by the sight of Rouen cathedral, which one could see, complete – the houses all round were absolutely flat and one had a magnificent view of the cathedral; nowadays, of course, the city has been rebuilt and the cathedral partly masked.

Twenty-first Army Group Headquarters took over a hotel – not unlike, in height and general size, the Dorchester in London. The anti-aircraft side of 21st Army Group, which was known as GHQ AA Troops (always called GHQ Ack/Ack Troops) was positioned very close – five minutes' walk – in a building in a nice little street called avenue de Gaulois. The liaison officer between 21st Army Group Headquarters and GHQ AA Troops was the Hon. Michael Berry (now Lord Hartwell). He attended regular meetings in which, amongst other things, we were briefed by the intelligence officer with a large map about positions of the various forces. I was given a big store-room where I could deposit all my aircraft recognition material – silhouettes, models and books of information. Apart from that I shared the office of Major Stratton, who was in charge of training. I respected his knowledge of staff work and his ability to answer any question put to him at meetings. He enjoyed my attempts to be soldierly, and we both laughed a great deal. We also developed the knack of looking instantly regimental should any VIP come in unannounced.

There was the little problem to be sorted out of where we were going to live; various Belgian families had volunteered to put up officers and it was really a question of who went where. I asked to be given time to do a little personal reconnaissance, as I was desperately anxious to find a billet where there was a piano. I struck lucky, because down some steep steps just off the avenue de Gaulois was a group of houses, one of which was marked on our list of possible addresses. I knocked on the door and a charming elderly lady called Madame Deflandres opened the door; she spoke quite good English, and asked me in. Up the stairs I went and in her drawing-room was a grand piano, a Pleyel. I asked her if I might play it and she was delighted because she was very musical. The piano turned out to be a very beautiful one and I made that my home – I'm almost ashamed to admit it – until VE Day. I also struck up a friendship with a lady who lived next door to our office, who also turned out to have a good piano.

Then there was the officers' club, which was an awfully useful meeting place for us soldiers, and one of the first people I ran into was a girl with whom I had literally grown up in old Bristol days, Mary Fedden, who has since become very well known as an artist. Mary, as it turned out, was driving for Jimmy Nuthall, who was then a VIP in the NAAFI, and I instantly recalled that Jimmy Nuthall had beaten the Hon. Peter Aitkin in the semi-finals of Junior Wimbledon in 1929 (the year I played). Anyway, I invited Mary Fedden round to see Madame Deflandres. Mary, incidentally, spoke very much better French than I did and started off in French, but when she discovered that Madame Deflandres spoke English I'm afraid, like most English people, Mary became lazy and we always used English after that.

For a day or two, frankly, it seemed the best thing to do was to relax, sort out all my aircraft recognition material, look as intelligent as possible and do as much piano playing as I could. My van officers knew how to contact me, and one did at once – Captain Thomson, who had mislaid some silhouettes.

One morning at the meeting there was a question of some special small-arms ammunition to be brought from England and it was agreed that as I seemed to have some time on my hands, I should be sent off to get it. It was arranged that I should fly to England and bring the equipment back by ship. In due course I found a seat on an Avro Anson and flew across to Northolt aerodrome. I had been told where I had to pick up the equipment. When I got to the place where the ammunition was supposed to be, I was told that it wouldn't be ready for a few days; this delighted me because it meant that I could look up one or two old friends. I discovered that my musical benefactress, Lady Ravensdale, was in London; she took me out to dinner at the Savoy Grill and we had a very delightful evening. I'm afraid I didn't look very smart, but it was wartime and dressing up was optional; people were only too glad to be alive.

In due course I went to the spot, which was somewhere south of the river, picked up the treasure trove and took it in a locked van, which was loaded onto a ship at Tilbury. There were several hundred Canadians on the boat and I enjoyed meeting them. The only trouble was that the sea was very rough; there was a force eight gale blowing and, other side-effects apart, it slowed down our progress. We were actually a week on the sea, admittedly only about two days getting across, but at anchor another four days, a mile out, unable to land.

When we did finally get ashore I made a slight miscalculation, because I didn't realize that my van had to go back to England, so I had to re-load this very special small-arms equipment into another van, one which I more or less commandeered; fortunately there always seemed to be spare vans knocking around. But there was no driver, so I decided to drive it myself to the nearest airport and unload the equipment, with the help of various people, and fly it to Evère airport at Brussels – this time in a Dakota. I telephoned the office and a van was sent to pick up me and the precious cargo. When I arrived, the particular officer responsible for small-arms equipment was very grateful to me and when I handed over the parcels (which seemed to weigh a ton) he thanked me for accomplishing the mission so thoroughly. I apologized for being such a long time and explained we had had this terrible storm.

However, when the parcels were opened an appalling discovery was made – instead of this special small-arms ammunition, it turned out that the boxes contained nothing but tins and tins of Blanco! The officer was very annoyed with me, but I explained that I carried out every instruction and it was in no way my fault. When I told Dick Stratton, the major in my office, he roared with laughter and thought it was quite the funniest thing he had heard for a very long time.

One morning Dick Stratton told me that he had received information that an alarming number of troops were reporting sick with various diseases; quite a number of them were connected with riotous living and the fact that the girls had given our troops too hearty a welcome on liberating their city for them! Would I go down to the army cinema unit and see the chap there and get some films on hygiene 'and that sort of thing'. The film officer would know exactly what I meant and there was no need to labour the point. (I intended using basic English and no beating about the bush.) I found out where the army cinema unit was and knocked on the door, but to my surprise a female voice said 'Come in'. I went in and there was an ATS senior commander, a very charming girl with blonde hair, blue eyes and a marvellous smile. I said that I was Captain Cooper from GHQ AA Troops and she was all eagerness to help: did I want films? I said: 'Well, I did actually.' But when she asked what kind of films my courage failed me completely and I didn't know what to say. I stammered that entertainment films would do splendidly and she said she had some fine Marlene Dietrich films, which she thought were admirable for the troops – I thought privately it was the very last thing I wanted, but I simply couldn't face up to saying what I had really come for. This lovely lady, whose name was Senior Commander Greig, gave me the films, which I took back to Major Stratton. I told him the whole story. He wasn't awfully pleased and said he thought I should have got round it somehow. 'All right, but you come with me tomorrow morning and you ask for them,' I replied. 'You'll see it's not as easy as it looks, because this girl has quite exceptional charm and it's a kind of subject that I simply couldn't associate with her.' 'Coward,' he said.

The next morning we set off together and when we got to the office Dick Stratton was completely tongue-tied and didn't know what to say. We were then both ushered into the colonel. Dick scribbled about three words, which the colonel read and acknowledged with a quick nod, and then said he thought it would be a splendid idea if we all went and had a drink. So Senior Commander Greig and Colonel Bartlett and Dick Stratton and I went off to Le Serf in the Grande Place and drank champagne cocktails. I don't know if the hygiene films ever reached the troops, but I got to see more and more of Senior Commander Greig, whom I found enormously entertaining with a very infectious giggle.

When VE Day eventually came and it was time for us all to move up and occupy Germany, I said a rueful *au revoir* to Senior Commander Greig, hoping that somehow we might meet again in Germany. We were given opportunities for saying what kind of work we would like to do and I, of course, opted for something to do with entertainment – anything in the music line or theatre line that was going would interest me. I was sent to a town called Herford in Westphalia, which was the base of 21st Army Group (Rear) and the home of the welfare department, which included entertainment. I found there was a harmonium in the chapel there and I volunteered to play for the services (the main organ was out of action). At the first service I was in the middle of verse three of 'O God our help in ages past' when I turned round and who should I see in the front row – Senior Commander Greig, singing her head off. This seemed absolutely marvellous – I've never pedalled so hard in my life – I nearly bust that harmonium. After the service she waited behind and we had a talk and arranged to meet for dinner in the mess.

My small billet was without a piano, but I decided that now I was in Germany, where the finest pianos were, I must get hold of a Steinway. I made an excuse of some sort that I needed some equipment and took a lorry to Hamburg. There I visited Steinway's, armed with a large supply of coffee brought from England, because that was the one thing I knew they hadn't got. In return they would loan me the use of a Steinway as long as I promised to return it.

I proudly brought a lovely Steinway down to Herford and installed it in my billet.

When I next met Jean Greig, as her name turned out to be, I suggested that she came and had coffee one evening, because I'd got a new piano and I'd rather like to play to her. It was a beautiful piano and I started playing the eighteenth variation from Rachmaninoff's *Rhapsody on a theme of Paganini* and I really made the piano sing that night. When the orchestra is supposed to come in I made the piano sound like about five symphony orchestras.

Unfortunately the time was soon due for Senior Commander Greig's demobilization. We promised to keep in touch by letter, which we did, and made one interesting discovery before she left – that we both knew Lady Ravensdale, so we did have a point of contact. Apart from that she told me very little about herself or her background, but gave me a telephone number, so that when I next came to England I could ring.

On my next leave I rang the number and Jean Greig agreed to meet me and take me to meet her family. She said they lived at Thatched House Lodge in Richmond Park. Jean met me at Richmond station in a car and we drove to the park. It was dark and the huge iron gates were locked. Jean produced an enormous key and insisted on opening the gates herself. 'It isn't strength but a knack that you need; besides the man in the cottage knows me and in wartime they don't like strangers.' Once inside the park I registered alarm. 'This all seems frightfully grand, what is your father?' Jean replied: 'Oh, he's a sort of park-keeper.'

But when we got to the house I could see it was not exactly a humble park-keeper's house; it was a large and quite sumptuous place. I looked very scruffy, my boots weren't even clean and I asked if I could go to the loo as soon as we got in, to tidy up. There I became absolutely petrified with fear and remained for about half-an-hour. Eventually I heard a voice from outside; it was Jean saying, 'Do come out, the family are longing to meet you and they are not a bit frightening.'

Out I went and met Jean's parents, who turned out to be Sir Louis and Lady Greig.* The Greigs couldn't have given me a warmer

* Sir Louis Greig was Deputy Ranger of Richmond Park, and a Gentleman Usher at Buckingham Palace – I only discovered later that King George VI was in fact Jean's godfather.

welcome. None the less I felt highly embarrassed and apologized for my clothes and was very thankful when the evening was over.

I knew I was going to miss Jean when I got back to Herford from my leave, but I didn't realize quite how much – I think it was her lovely, silvery giggle, and her interest in everything that I did that made life seem terribly worthwhile.

There was for the troops, naturally, an inevitable reaction which followed the relief with the end of hostilities in Europe. People soon tended to become bored. Some were lucky and managed to land jobs that were very akin to their own work. I, in fact, in the general distribution of jobs that came under army welfare, was unlucky – I was made second in command of canteens. The representatives in charge of the various vans, such as the Church Army, the British and Belgian Red Cross, and the Salvation Army, knew their job and all they required was to be told which area they had to cover. They attended meetings where they could air any problems that might arise, or where we could discuss any complaints that reached the office from the field.

I needed something to occupy my attention, and decided – I don't know quite how – that I would introduce some evening concerts called Saturday night proms. There was a room above some offices in Herford which would take about seventy to eighty people with a piano in it and I had record-playing equipment installed. Every Saturday I gave my 'prom', which consisted of, say, my analysing a symphony, or a movement of it, showing them what to listen for, and then playing a movement of it on the gramophone: or I might do the same with a piano concerto; or I might play a few piano solos myself. I hadn't too much at hand in my repertoire, but if I aired some of the old war-horses with more ardour than accuracy, no one cared. These Saturday night proms caught on in a big way. From audiences of about twenty they swelled to one hundred. We had troops sitting on the floor and even under the piano; in the end we had queues right down the street and people had to be turned away.

As well as that there was the YWCA canteen, which had an excellent piano and I gave regular concerts there. Then there was another, much larger hall in Herford. Having met several members of the Berlin Philharmonic Orchestra, I managed to persuade them when they were doing a tour down in our area to come and give us a concert. I wrote the programme notes and arranged the programme with the conductor, who was then Celebidache, a delightful and brilliant man. This was fun, but much more fun when Jean had been around to inspire me and help me with the choice of music. I kept in touch by giving her a weekly report of my activities. Regular two-way communication was maintained.

Eric Maschwitz was then in charge of entertainment and one day he met me in the mess: 'I think I've found a way of getting you out of that miserable job of yours in canteens.' I eagerly pricked up my ears and asked what it was. 'British Forces Network in Hamburg need a musical director and without bothering to ask you I've put your name forward and they've accepted it.' 'So it's all signed and sealed?' I said excitedly. Eric replied: 'By no means, I'm afraid, because I am not your boss. You have to get permission from your CO to release you from canteens. Once that's done, you're clear to go. Perhaps you had better leave it to me and I'll try and fix it.' I didn't hear any more for two days and then a very doleful Eric met me; 'I have bad news for you. Your colonel in charge of tea and buns is reluctant to let you go; he says you are doing a good job and he doesn't feel at this stage he can spare you.'

You can imagine my feelings of intense disappointment, because instead of this leap back into the music profession, here I was, stuck with my confounded canteens. However, I had heard that my friend Trevor Harvey was in the neighbourhood. He had been in the BBC before the war and had a great deal of broadcasting experience, so I suggested his name. I didn't quite know where his unit was, but they managed to contact him and he got the job. It fitted like a glove, because Trevor was already a conductor and he had knowledge of administration in broadcasting. Being the good colleague he is, Trevor Harvey returned the compliment to me by inviting me up to Hamburg to broadcast whenever I liked and could get off. It's quite a long way from Herford to Hamburg, so visits were rare.

But there was one incredible occasion that will always stick in my memory. I arrived and was greeted by Trevor Harvey, who said they had a crisis on their hands. A half-hour spot called *Piano Playtime*, where the pianist plays dance music, was due on the air in a few minutes, but the pianist had fallen sick and they had no replacement. Trevor said he knew I could sit down straight away and do it – but would I? I agreed, but first retired to put my hands in hot water. Then I was greeted by the producer, Arthur Langford; I asked him to sign to me when to start and when to stop. I think he was very surprised, because although he knew that I was a classical musician, he had no idea I had a passion for playing the tunes of the Twenties and Thirties – still less that I would reel them off with no rehearsal after a long journey.

The other excitement was that the next day Trevor Harvey said he had some auditions and asked if I could stay and listen. He told me there was a singer coming from the RAF, one Leading Aircraftman Evans, G. (one of the lowest ranks). There was quite a little group of us seated around and LAC Evans started off with 'Water Boy'; before he had finished everyone was deeply moved – it was quite obvious that here was a voice in a million. Trevor Harvey afterwards arranged for him to go to Theo Hermann, a well-known singer in Hamburg, where he was able to have expert training. An incredible, but true, story and I'm always so glad to have been in on the 'birth' of Sir Geraint Evans – one of the greatest operatic singers of our time and one of the nicest people.

The next day I gave a classical broadcast recital before returning to dreary old Herford.

But when at last the time came for my demobilization, I didn't leave Germany immediately: I accepted an invitation from the Control Commission for Germany in Lübbecke (civilians who came out to take over administration as the army was demobilized) to organize concerts for them, in particular the Saturday night prom. I did these for a while, fairly successfully, and managed to get another lovely piano. However, I failed to recapture the army's warmth. Nor could I expect to.

Soon afterwards I had an urgent letter from Jean saying that a very important job connected with Vaughan Williams had come my way and she had pencilled an acceptance, if I could leave the Control Commission. There was no problem, because in any case I had agreed only to start them off. They generously granted me an immediate release.

6

Peace, Partnership and Progress

I arrived back in England in the first week of September 1946. The first thing I did was to contact Jean and take her out to lunch. I'd made a little money in the CCG, so I made it a bumper occasion and we went to the Mirabelle.

Jean wasted no time in coming to the point of her story. 'You remember meeting Cyril Smith and Phyllis Sellick in Brussels and you said you lent Cyril the use of your piano? Well, at the Albert Hall in two months' time, on 22 November, there is the St Cecilia's Day Festival Concert in aid of the Musicians' Benevolent Fund. They want to do the Vaughan Williams Piano Concerto, but instead of using one soloist, the organizers want it arranged for two pianos with orchestra and want you to collaborate with the composer, Vaughan Williams, in making this two-piano version specially for Cyril Smith and Phyllis Sellick. Sir Adrian Boult will conduct.'

I was thrilled, because I thought it would give me great experience in getting back to music and with any luck I would get my name on the programme of the concert at the Albert Hall, which was being given in front of the King and Queen, and many musical celebrities.

Jean said she'd been in touch with Cyril and Phyllis and they wanted me to go down and see them and talk about the concerto. They lived quite near Richmond Park, which Jean said was very convenient – I shuddered at the thought of the words Richmond Park, but said nothing. Anyway, we visited the Smiths and they told me all about the plan; one thing they stressed was to make the concerto playable, because Vaughan Williams, bless him, was not a pianist and, great composer though he was, he didn't entirely understand there are certain things that just don't lie comfortably under the hand.

There used to be a famous haunt of musicians called the MM Club

(Mainly Musicians Club). It was next to the Oxford Circus underground entrance in Argyll Street; judging by the number of steps that took you down to it, it was almost as far below ground as the railway station. Its very seclusion attracted musicians, specially composers – Britten and Vaughan Williams were both members. It was at the MM Club that I had my meeting with Vaughan Williams to discuss the concerto. He was coming up specially from his home at Dorking and arrived a bit late. I introduced myself: 'I am Cooper, sir, your collaborator.' He was full of apologies, hoped I wasn't in a hurry and asked if I would have lunch with him. 'Such a nice place this; order yourself a drink and I will rejoin you shortly', and he made for the loo.

Over a leisurely lunch Vaughan Williams spoke in the most friendly manner, as though we were old acquaintances. He then said how sorry he was that the first performance of *The Bridal Day* had to be cancelled by the war, and how well he remembered my playing of the piano part at the first play-through in the spring of 1939.

Had I seen anything of Jean Stewart? I told him the only musicians I had seen since Germany were Cyril Smith and Phyllis Sellick. Vaughan Williams said they had recently given a brilliant first performance of his Introduction and Fugue for Two Pianos, which he wrote specially for them. 'They sometimes find your piano writing difficult,' I ventured. 'Nonsense! Cyril and Phyl can play anything.'

Then Vaughan Williams turned to our collaboration in the concerto. He said he would give me a free hand to re-arrange the single piano part for two pianos. If I ran into difficulties I was to write to him and he'd send back a suggested solution. After lunch he gave me a printed piano score with the bars numbered. He had another one similarly numbered, and said I must always mention the bar number for quick reference.

As a parting compliment I said: 'I hope you still enjoy your beautiful song "Linden Lea" in spite of its popularity.' Vaughan Williams's reply is worth noting by aspiring singers: 'Why does everybody sing it like a dirge? It's meant to be bright, rather quick, and full of country air.' Poor V.W.! Twenty years after his death famous singers still grind it out soulfully, apparently searching for hidden meanings in every syllable.

As far as staying in London was concerned, I had the choice of several 'pads' where I could go for the odd night or two, and I rang the changes so as not to become burdensome.

But for this delicate piece of musical plastic surgery I needed a hideaway at least a hundred miles from Richmond Park. I telephoned some friends near Shepton Mallet and explained everything. The answer was, 'Come at once – nice to have you.' I left my address with Jean, armed myself with manuscript paper and left for Somerset.

By now Jean and I were emotionally involved and I sensed that Jean wanted me to push forward and propose to her. I was diffident, because there was little money in the bank and I couldn't picture what her father would say at the thought of his daughter marrying an impecunious musician, without any apparent prospects. So I stalled and stalled.

Then one day I had a letter with a typical piece of feminine blackmail. In it Jean said that she didn't know what my plans were, but if they didn't involve her in any definite way, she'd had an offer to ferry aeroplanes to Moscow, and as she'd always rather fancied being an air pilot, would I mind if she trained for this? I telephoned straight away to Thatched House Lodge and invited Jean down. I met her at Bath station and I proposed to her on a bus between Bath and Shepton Mallet. She accepted very quickly, because she felt this would probably be the first and only chance before I became engulfed in the Vaughan Williams. I was engaged to be married: I couldn't believe it.

Jean had cousins at nearby Castle Cary, with whom she went to stay. So with her on hand, the work on the Vaughan Williams progressed so smoothly and sweetly that in a fortnight it was done. Several times I sent queries to Vaughan Williams; invariably by return of post came the almost illegible but admirable solution.

The next thing was to get Cyril Smith's and Phyllis Sellick's approval. So Jean and I travelled to London with the new score and went together to the Smiths' house near Richmond Park. They could hardly disapprove in front of a newly-engaged couple. Having cast their quick and expert eyes over the music, the score was put away and a bottle of champagne opened.

Jean suggested that we shouldn't see each other for a few days or announce the engagement to her family until we had bought the ring and could present the news as a *fait accompli*. So I went to one of my pads, some friends in Medway Street, Westminster, for a little quiet thinking. I wrote to Vaughan Williams at Dorking to say that the arrangement of the concerto was complete. By return of post I received a letter of gratitude from him, enclosing a cheque for £25 – my first job since the end of the war.

When the concert took place a few weeks later I was delighted that the Vaughan Williams Two Piano Concerto went down so well – both with the audience, and in the press the next day. I was equally delighted to note that my name was on the programme.

While staying in Medway Street I thought about looking up some of my friends from the pre-war period, but many of them were out of London. Primrose Yarde-Buller had married Earl Cadogan in 1936 and I hadn't really seen anything of her since then. Virginia Gilliat had married Sir Richard Sykes in 1942 and was living at Sledmere in Yorkshire. Her parents, Lily and Jack Gilliat (who gave the marvellous party which started off my ambitions to become a concert pianist), had moved to Sunningdale.

Mrs Wessel, originally Lady Churston and mother of Primrose Yarde-Buller, was now, I discovered, The Duchess of Leinster. She was in London: she had a house in Hamilton Terrace, St John's Wood, and also had the use of another house opposite, which had been lent to her by a friend who was abroad. Jo Leinster was running both houses as a sanctuary for rich, but temporarily homeless people, most of whom had been bombed out during the War. They had to be rich, because Jo Leinster herself badly needed money and so her prices were very high.

I wasn't able to get hold of the Leinster telephone number, so I decided to go to Hamilton Terrace and call. The fact that Jo was now a duchess had made no difference to her – she was just the same and full of warmth and friendliness. She asked about everything that I had done since we last met before the war. I told her; also that I had just become engaged. When Jo Leinster asked where I was living, I said I was homeless at the moment. She said that could soon be solved: 'I have a nice little suite of rooms in the house opposite. Why don't you come and stay here as long as you like – until you get married if it suits you?' I thanked her, but said I couldn't begin to afford what she must charge for these very luxurious apartments. Immediately Jo said: 'There's no need to worry about that; I will charge you a nominal rent and regard this as my contribution to your career, which has been so cruelly interrupted by the war.'

She showed me the suite of rooms, already exquisitely furnished, which included a bedroom, study and a very large sitting-room. All it lacked was a piano. I assured her I could easily have mine moved in. Meals were served in her dining-room across the road and she still had her French cook, Rachel, so I knew that I'd rapidly be putting on weight. Jo suggested I moved in immediately. I went back to Medway Street, collected my suitcase of belongings and took up my new residence in the ground-floor flat of 90 Hamilton Terrace, NW8. Late that night I rang Jean and asked her to tea the following day.

I decided to leave my Steinway in Somerset for the moment, just in case plans were to change, and bought (on hire purchase) a concert grand, which was going cheaply on account of its very heavy action. I thought this would be an asset for me in regaining my lost technique. It would look and sound wonderful in its new home. Steinway's promised delivery within a week. My upright piano was still at Harlyn Bay (I eventually gave the 'Somerset' Steinway to a piano-tuner there).

No. 90 had a housekeeper, a Scots lady called Meg, the antithesis to the Duchess in every way except one – both had hearts of gold. (In case the reader hasn't already guessed it, I confess to my passion for being cosseted, spoilt and loved.) Cups of tea or coffee were on constant offer.

I now longed to show Jean Greig what I had been up to and I could hardly wait for tea-time. When Jean arrived I showed her into what I now called the music room. She took one look at the lovely room and gasped – she wasn't expecting anything quite so grand. I suggested to Jean that if she could come up in the morning we'd choose an engagement ring and then go down to Thatched House Lodge together and announce our engagement.

This is exactly what we did. Sir Louis and Lady Greig appeared to be delighted, and a dinner party was arranged in our honour.

The Sunday after I had moved in to Hamilton Terrace, Jean rang and asked if I was free that afternoon, because she would like me to go down to tea at Thatched House Lodge. She said it was a rather special tea-party, but she couldn't say anything about it on the telephone; she would collect me by car at 3 o'clock. So I popped on my one and only suit, brushed my hair smartly and went down to Thatched House Lodge with Jean. On the way I was told that Queen Mary, accompanied by her daughter, Princess Mary, would be coming to tea. I remembered having played to Queen Mary and being presented to her during the early part of the war, at Bristol, and noting how friendly she had been. So I wasn't too worried.

Sir Louis was very tense, waiting for the moment for the park police to ring to say Her Majesty had arrived at Robin Hood Gate. When the telephone rang he rushed out to the door to wait to greet Queen Mary. We remained in the drawing-room: the door opened and we all stood as Queen Mary entered and behind her Princess Mary with Sir Louis. We bowed and curtsied respectively and, after a few minutes' small talk, went into tea. I noticed with interest how Queen Mary tucked into scones and cakes with relish and at the end of tea smoked a cigarette. Then we went into the music room and I played to Queen Mary. After I'd finished the first piece she said: 'I remember you; you played at Bristol during the war and I spoke to you and asked how it was you played everything by heart. I remember well. Play me one of the pieces you played at Bristol.' I played 'Jesu, Joy of Man's Desiring' which she liked very much and I played one or two other pieces, including a Rachmaninoff prelude. Then Queen Mary said, 'Now play me something of the kind Mary and I always turn off on the wireless.' So I played to her a little bit of Poulenc and she said, 'Oh no, much more modern than that.' 'Ma'am, I don't go more modern than that,' I replied, and she said that was a relief.

Her Majesty expressed great delight in the occasion and asked if she could have a repeat performance in a few weeks' time. Apparently private royal visits were always cloaked in secrecy as a matter of protocol. But she herself wasn't starchy or stiff; that was her public image.

Afterwards, on the way back to Hamilton Terrace, Jean made an amusing confession. The piano at Thatched House Lodge didn't belong to the house. Sir Louis' sister, Aunt Anna, had lent it as soon as she received the SOS that a musician was visiting the house. Aunt Anna wanted her piano back, so Jean said she would buy one. She bought a presentable second-hand Blüthner with a soft tone – Sir Louis couldn't bear anything loud.

This precipitated the one near-row that was to clear the air and establish real friendship. I had been staying at Thatched House Lodge. On the Monday morning, just as Sir Louis was leaving for Buckingham Palace, Aunt Anna's piano was blocking the front door; Sir Louis went to the back, only to find Jean's Blüthner was being moved in and was blocking the back door. 'It seems I am a prisoner in my own house,' said Sir Louis half-humorously. He gave me a lift to London. When he remarked he was glad that I had my own piano at Thatched House Lodge I replied: 'It's not mine. It is one that Jean has bought.' Sir Louis said, 'I really can't have Jean buying pianos for you, you know!' I replied: 'I cannot think why she did, as I already own three pianos.' Sir Louis seemed surprised and greatly relieved. After that there was a noticeable improvement in our relationship.

My mother and father had moved back from Harlyn Bay to Westbury-on-Trym and I thought it was high time that they met Jean. So we went down and stayed a few days with them. To my great relief they took to Jean immediately. My father, who was very difficult to please, obviously found great joy in her enthusiasm and her lovely looks. He was by then slightly deaf and you couldn't make confiding remarks to him; but he took me aside (out of other people's hearing) and said, 'Bravo, my son, you've picked a winner.'

While I was in Bristol I called at the BBC, where I had a number of friends, and in particular talked to Nicholas Crocker; he was going to run some 'smoking concerts' in the West Country and agreed that I should be the pianist for the solo singer and have a solo piano spot to myself. The main ingredient of these smoking concerts was the male voice choir. In those days, especially in Cornwall, there were some magnificent male voice choirs, of which the local inhabitants were very proud. It was arranged that sometimes my piano spot should consist of an improvisation – I might even wrap up a tune in the style of a certain composer – do a 'hidden melody' in fact.

Each week I went down by train to the West Country and performed in one of these smoking concerts, presided over by an affable Cornishman called Bernard Fishwick – a local celebrity. The concerts were a great success; they were 'live' of course (taping of programmes hadn't yet become a habit) and they were all very well attended, even in remote places such as Mousehole. The audience had a chance of joining in choruses which, encouraged by Bernard, they took. So their lively participation added much to the total effect for listeners at home.

The train journey was very easy because Hamilton Terrace was only five minutes' walk from Maida Vale tube station, which itself was only two stops from Paddington and the main-line station that took me down to Devon and Cornwall. I decided to change my name for these broadcasts, because they were so very light in nature, and as I was going to give a series of London recitals of a very classical and serious kind, I didn't want the critics in advance to typecast me as a 'light' pianist. I chose Roger Elliott as my name – Elliott being my mother's maiden name and being the first name that came into my head. My pseudonym occasioned one rather amusing little episode – the BBC had a letter from one of my old fans in Wells, who said that though he quite liked Roger Elliott he remembered a pianist in the army called Joe Cooper, who could 'play Roger Elliott off the platform'!

Each week was enlivened by the presence of a distinguished solo male singer: Owen Brannigan, Henry Cummings, Frederic Harvey, William Parsons, are all names that spring to mind, with Owen Brannigan easily my favourite. One week at Plymouth (with Henry Cummings) we got into trouble with the weather; after two days of continuous heavy snow with gale-force winds, Plymouth was completely cut off. That wouldn't have mattered if Jean and I hadn't arranged a large cocktail party at Hamilton Terrace a few days later. I got Jean on the telephone and told her we couldn't get out of Plymouth at the moment – the trains couldn't get up the notorious hill and the roads were blocked by heavy drifts. Eventually the railway line was cleared and I just got back in time for the cocktail party, although I had had to leave Jean and her very kind mother to handle all the arrangements.

In between my visits to the West Country I kept practising hard on my Steinway concert grand; it did look as lovely in its new surroundings as I thought it was going to – and its tone was magnificent. Jean noticed a certain reluctance on my part to commit myself to naming a date for a first London recital, so she teasingly made the little threat that she wouldn't marry me until I had given my first London concert – she thought that would act as a necessary inducement.

19 Discussing a point with Claudio Arrau.

20 At the Mansion House with Lady Ravensdale.

21 Leaving Toulon in *Cormorant*.

22 Joe and Jean on the Thames at Newbridge.

23 Tense moment on *Here Today*.

24 Interviewing John Betjeman in the same series.

25 Croquet instruction for Carol and Joe from Uncle Dunk.

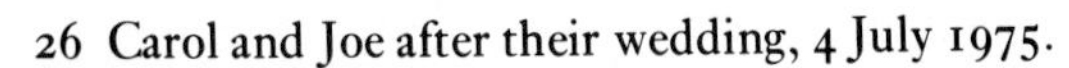

26 Carol and Joe after their wedding, 4 July 1975.

27 Joe and Carol with Joan Drogheda (photographed by Garrett Drogheda) at Englefield Green.

28 Joe on Maestro Solti's bicycle somewhere in Italy.

29 Suti-Mia's great moment.

30 Carol and her Arab mare, Lalibela.

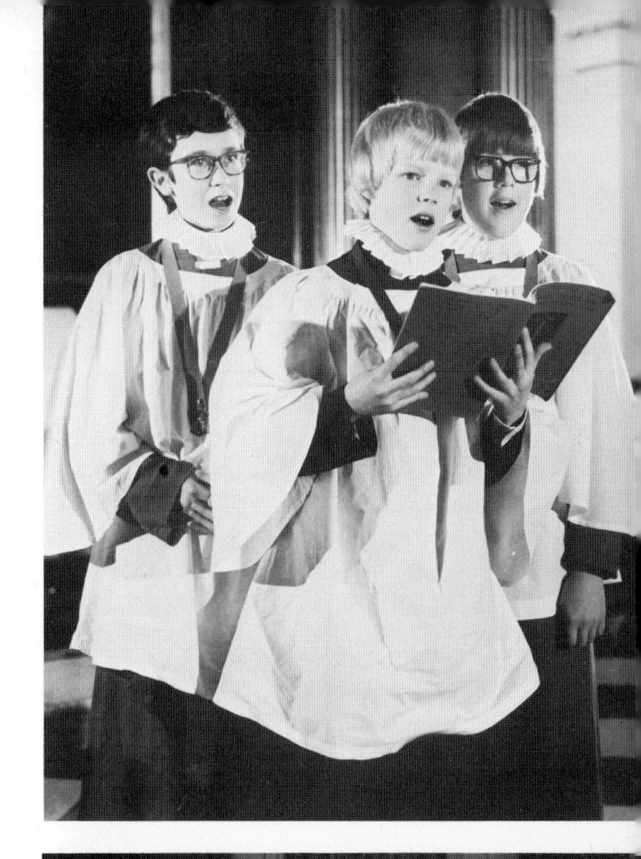

31 Prizewinners of the Rediffusion Choristers' Awards, St George's, Hanover Square, 1978.

32 The same competition – Joe signing his autograph for one of the prize-winners, Stephen Cooper of Ipswich (no relation).

33 At the Royal College of Music with the Queen Mother, November 1976.

34 Richard Baker, Dorothy Tutin and Jel rehearsing Horovitz's *Toy Symphony* at Covent Garden.

I was very anxious to get in touch with Jean's and my mutual friend, Irene Ravensdale; she was a great globe-trotter and was very often away. One morning I telephoned her and found her at home. Jean and I went over and had tea at her house in The Vale, Chelsea. We told her all our news and she was so thrilled. We also told her that I was planning to give that postponed concert (for which she had so kindly put up the money) in the coming October (1947), and the marriage was planned for November.

Irene said she was particularly glad we had got in touch, because a pianist she had heard great things about was coming to give an afternoon recital at Covent Garden shortly and she was going to give a tea party for him and would we come. His name was Claudio Arrau. This struck a chord in my brain – I remembered that members of the Berlin Philharmonic, especially the principal cellist, Münch-Holland – had spoken so often to me of Arrau. He said of all the younger pianists they had had living in Germany, Arrau was easily the best. He was much missed when he went to live in America.

With great excitement we went to that concert and to the tea party afterwards. Arrau's playing was of a tremendous order – he had a glorious technique and an incredible command of tone. He seemed to me the complete pianist and I was terribly excited by the occasion. At tea we were sitting side by side on a sofa; as an opening gambit I asked Mr Arrau how long he was going to be in London. He said for a week, because he was about to record the Brahms D minor Piano Concerto at EMI Studios; he was worried because he hadn't got a piano to practise on. I realized very quickly that the EMI Studios were only a few minutes' walk from Hamilton Terrace, so I dared to suggest that I had got a Steinway concert grand and I could put it at his disposal. He was enormously grateful. I gave him the address and telephone number and he said he would be there about 10.30 the next morning.

Well, the next morning at 10.30, no sign; 11 o'clock, no sign; and I began to think I had been forgotten and I had a terrible sense of let-down. About 11.30 a taxi rolled up and I saw Arrau get out of it. I went to the door and showed him in; he had a miniature score of the Brahms D minor. Meg brought in some coffee and he said he only needed one thing now – to be left completely alone. I said it couldn't be simpler, but he asked where I was going to practise. I told him there were other pianos I could easily go to and I wouldn't disturb him or come near him; but I would come and tell him when it was lunch-time. Arrau said: 'Actually, I'd like to practise through the day. Could you collect me about 4.30?'

I left the room and decided to go to the EMI Studios to time the walk, just to see how long in fact it took, in order to allow us plenty of time for his recording on Wednesday. Having done that I came back and heard sounds of the Brahms No. 1 coming from my room; I sat quietly on the stairs outside and just listened. I thought, how does he do it? How does he make that fantastic technique sound always like a steady stream of glorious music pouring from the piano?

At 4.30 p.m. I went in and Meg had some tea ready (I discovered Mr Arrau had a passion for 'English tea' as he called it). He asked if he could come back and do the same thing next day, and perhaps I would accompany him to the recording studios on Wednesday. I said it would be a great honour and pleasure for me to do so.

The next morning Arrau arrived punctually at 10.30 a.m., and although I was bursting to ask him some questions about piano technique, I could quite see he wanted to be left alone. At 4.30 p.m. Meg again produced some tea. Arrau said the next day he would come at 2 o'clock for the studio recording at 2.30 p.m. On this occasion he said he would like to sit alone for a few minutes and read through the score, and when it was time for us to walk round to the studios, would I very kindly come in and collect him. His manner was that of great humility, without a trace of bombast.

A few days afterwards Arrau was due to play Beethoven's 'Emperor' Concerto at the BBC Maida Vale Studio No. 1, which had an audience gallery. He took Lady Ravensdale, Jean and me as his guests. That performance was equally magnificent; I only wish it could have been recorded then and there, because I am sure it has never been played better before or since! The same goes for a performance of the Brahms B flat Piano Concerto which he gave a little later. Again he was in absolutely peak form; there wasn't a hitch or a sign of a wrong note. I cannot pay him a higher compliment than by saying the enormous four-movement work seemed short. He could have repeated it and the audience wouldn't have moved.

When I was walking Arrau to the EMI Studies for the recording which he was to make of the Brahms D minor Concerto, I remember him telling me that he wouldn't be coming back to London for many months, but he would like to see me again. I told him that I was getting married in November and he said he would be coming over some time around then and hoped to bring his wife, Ruth, and also his two young children, because they had never seen London. And he thought he would organize a merry meeting at the Savoy Hotel. 'Get my moves, if you will, from my agent, Harold Holt, who knows my exact itinerary.'

From then on it required no effort from anybody to make me sit down at the piano and practise six hours at a stretch; in fact Meg used to come and bang on the door and say, 'Your lunch will be getting cold, Mr Cooper.' I had been very tense since I arrived back in England and in order to try and soothe my nerves I had been smoking more and more cigarettes, until I got up to about forty a day. After Arrau had gone I made a resolution: I smoked a cigarette, stubbed it out in the ashtray and said, 'That is the last cigarette you will ever smoke in your life.' And I have kept the vow ever since. For one thing it was a way of saving money, urgently required; and for another it was a little victory over myself. As I was a non-inhaler it didn't take long to get the habit out of my system. I later smoked the occasional small cigar (now also abandoned).

There was one pressing worry: Jean had insisted on my giving this recital before we got married, so what was she going to do in all the hours I was practising? From now onwards until the recital, apart from short breaks, I was never going to leave the keyboard. What were the Greigs going to say about a prospective bridegroom who never bothered to take his bride-to-be anywhere, or even see her? This wouldn't do, so I hit on a plan. Although Jean loved music and even had her own collection of records – her taste was conservative but good, ranging from Beethoven to Rachmaninoff – she couldn't read music and she didn't really understand time or rhythm, didn't even know what the notes were on the piano. So I asked her if I might teach her the rudiments of music. She said she thought she would never be able to grasp them, but I persuaded her that I would like her to try. In point of fact she picked up the basics quite well, especially the rhythmical side; she learnt to count the bars, whether they were in three or four, or even ultimately in seven, and with the aid of a pencil she learnt to conduct them.

Then I taught Jean elementary sight-reading, and she could soon play a few simple pieces. Next I asked her if she would be kind enough to turn the pages of new pieces while I sight-read through them. This would give me an overall 'picture' of the work, without having to leave out notes while I fumbled with the turning. I was startled to find she could do this, and she could even judge the exact 'right' moment when to turn (most pianists read ahead of the bar they are playing). Eventually I asked Jean if she would test my memorizing. I would play a short section, pointing out as I went various beauties and subtleties of harmony, melody or rhythm. Then I would give her the copy and ask her to see how much I could remember. Here I surprised myself. I often got it right first time. I remembered reading that Schnabel liked to learn by teaching.

So, extending very gently Jean's capacity for sustained interest, and finding that it grew as her own knowledge of the craft of music grew, I proceeded to memorizing pages, then finally whole pieces, by this method. In fact the whole of the programme was learnt this way.

The next step was to try the programme out on various long-suffering friends and I even managed to organize a few concerts for charity – giving my services, but gaining vital platform experience.

I can't remember why the Cowdray Hall was booked for my first recital rather than the Wigmore Hall; it is possible that the agent may have recommended the Cowdray as being smaller and therefore easier to fill, and also perhaps less frightening – more in the nature of the nursery slopes for a first recital. With it was the combined advantage that the critics liked it as a hall, so that I was fairly well assured of *The Times* and the *Telegraph* turning up – the papers that really mattered so far as music criticisms were concerned.

On the day of the concert I had a good run through of the programme, enjoyed the acoustics of the hall and found the atmosphere very congenial, so when I came back in the evening I was not nearly as nervous as I'd expected to be. I asked Jean to keep any well-meaning visitors out of the artist's room, both at the beginning and at the interval, saying very politely would they come round and see me afterwards. I personally can't bear meeting people until I've finished a concert, because I find it puts me off and I lose concentration.

I was greatly comforted by the presence in the audience of many stalwart friends from either the army or Harlyn Bay days, or even musical friends not predisposed to be too critical. As I turned to bow I purposely didn't try and pick anyone out, least of all the critics, whom I managed to dismiss from my mind altogether. I think I played reasonably well – I certainly didn't let myself down, but many things could have been played a great deal better. But for the first recital, all things considered, it was not discouraging. The next morning *The Times* and the *Telegraph* had nice things to say – in fact they were sufficiently encouraging for me to be able to quote bits of them and also give me the feeling it was worth while going on and next time booking the Wigmore Hall. (The main object of the exercise with these London recitals is to acquire enough notices to make up a brochure which the agent then sends round to the music societies to try and obtain engagements.)

The Times made one helpful criticism, having said that my playing was characterized by rich imagination, it said that I must develop the habit of listening more carefully to my own playing. It's a good idea to read criticisms, because, even if they hurt, one can always learn something from them. My concentration was by no means complete and I often wasn't listening to myself, and so I took this very much to heart and felt that *The Times* had in a way given me a free lesson. Back in the practice room, helped by Jean, I cultivated the habit of listening to myself as I played.

In those days *The Times* used not to reveal who the critic was, so I don't know who wrote that notice, but the *Telegraph* has always given either a name or initials, and under my notice are the initials F.B. which stood for Ferruccio Bonavia, who was a very experienced musician and critic. I think he was also a very kind man; he gave me the sort of notice every tiro dreams of – better than I deserved, I thought to myself.

We had soon to put the thoughts of this first recital to the back of our minds and turn all our attention to our wedding, which was a fortnight later. Lady Greig had already been busy getting the invitations out and ordering a large marquee to cover the tennis lawn in the garden at Thatched House Lodge.

We were to be married on 15 November 1947 at St Andrew's Church on Ham Common, which adjoins Richmond Park. The vicarage was supposed to be haunted and the vicar, the Reverend

Ernest Beard, used to talk quite openly about his ghost as though he really believed in its existence. Because of this Jean wasn't keen on going to the vicarage to choose the hymns for the service. I tried to avoid it, but Mr Beard said he would like us to discuss the music with him. So we went to the vicarage and Mr Beard showed us into his study. In the middle of choosing the hymns Mr Beard suddenly stopped speaking, opened his eyes wide and looked up to the ceiling. Then he said, 'Oh dear. He's here.' 'I don't see anybody Mr Beard,' I said. 'No, one doesn't *see* him,' he replied, 'but it's our old friend – he's around, I'm afraid. I'm sorry about it, but don't take any notice. Let's proceed.' I looked at Jean and she was obviously very worried indeed. We made our final selection of hymns and Mr Beard said: 'I think that's all. But having cooped you up in this little study, I must show you my big drawing-room.' He showed us into a lovely room, with a piano at the far end. I said, jokingly, 'I'm going to play a few chords on your piano and see if I can frighten your ghost.' I sat down and played the opening few chords of Rachmaninoff's Second Piano Concerto: as I did so, from the other side of the drawing-room door came a tremendous noise of crashes, bangs and wailings, I stopped and rushed to the door. I thought, this must be a practical joke. I flung the door open – nobody there.

Jean was as white as a sheet and I felt shivers down my back. Mr Beard simply said, 'Now you see what I have to put up with.' We left the house as quickly as possible, glad to be in the open air. The matter was not referred to again, but we read in the papers several years later that the ghost had been exorcized.

As best man for my wedding I chose one of my friends of long standing, Martin Hardcastle, who you may remember was a master at Clifton and whose father had been Archdeacon of Canterbury. Martin had all the good Christian virtues of kindness, honesty, patience and love, and he was above all a calming influence. Everybody who has come into contact with Martin Hardcastle would agree with me. When you add his infectious sense of humour, which had people in stitches when he was doing his acts on the stage in the Canterbury Chestnuts, you will realize that I couldn't have chosen anybody better for best man.

We had lunch quietly together before the wedding at the nearby Dysart Arms, only about ten minutes away from the church. While speaking to some people in the car park, before leaving for the church, I unfortunately left my top hat (which I'd hired from Moss Bros) on the top of Martin's car. Martin, not realizing the hat was there, started moving the car and, backing rather suddenly, the hat ricocheted into the middle of the road and was squashed flat by a passing bus. So the bridegroom was without a top hat – as the photograph shows. Of course, I had to pay Moss Bros for not returning the hat.

Jean's sister, Bridget, was chief bridesmaid and we also had a small girl bridesmaid and a little page, a small nephew of Jean's who looked very smart in a kilt. Unfortunately he had to leave the church in rather a hurry in the middle of the service, and as he returned the uncle accompanying him remarked, in a voice rather too loud, 'Too late!' Apparently the page was not wearing his kilt in the true Scottish fashion and certain adjustments had to be made which took up valuable time – and the inevitable result ensued.

My former music master at Clifton, Sir William McKie, then Organist of Westminster Abbey, sent down the pick of his choirboys from the abbey, to join in with the already excellent choir at Ham Church. The overall effect was astonishingly beautiful.

Jean had specially asked her former colonel in the Army Film Unit, Sir Basil Bartlett, to propose the health of the bride and bridegroom at the wedding reception. He made a hilarious speech and changed an atmosphere which up to then had been slightly forbidding into one of enormous enjoyment. I replied with a similarly light-hearted speech.

Before the wedding there had been much activity in Westbury-on-Trym. The trouble was that my father's health had started to fail rather rapidly and my sister, who had recently returned from India and was living at Westbury-on-Trym, telephoned me to say she was going to make a great effort to get our parents to the wedding. Mollie, who has always been a great supporter of mine and a lady of enormous spirit, pointed out that father wasn't likely to have many more jaunts, so he might as well have a jolly good time at the wedding, rather than stay at home and mope. 'Don't you worry. I'll get the family there; I'll have them looking smart and we won't let you down.' You can see from the photograph that both my mother and father looked in fine form.

Some time after the wedding my father told me that from the moment he arrived at the reception at Thatched House Lodge he didn't remember anything at all and he was acting entirely on reflex; his mind went a complete blank. I asked if he had already had a glass of champagne and he said, 'No, funnily enough I hadn't. But I suppose the excitement of the wedding was just too much for me.'

We spent our honeymoon at a hotel in the New Forest, which was owned by some friends of ours who generously gave us a fortnight's stay as a wedding present. We had been lent a car which was suitably daubed with rude messages, which we didn't know about until we stopped. Much as I enjoyed our honeymoon, I used to dread the breakfasts, especially the first morning when, as we came into the room, everybody giggled and muttered. I felt acutely embarrassed, and on looking back can't think why I didn't ask our very nice host and hostess if we couldn't have our breakfast in bed.

Just five days after our wedding, on 20 November 1947, of course, Princess Elizabeth (as she was then) married Prince Philip; while we were honeymooning in the New Forest, they were honeymooning nearby at Lord Mountbatten's house, Broadlands.

Before we married and in spare moments between practising, Jean and I had bicycled around areas of London where we would like to live. We hit upon a mews called Roland Way, which runs parallel to Roland Gardens, just off the Old Brompton Road; the old mews houses had been gutted and were being re-built. They were for sale at a very reasonable price, but getting a mortgage, or a loan from the bank, would have been difficult as I hadn't started to earn regular money. After a long discussion with Jean's parents, her father most kindly agreed to put up the money, on which I agreed to pay him regular interest.

The next problem was where to go in the intervening months after our honeymoon, until the new house was ready. A cousin of Jean's rented us a small flat in her house in Sussex – about two miles from Midhurst. Luckily there was a piano available.

The very first day when Jean had to produce her first lunch, I was practising the piano hard. I thought I'd better not say anything, but I looked at my watch and saw the time was 3 o'clock. Eventually Jean poked her head round the door and called, 'Lunch', in a casual-sounding voice, as though the time were about five to one. But after the lunch, which was a very good one, Jean said she'd had the most appalling struggle; it was the first meal she had ever cooked. It was a real example of coolness in a crisis. I was to see many more examples of Jean's unflappability under all sorts of conditions in the coming years.

Enjoyable as the country air was and the scenery, I think if we'd stayed very long in Sussex we would have both become very happy cabbages. A concert career demands intense concentration and somehow it seemed so pointless to be worrying about work when you were surrounded by glorious countryside. Admittedly a pianist needs quiet to practise in. He also needs to be at the hub of the musical wheel and to be in constant touch with 'live' music and musicians.

We used to go up to London quite often by Green Line to see how the Roland Way house was progressing. When it was just about ready we packed up and went and spent a few days at Thatched House Lodge, to be on hand to make final arrangements.

We had a slight piano problem as there would never be room for a concert grand at our new mews house. So I sold the Steinway to Reading Corporation, who gave me quite a good price, and the piano was installed in Reading town hall. Jean sold her Blüthner piano to Nora Reynolds-Veitch, a friend of the family who lived in White Lodge (now part of the Royal Ballet School).

Having made these two sales I lost no time in going to see my old friend at Steinway's, Frank Usher, and told him I wanted a small grand piano. He had a six-foot four-inch piano that had been damaged in a fire. He promised me it had been completely reconditioned, but because of its history I was able to buy it cheaply. We also bought a lot of furniture in the Fulham Road.

We were both very excited when the day to move in arrived in early March.

The front door opened straight into the living-room, so we decided we would put the piano in one of the rooms upstairs, where I could be left in perfect peace to practise. I had booked the Wigmore Hall for a recital in May and had a completely new programme to learn, so I didn't have too much time. Also Jean had to run the house and get used to domestic life, so our new home became a hive of industry.

Louis Greig, having got quite used to the idea of the Coopers as a unit, used to visit us regularly on his way down to Richmond Park after doing his various jobs. He was a very busy man, with several directorships, apart from his honorary Palace work. But having got over his very understandable misgivings about musicians, he now began to take a great interest in my future and offered to help in any way possible with contacts for my career. He introduced me to people with money and power in various walks of life, who could prove useful in building up my career.

It doesn't matter where the help comes from for a concert artist, but when he's setting out on his career he has to have help, unless he is blessed with a large bank balance. The fact that I was married to Jean didn't mean I was marrying money – Jean had a little pin-money as a dress allowance, but otherwise she was as poor as I was.

One morning Nora Reynolds-Veitch telephoned Jean to ask if I could give a recital on the Blüthner at White Lodge and she would invite as guest of honour the ageing Princess Marie-Louise, who loved music. Nora insisted on paying a large fee. It was a very smart gathering and I was extremely nervous, so I asked if it would be all right if Jean and I didn't attend the dinner party: I couldn't bear the thought of chattering and having to eat a large meal before giving a recital. Nora sweetly understood, so Jean and I sat very quietly in another room while the guests dined.

When it came to the time for the concert, Princess Marie-Louise was in a talkative mood – she was getting on in years and the conviviality of the dinner party had made her rather excited. The Princess talked intermittently while I was playing, which rather spoilt the atmosphere. I ploughed on manfully and felt the audience very much on my side. When I was playing a very quiet piece – Debussy's *La fille aux cheveux de lin* (The girl with the flaxen hair) – Princess Marie-Louise turned to Sir Ulick Alexander, Keeper of the Privy Purse, who was sitting beside her and said, 'But you did promise me that bathroom, Ulick'; the remark was audible all over the room, but the rest of the audience pretended not to hear. However, my concentration was totally upset and I finished the recital with an extremely noisy piece of Debussy's, *Feux d'artifice* (Fireworks), against which nobody's voice could be heard.

Nora Reynolds-Veitch was very upset afterwards and said she didn't know how to apologize enough. But I pointed out it was all good experience for me. Nora said that Princess Marie-Louise had been very lonely since her sister, Princess Helena Victoria, died, and one had to make allowances.

One problem about playing the piano at Roland Way was that the sound reverberated against the houses opposite and you could hear the practising quite clearly from the street below. Because of this I always kept the windows tightly shut and often practised with the soft pedal on. The piano could still be heard, but fortunately for a long time nobody made any complaints. Then a new neighbour arrived next door as a temporary resident – she was caretaking the house until some other people moved in. If I played after 10 o'clock at night, understandably the good lady objected and used to bang on the wall. I called one day to apologize for my piano practising and she said, 'I don't mind as long as you stop at 10 p.m. – otherwise I bang on the wall with this little shoe which I bought in Poitiers.'

A few days later we heard from Harold Holt that Claudio Arrau was arriving in London, so we left a message at the Savoy with our new telephone number. Claudio rang and asked if he could come round that evening and practise, as he had an important broadcast the next day. We were thrilled to hear his voice and said of course he could come. I warned Claudio he would have to stop playing at 10 p.m., because of our neighbour, and he asked me to watch the time and tell him when to stop. He went upstairs and started practising – as usual glorious sounds poured from the piano; of course we were listening, although we pretended we couldn't hear.

There was one passage that seemed to be worrying Claudio and I was so engrossed in the various ways he played it, over and over again, that I forgot to keep an eye on the time. Suddenly there was a most enormous crash on the wall – it couldn't have been the shoe from Poitiers. Claudio stopped at once and rushed downstairs; he'd never heard anything like it!

The next morning our neighbour knocked on the door and said, 'It's bad enough with you practising, but I really cannot put up with your pupils.' I apologized, but told her it hadn't been a pupil playing, but none other than Claudio Arrau, who was classed amongst the six greatest pianists in the world. The lady went scarlet. She never banged on the wall again.

Shortly after his broadcast Arrau was leaving for the Continent and then he was going to meet up in London with his family – his wife, Ruth, and his children, Carmen and Mario – and we would then have a party. Just before he left, Claudio said to me that next time he very much wanted to hear me play the piano. I was very honoured at the suggestion and wondered if this might provide an occasion to get a few hints and tips that I so badly needed on piano technique.

My next London recital was due at the Wigmore Hall in May 1948 and I had planned, amongst other things, to play the Schubert Sonata in A minor, Op. 143, and this is the work I earmarked to play to Arrau on his next visit. I knew that he was a great Schubert lover and this sonata soon worked itself into my own system and heart; I thought of Arrau's rich tone and I tried to think as I played it of various movements that I saw Arrau make when I watched him at his recitals and concertos; I tried to incorporate them as best as I could into my own playing.

When I first met the Arraus *en famille* I was struck by Mrs Arrau's dark hair and blue eyes, a rare and lovely combination. I was also very struck by her serenity and a kind of inner peace that ran right through her character. I think this was probably very necessary, because there is no question that Claudio had the true musical temperament, and the two children were some of the liveliest I have ever met. They wanted to be shown all the usual London sights and among other places we went to was Windsor Castle. Claudio, by the way, knew almost more about Windsor Castle than the guide who took us round; quite apart from being a wonderful musician and pianist, he is an extraordinarily well-educated and well-read man and can talk on practically any subject, in about half a dozen languages.

We all enjoyed the Windsor visit, but I was intensely nervous at the prospect of having to play to Arrau the following day. Yet somehow his manner was reassuring and once I had started I soon concentrated completely on the Schubert Sonata, to the exclusion of all else. I don't wish to flatter myself, but when I had finished Arrau was complimentary. He seemed taken aback and his very first words were: 'But you play exactly like I do.' I said jokingly: 'I'm a sort of parrot character and I can imitate people, but it's very much you second-hand.' Arrau replied: 'It's very nearly me first-hand, but you haven't got it all right. I would love to help you with one or two points.'

At first I thought Arrau was saying all these nice things to me just to give me confidence, but later I discovered that he had told all sorts of people in the musical world that I was a pianist to be watched, because I had an unusual talent. Anyway, he had offered to help me – that was marvellous, and he did. Not then, because the children had to be attended to; but later he gave me a lesson and showed me all the things I wanted to know and that I hadn't got quite right. Funnily enough, it was rather like continuing lessons with Egon Petri, because what they had to say was very much the same and concerned the use of the upper arm – in fact the back and upper arm, right down to the finger tips, the finger tips being the sentinels which had to be strong and independent. But Arrau emphasized over and over again the need for freedom in the arm. He used to say: 'You must feel you are dropping loose, heavy weight onto the keyboard.' For strengthening the fingers he was a great believer in the dummy keyboard. He also carried around a little rubber ball which he used to squeeze in his hand, and a small spring which you squeezed tight. But he never gave the metal spring to any pupils until they were very advanced, because fingers must always be practised with a free arm and the spring tends to stiffen the arm unless it is very carefully used.

My Wigmore Hall concert was on a Saturday afternoon. We had quite a good house, buttressed by a number of friends and relations who came to support me. We broke about even, which was important, as I was now financially on my own.

The hall had been reserved for me to have a morning rehearsal session; you can imagine my dismay when I arrived on the stage to start rehearsal, to hear the sound of a piano in the artist's room behind. Chopin studies were being played, but not at all well. Somebody was fumbling their way through them and I felt whoever it was had absolutely no business to be there – in my rehearsal period. With more haste than judgment I opened the door of the artist's room to find a very old man sitting there, with hands that looked arthritic and feeble. I said rather tersely: 'I'm awfully sorry, but the hall is mine for the morning.' He replied in a heavy foreign accent that he was so sorry to disturb me – as he spoke his face suddenly seemed familiar. I quickly looked round the artists' photographs that adorned the walls of the room; staring in front of me, just by the piano, was a photograph of Alfred Cortot. I gasped and realized that this was Cortot himself.

'Monsieur Cortot, I recognize you, I do apologize,' and I made endless excuses for my rudeness. 'Not at all, not at all,' he said, and then asked me what I was playing at my recital. I told him one of my pieces was the César Franck Prelude, Chorale and Fugue: straight away he started giving me a few hints and suggestions. I was astounded – to have a free lesson from the great Alfred Cortot! I had long studied his own recording of the César Franck, but to hear advice from the great man himself was extremely moving. What was even more moving was to see how pathetically old and withered he had become.

Inspired by this strange encounter with one of my immortal heroes, I played the recital with unaccustomed confidence and received very good press notices.

Incidentally, William McKie had written to me from Melbourne years ago and said I should go and study with Cortot in Paris as soon as I came down from Oxford. But I had heard on the grapevine it wasn't as easy as that; you were apt to be palmed off with assistants and not the actual man himself, unless you were extremely lucky. I didn't take the risk; but I often wish I had. I later told Arrau about all this, who was an enormous admirer of Cortot; but Claudio did make one interesting observation. He said if I'd gone to Cortot himself I would have been all right, but Arrau knew of too many pianists who had been to Paris and just been put on hours, weeks, months, of finger exercises and scales; they had come back with very good finger techniques, but no desire to make any music. Arrau always stressed that technique and music must mostly be learnt together; you can't really divorce them.

But back to the Wigmore. In case the reader should think that I found these concerts easy, I would like to stress that they were an enormous strain. I have mentioned several times that I was very nervous, but I haven't spoken of the after-effects – after each recital I was totally exhausted for at least three days and I wondered if this reaction was quite normal. I suppose I was simply paying for the amount of tension I'd harboured before the concert. I was still really a reluctant concert pianist, with very little experience of public playing, and suffering what the French call *le trac* – known in English by the horrid word 'stage-fright'.

Luckily for me, Jean's enormous resilience and her ability to laugh, both at herself and at me, encouraged me also to be able to laugh at myself, so gradually this post-concert exhaustion wore off. So many things seemed to happen to make us laugh in our life that when we weren't actually worrying about concerts, a great deal of the time was spent giggling. The first example of almost uncontrollable hysterics came when Mr Jones, the accountant we decided to employ, came for his first visit to Roland Way to examine earnings for tax purposes. Jean had to go out shopping, and she left some scones in a low oven and said she would be back in time to get them out and make the tea for us.

Mr Jones and I were busily working through the accounts, when I suddenly noticed a smell of burning coming from the kitchen. I went to the kitchen and found smoke pouring from the oven: the scones appeared to be absolutely burnt to a frazzle, so I quickly turned out the oven and put the scones in the dustbin. I returned to Mr Jones and said there had been just a little domestic crisis, nothing really, and we went on with our figures.

A few minutes later, Jean came rushing in through the front door and went through to the kitchen to prepare the tea – I had no opportunity of telling her of the disaster. But the next thing I knew was that about twenty minutes later she came in with the tea – lo and behold, there, buttered and jammed, were those dreadful scones. Jean had taken them out of the dustbin and scraped off most of the black very effectively, and proudly – even defiantly – produced them. I had to retire from the room, shaking with laughter, tears pouring. I quickly composed myself and returned. But then I saw Jean shaking and giggling and she had to leave the tea party. Mr Jones remarked in his nice Welsh accent: 'It seems to be all coming and going, doesn't it? But it's a very nice tea – lovely scones you've got.'

The concert agents, although very pleased with the notices of both my London recitals, said I should give at least two more to establish myself. Meanwhile, without saying anything to me, my sister Mollie was working away in Westbury-on-Trym, making sure my name and press notices were brought to the attention of people in the area who might be able to offer me work. She went and bombarded the local impresario in Bristol, the late Charles H. Lockier, who commented to Mollie: 'I once turned your brother off the platform when Rachmaninoff had been giving a recital – the little devil had the impertinence to sit down and play Rachmaninoff's piano.' But behind a forbidding exterior Charles Lockier was really a very kind person, and I later got to know him well. Mollie went in to sell me and very nearly failed; but my sister was nothing if not persistent. She kept on pointing out the notices and said she felt sure I wouldn't let myself or Mr Lockier down if he would put me on in Bristol. Quite suddenly – probably in order to get rid of my sister – Lockier agreed. On Wednesday 17 November 1948 at 7 p.m. I played at the Central Hall, Bristol (the Colston Hall had been burnt down in 1945 and had not yet been rebuilt).

The concert, thanks to Charles Lockier, got a lot of advance publicity and was announced as 'Important reappearance in Bristol of the distinguished pianist' – though in fact I'd given practically no concerts in the area, except private ones at Clifton College. On the night we had a huge turnout and the Bristol press were very kind to me next day. My sister kept a dossier which, as I write now, I have in front of me, with the programme, programme notes and the reviews; and also at the back of the file, what all the local musical bigwigs had to say.

So my sister had started up what you might call a 'second front' from which one could develop perhaps music clubs in the area. I was soon made a life member of South-Western Arts. Most important of all, my success pleased Charles Lockier – he was delighted with the full house. He paid me a fee and he made some money. That meant, although of course I didn't know it at the time, that he would be looking for an opportunity to put me on in some more important capacity, with an orchestra.

It's amusing to read that the highest priced ticket at this 1948 concert was 7/6d and the cheapest seats were 2/6d – how times have changed.

7
The Giddy Heights

Looking back over my progress so far, I feel that the omens were good. For one thing I'd had the luck of having good notices for the London recitals; and then again I'd had the immense good fortune to meet Claudio Arrau and get so much practical help in piano playing from him and encouragement to go on for all I was worth.

Also, I had hit on this new learning method – working with Jean and sharing the interest of the work, which enabled me to go on for far longer and take in all I was doing more deeply into my subconscious than if I'd been left on my own. Of course, six years was a long time away in the army, but this didn't deter us. Between us, Jean and I were determined to storm the heights – even the Royal Albert Hall and the Proms, which only a year ago had seemed beyond our wildest dreams, could now be envisaged with equanimity. There was no conflict of interest at all; indeed we had only one idea – to try and go to the top.

So next I set about trying to build on the success I had achieved. I was lucky to get some marvellous breaks. I took a BBC audition, successfully, and work came flooding in from there – almost every week at times. I had engagements with the Bournemouth Orchestra, the Boyd Neel Orchestra, and for a BBC studio concert with the London Symphony Orchestra. The next year, on 22 February 1950, Charles Lockier engaged me to play the Mozart Concerto in F major, K.459, making my début with the Philharmonia Orchestra, in Bristol (again at the Central Hall), conducted by Anatole Fistoulari.

The accent was very much on piano concerto dates and I had to mug up, at great speed, no less than seven piano concertos that were new to me; but using the method that Jean and I had evolved, I found that I could streamline this system more and more and could really memorize quite quickly, which was very lucky for me because my repertoire had been extremely small.

The only blot on an otherwise very happy 1949 was the death of my father in November – he had been failing for some time and I am always happy to think that he enjoyed the part of the wedding he remembered and did have a final fling. In due course my mother decided to sell the house at Westbury-on-Trym and to make her headquarters at Harlyn Bay. My sister came to London to take a job. Nobody wanted the family Morris (nicknamed Mobo), so Jean and I were offered the car, on the condition that Mollie could use it when she wanted. Although Mobo was old, she had plenty of life in her, and bicycling around London could be tiring and sometimes very dangerous; also, until then, I had been entirely dependent on public transport for reaching engagements out of London. So Mobo was a godsend.

Noting that concert work in the summer months tended to be rather thin (in those days festivals, unlike now, were few and far between), and in order to supplement my income, I applied for an audition with Harold Fielding – he ran summer shows and concerts in the various holiday resorts throughout the country. I went along to Fielding's office and played him the Chopin Polonaise in A flat and one or two other pieces. He said it sounded nice and flashy and he could use me, but pointed out I would be low on the bill. That didn't worry me at all – it was money and experience I was after. I did a tremendous season – in fact I undertook several seasons of Fielding concerts. I remember playing on bills with Peter Brough and Archie Andrews, Leslie Sarony, Robb Wilton, Anona Winn, Gilbert Harding, Jack Train and Ethel Revnell. I was always the one that people hadn't come to hear – this helped to teach me platform concentration more than anything else, especially because the audience audibly showed impatience if I played for too long. Among the bevy of stars I met backstage, Kenneth Horne stands out in my memory for his kindness and total lack of swank.

I was engaged for a Fielding concert at Harrogate, so Jean and I decided to go in Mobo and in order to save hotel costs (it was mid-summer) we took a tent and camped on the Yorkshire Moors. This was very delightful, so we extended the idea and went with our tent to all sorts of places.

But disaster struck at Llandudno, North Wales. We were very near a farm and we got the farmer's permission to pitch our tent on a field high up, overlooking the sea; he warned us there were cows in the field, but said if we kept to a particular corner they wouldn't disturb us.

We duly pitched our tent, and I changed into my tails – it always seemed rather funny to be wearing evening dress in the middle of a field – and trundled down to Llandudno in faithful Mobo. The concert went well and we returned to our tent, relieved to find no sign of any cows. It was a gorgeous summer night and we settled down and went to sleep. Jean always slept far better than I did – I was a very light sleeper and the slightest noise would disturb me. In the middle of the night, I was suddenly aware of munching going on – obviously a cow, rather close, munching grass. The next thing I knew the cow had come right through the tent, lifting the tent with her, and had gone off with it. I woke Jean rapidly 'Darling, we are under the stars.' 'This is no time for poetry,' Jean mumbled, 'for goodness sake relax, and let's sleep.' 'Wake up and look up,' I told her. Jean duly woke up and looked up and there, to her amazement, were the stars above. Then she saw in the distance a ghostly, shambling figure of the cow, wrestling with the tent and trying to get clear of it. How the cow didn't tread on us is a miracle. We must have looked a funny sight. Jean immediately got under the bedclothes, saying: 'We might be seen, it's really indecent.'

By the time the poor cow had disentangled herself from the tent I'm afraid the canvas was unserviceable. Next day we bought a new tent in Llandudno and reported our bizarre experience to the farmer. When he eventually stopped laughing, he kindly showed us to another field which had no livestock in it.

In March 1950 I was engaged to play in Brussels; the concert was very successful and it resulted in a tour of Belgium and Luxembourg in January 1951. I got good notices at Luxembourg, Liège, Brussels and Bruges, and was delighted to have had a success abroad – this was very important; we were beginning to open out on the international scene.

The Harold Fielding concerts went on for several summer seasons and I began to be included in his more serious music concerts. One memorable occasion was a concert in the Isle of Wight; on the ferry between Portsmouth and Ryde I noticed a pretty girl, who couldn't have been more than fifteen at the most. She was accompanied by a man and a woman whom I assumed were her parents. The girl was extraordinarily self-possessed and I wondered if she could possibly be taking part in the concert too. When we got to Shanklin, where the concert was to take place, there sure enough was the girl. I discovered her name was Julie and the older couple were Ted and Barbara Andrews. Julie Andrews sang at that concert like a lark, trilling away at least four or five notes above top C. I even became a little anxious for her voice and wondered if at that tender age she should sing such very high notes. But she had such assurance and charm and her voice production was so natural that I needn't have worried. I keep the record of her singing in the cast of *My Fair Lady* as a precious souvenir. As I listen, I can still see little Julie on the boat – her life with its triumphs and disappointments still before her. In case you haven't guessed it, I am a fan.

The Royal Festival Hall was opened on 3 May 1951. Eric Thompson of the Arts Council was asked to arrange a series of informal afternoon recitals. I was astounded to find myself included in the list of artists. The object of the exercise was to enable the public to view the hall – the prize exhibit of The Festival of Britain – and listen to some music at the same time, if they so wished. People could wander in and out as they liked; they were in fact very polite and caused no disturbance to the performer. I enjoyed playing there. From the platform the sound was warm, and one seemed to have power in reserve. General critical opinion, however, was agreed that the sound in the hall was lifeless, the tone of the piano metallic and lacking in body. I will not repeat what singers thought about it (it has been vastly improved since then).

I made my concerto début there with the London Symphony Orchestra in November 1952 with a little-played work, the Fourth Piano Concerto of Saint-Saens.

Just about then the sad news, that only the Greig family had known, started to spread around the Court circle – that Jean's father was dying of cancer and had only a few months to live. He was himself a doctor and knew and accepted his fate philosophically. 'I am just going to have a little chat with God,' he used to tell visitors, in a tone of voice that suggested the next sentence might be 'Wimbledon will soon be round again' (he was Chairman of Wimbledon All England Lawn Tennis Club). He wanted no sympathy, no regrets. For my little part I was happy that he lived to see me make good. The night he died I was actually making my début with the Hallé Orchestra in Manchester. The day before I had seen him and he had wished me luck.

Sir Louis brought the same guts to dying as he had to living – whether it was piloting an aeroplane, being taken prisoner in the 1914–18 War, being a Scottish Rugger International, partnering King George VI (then Duke of York) at Wimbledon, or even (so it is said) taking over a broadcast speech from King George VI when the King was suddenly reduced to silence by an attack of stuttering. Two words on Group Captain Sir Louis Greig's tombstone at Ham Common say what all his family and friends felt: he was 'GREATLY LOVED.'

One day the telephone rang and it was Charles Lockier from Bristol; he asked me if I played the Tchaikovsky Piano Concerto No. 1, because he said if I did, a soloist had fallen out through illness and he could offer me two dates – one at Cardiff and one at Bristol, at the newly opened Colston Hall, a fortnight later. I said unfortunately I didn't play that concerto, although of course I knew the music. Lockier said: 'Do you think you could learn it?' So without really thinking I said, 'Yes, I'll have a go.'

If I had really thought about it, I think I would have turned it down, because the Tchaikovsky First Piano Concerto is one of the most difficult, technically and musically, to bring off. Also, I was playing with the Liverpool Philharmonic Orchestra with a conductor I didn't know, Hugo Rignold, and no allowances were going to be made for the fact that I had learnt the concerto quickly.

It's quite simple to tell you what happened and it's a confession. I prepared the concerto in a fortnight and it was memorized, Jean helping me for all she was worth, coming into the practice room and abandoning the kitchen to look after itself. Three days before the concert I could play the work through confidently, with an assistant playing the orchestral part on a second piano. But when I got down to Cardiff I suddenly panicked – I can remember now, sitting on the grassy bank outside the hall when I was due for rehearsal, saying to Jean, 'I can't go through with it; I feel unwell.' Jean, very quick in her responses to crisis, took out the little pocket mirror of her powder compact: 'Look at your face in this; do you look unwell?' I had to admit my cheeks looked quite rosy. 'If anyone is going to tell Hugo Rignold you are unwell it's you, not me. It's your job,' she said.

So in I went and got through the rehearsal as best as I could in a state of great fear and uncertainty. Charles Lockier was down in the hall; he had come over from Bristol and said to Jean (who didn't tell me until afterwards), 'He doesn't seem so happy in this one.' Jean reminded him that he had taken a gamble.

The evening came and went. Hugo Rignold was obviously displeased with my performance and had every right to be. The press notices differed: one said I was good and one said I was bad. The next day we went over to Bristol to the Colston Hall and had a second shot at it. I must say it went better, but there was still, of course, uncertainty and a feeling that any moment my memory might break down. After the performance, Hugo Rignold called me into the conductor's room and in a friendly but critical way showed me in the full score some of the weaknesses of my performance. When I told him I had lost six years in the war, Rignold said, 'I wonder why you bother at your age to go on, when there are so many successful pianists doing the rounds of the provinces. Couldn't you do something a little less nerve-racking than learning concertos at your time of life?' I felt this was not unkindly meant. In fact I accepted it as a challenge: it made me resolve to master that Tchaikovsky concerto and really make it mine; 'Who does Mr Rignold think he is?' I said to myself.

When I applied for a Prom audition the next year I deliberately took as my concerto the Tchaikovsky B flat minor and I got through the audition. I had practised all the technical passages until they actually shone and glistened and the Tchaikovsky concerto fairly rang round the Albert Hall, empty save for the panel of judges; a discreet Eric Gritton played the orchestral part on a second piano and gave me the most wonderful help.

Having passed the audition on the well-known Tchaikovsky No. 1, the BBC thought that they would give me the then unknown Tchaikovsky Second Piano Concerto to play for my Prom début in 1953. They said quite happily: 'If you go along and see Mr Basil Cameron he will give you our cuts.' Oh, so the concerto was to be cut – how strange! Anyway, I called on Mr Cameron, who said: 'Some of these cuts Moiseiwitsch made, some of course were the published Siloti Edition. It's an awful mess in the score, but I'll try to help you sort it out.' He produced a score with all these cuts marked up, which he lent me. Finding I couldn't get a score of the Tchaikovsky No. 2 in London, I sent a telegram to Claudio Arrau and he sent his copy over from New York, which I lightly amended in pencil. However, eventually I managed to get a copy of my own, but not before I had memorized the concerto from Arrau's copy.

The Prom day came and the rehearsal went well. I left the hall almost unnaturally buoyant, especially as my friend John Lade (of BBC 'Record Review' fame) had been there and was pleased. However, by lunch-time I was panicking and miserable. Jean said: 'It's no use practising any more; this afternoon we'll go for a drive.' So we went down to Barnes Common, a very pretty spot. Jean saw a weather-boarded cottage with a large notice marked 'For Sale'. For some time we had been wanting to get out of our Roland Way house, because people had been complaining quite openly about the sound of Tchaikovsky echoing up and down the mews.

Jean stopped the car and almost in a nurse's voice said, 'Shall we go and have a look at it? Shall we just look in at the windows?' 'I don't want to,' I said. 'Oh yes you do; I think you'd absolutely love it.' So we wandered round the garden and looked in. I said the rooms looked awfully pokey; but I had to admit it was in the most beautiful situation, right in the middle of the common, in its own garden and facing south. Jean said: 'I think it's absolutely fascinating. Anyway we'll go back now, and tomorrow we'll come down and investigate further.' It was a good bit of pre-concert therapy on Jean's part.

The Prom came and went. The notices were excellent. I admit that I took some risks that didn't come off and in the last movement there were several mistakes, but the general effect seemed to please both the public and the critics. Relieved that it was over, we came down to Barnes Common again and had another look at the house. Seeing that Jean was captivated with the cottage, we called on Percy Tipping, the agent named on the board, and got permission to look over the property, which turned out to be three cottages turned into one. After much thinking about it, we decided it did seem almost ideal.

We hadn't too much time, because in the winter I was due to go to India with André Navarra, the French cellist, on a long tour. So I made a proposition to Mr Tipping: 'If you can make a small profit on the sale of 25 Roland Way – say £250 – the deal is done. In other words, sell Roland Way and we will buy the cottage' – then called The Rosery, a name we later changed.

All the paperwork was tied up and we employed the builder who had renovated the old mews house, Mr Bonner, to re-build the Barnes Common house. When I say re-build, it really was almost that; without the services of a surveyor or an architect, Jean just pointed at a wall and said, 'That must come down,' and then she would go upstairs and say, 'That must come down.' She wanted to make a lot of small rooms into several big rooms. In her enthusiasm she never stopped to think whether the whole house would fall down if you started removing walls. Anyway, the good Mr Bonner went faithfully ahead; the next thing we heard was when we were out in India and we had a telegram from Jean's mother, who was very kindly master-minding operations in our absence. The text read: 'Discovered six-inch drop in upstairs drawing-room floor when wall demolished. Please cable instructions.' Jean immediately cabled back, 'Get on with other work. Decision awaits our return.'

The tour was very exciting, but the only disappointment for me was that I had hoped to make it a sight-seeing tour, as well as doing a series of concerts. But unfortunately Navarra wanted to try out several different programmes, which he was obviously playing in various parts of the world afterwards – so instead of being able to tour around India with just one programme, we had three on the go. So I was constantly practising; as the temperature was about 100°F it was terribly hard work. I also found the keys of the pianos were all what is known as 'tropicalized' – glue cannot be used because it would melt, so everything had to be fixed with nails and screws, which tends to make the action heavy.

But we had nothing but happy memories of our visit to India. We started at Calcutta, which we found hot and rather smelly, but the concert went quite well. Then we flew across to Bombay, where in addition to playing with Navarra I played the Schumann Piano Concerto under the conductorship of Bernard Jacob, who, although an Indian, had, incidentally, been at Clifton College – a delightful man and a very good conductor.

Next we flew down to Ceylon (now called Sri Lanka). There was a great unintentional comedy act there. We were due to give a recital in a cinema at Colombo. The cinema screen-operator had gone off duty; when we arrived to give the concert in the evening the screen was still in position and hadn't been moved after the last film performance – there was no platform space available for our recital. Navarra said in his funny broken English, 'Where is the key? Someone can do it.' But we were told quite firmly there was only one man who was allowed to move the screen and he was not available (they were very conscious in India of 'each man for his job'). So we sat behind the screen, with Jean trying to keep me calm, and Navarra smoking continuous cigarettes and making jokes and practising. After a two-hour wait somebody had unearthed the screen-operator; the screen was wound up and the recital began. The audience had waited with patience and greeted us with cheers.

The humidity in Ceylon at that particular time of year was tremendous and I felt extremely limp. Navarra always told me that I played too loudly, but that evening I was evidently soft and rather dank in the first half. A friend of mine called de Saram, who had been at Oxford with me (and was the uncle of the cellist Rohan de Saram), came round in the interval and said he recommended me to have a small glass of whisky – 'It might help,' he added! I never drink as a rule either before or in the middle of a concert, but on this occasion I thought just a teaspoonful might do the trick – and it did, because I knew that in the second half my playing had some vitality, without any complaints from Navarra about drowning him. Neither the delay nor the humidity had the slightest effect on André Navarra's performance. It was always absolutely first-class.

We also gave a concert in, of all places, Poona – it is, of course, a joke name in England. I tried to explain to Navarra why it seemed to me so terribly funny giving a recital in Poona (with the traditional picture in one's mind of polo-playing, pig-sticking and tiger-shooting colonels), but I'm afraid the joke was a little lost on him. I was myself surprised to find in fact how much music there was in Poona.

It was while we were there that we met a man who was fanatically interested in Indian instruments of all kinds and invited us round to his house to demonstrate all the different instruments. We must have been listening to these instruments for four hours, and though we didn't really understand the music, we put up with it patiently, with looks of interest on our faces. But finally fatigue overtook us and Navarra said it really was time to go home because we had a concert the next day. But in the meanwhile, both

Navarra, who was a mimic, and I (as already mentioned, a parrot) had taken in fully all the sounds of these Indian instruments and also the garb of the players, and this was to prove very useful to me, at any rate, at parties when we got back to England.

After the visit was over we went our separate ways, Navarra back to France, and Jean and I went and stayed with some old friends of mine in Cairo, where we spent Christmas. They announced there was a fancy dress competition in Cairo which we should attend. I immediately thought I would do my Indian act, with a demonstration of musical instruments – believe it or not, I won the first prize!

Greatly stimulated by this, when we got back to England and were asked to a party by some musical friends of ours, cellists Douglas and Lilly Cameron, I volunteered to do a cabaret – Indian style – just to see if I could get away with it among a crowd of friends. When the moment approached for the surprise item I went upstairs and put on my Indian costume (which was made up by Jean with sheets and safety-pins, plus some net curtains as a turban). I darkened my face a bit with burnt cork. Then, Douglas Cameron, having disguised an old cello to look like some exotic eastern instrument, solemnly announced me as an Indian player, Amir Khusru, who was going to demonstrate authentic Indian music.

The curious thing was I had 'got' the Indian voice so well for the verbal description, and I believed in the whole thing so much (partly because we had only just come back), that nobody recognized me, and they listened seriously. The spoof bowed instrument, which I called a kind of sitar, fascinated them – and as for my singing, it sounded sufficiently strangulated and Raga-like. I also had a small tam-tam, which Indian beggars use to attract attention; this little drum, the only genuine prop, added an air of verisimilitude to the act.

It was only when I eventually took off my improvised turban and laughed, that the audience realized it was me.

When we first arrived back from India we had gone straight to Thatched House Lodge, Jean's mother's house, so that we could be with her and tell her all our adventures in India. Also, we wanted to hear how she had got on with the cottage on Barnes Common in our absence. She said she thought we would be very pleased with the result; together the three of us went over and had a look. Certainly an enormous amount of work had been done, but when we saw the gap in the drawing-room about which we'd heard – the six-inch difference in the level between the two floors, after the wall had been taken down – Jean said she would need a little time to think about what we should do.

But we decided that the only thing to get Mr Bonner, the builder, out of the house was to move in and this way expedite the rest of the work. In fact we had moved in on Mr Bonner once before, at Roland Way when the house wasn't completed, and we had found then how quickly things were brought to a conclusion. Again, it worked wonders here.

Also, Jean's imagination was greatly stimulated by actually living in the house; she made various changes, including having a bath moved from the kitchen (where it took up an awful lot of space) and re-fitted upstairs. More important than this was the solution to be found for the drop in the drawing-room.

In the middle of one night Jean suddenly woke and nudged me, 'Pillars,' she said. 'What are you talking about?' I asked. 'I've got it – pillars. We'll have two pillars each side of the gap, where the wall was taken down, and then we'll have a step from one level to the other. We'll make them look like Greek pillars.' And with that she turned over. 'Like a proscenium arch to a stage,' I suggested. But my audience was already asleep.

The whole idea was explained to Mr Bonner the next morning. He understood exactly what Jean meant and said he would give us some 'Corinthian/Doric' pillars, which he thought would look very nice; also an oak step. The change of level in the room would then almost look like a deliberate feature. Anyone would imagine the structural weight was being borne by these majestic-looking pillars, whereas of course it was entirely borne by the painted-over girder which Mr Bonner had hoisted across the width of the ceiling. When the room was complete the result was fascinating and has always remained a source of great interest for visitors.

Our new home turned out to be the perfect musician's house; on the ground floor I had a room twenty feet long, with plenty of space for two pianos and absolute peace and quiet. I couldn't disturb anyone and they couldn't disturb me. Above was the newly made drawing-room, where there was to be no music (that was the place to relax in), and the bedrooms; the main bedroom, also twenty feet long, had marvellous views over the common.

About the same time, George Foss, then Managing Director of Constance Spry, had bought the house next door, known as The Coach House. We soon became friends. In the garden were two bits of an old mill stone, because there had formerly been a windmill on the land behind the two houses. George Foss and I agreed to have half the mill stone each: he used his as the hearth stone in his sitting-room, and I put mine in the garden and made it into a step through a rose arch up to a lawn.

I discovered that the last miller on Barnes Common was called Joseph Trock, who died in 1836. I thought it would be a good idea to change the name of the house from The Rosery to Trocks Mill Cottage, especially as it seemed likely Mr Trock might have kept some of his workers in these small cottages, which had been joined together to make one house. Incidentally, there have been many friendly arguments among the neighbours as to exactly where the mill stood and it has never been quite agreed; one thing is certain – at different times there have been at least three mills on Barnes Common over the years, probably all in slightly different positions. There is a painting in the Tate Gallery of a Smock Mill on Barnes Common, dated 1805 and attributed to Constable.

One morning the front-door bell rang and it was George Foss. He said, with a smile on his face: 'I have a complaint: I can see you practising, but I can't hear you.' That was the best news I'd heard since we had moved in, because the one thing I always dreaded since Roland Way was causing disturbance to the neighbours.

George Foss and his wife, Iris, were the perfect neighbours; not only did George himself give us a great deal of help with our garden, but they were both extremely musical. If I wanted to try out a programme, I only had to get hold of them and they would bring a little group of friends to whom I could perform and thus give myself a practice concert. This is something every concert artist needs. What was even nicer was that George loved – and in fact insisted upon – the description of the music that I gave before I played each piece. He said he was one of the millions who loved music, but was no expert; so long as I didn't make my analysis too technical, he said he'd always be a fan of mine. That was something I was going to remember in the coming years.

When the Fosses moved we were lucky in having two equally

nice neighbours to take over their house – Dr and Mrs David Skeggs. David was a radiotherapist at the Royal Free Hospital (we discovered this years later). They were both young and good-looking, with two very attractive young daughters, Lucinda and Imogen. An informant told us that David used to get up at first light to work in his vegetable garden; we weren't about at that hour, but we often tasted his fresh vegetables.

David's wife, Anne, later started organizing a yearly concert in aid of the Red Cross in the beautiful chapel of the Royal Hospital, Chelsea (home of the Chelsea Pensioners). I gave a piano recital for her one year.

One of the first good pieces of news after we moved in to Trocks Mill Cottage was that I had been engaged for the next season of Promenade Concerts at the Royal Albert Hall, to play the Beethoven Piano Concerto No. 1.

My mother had given me as a present the Steinway from Westbury-on-Trym and it had been put in store ready for Mr Palmer to send it to Barnes as soon as I was ready. When the building works were finally complete, Mr Palmer came up from Westbury with the Steinway. So with that piano, and the Steinway I bought for Roland Way, I was fortunate to have two grand pianos in my splendid new music room. It turned out I was going to need two pianos, because concerto engagements were going to come in thick and fast in the following years and it was always useful to have two pianos on the spot. Either a pupil, or a keen amateur pianist, could come and play the orchestral part of the concerto on the second piano; this was a most important step and one every pianist should take, if possible, before embarking on rehearsing the piano part with the orchestra.

There was another good piece of news in store. I had met Walter Todds, who was a BBC talks producer, and we had done some pro-gammes together. Walter got in touch with me one day, saying he wished to put on a music quiz of a light-hearted nature and he wanted me to be the chairman. I didn't know what it involved, but I said 'yes' straight away, because I thought it would be just the kind of thing I would enjoy doing.

There was further news: Wilfrid van Wyck, the agent who had arranged the brilliantly successful Indian tour, asked Jean and me to call at his office. So we went to see van Wyck and told him how grateful we were for his arranging the tour. He came straight to the point and said: 'I can arrange further tours for you on quite a grand scale, but I'll have to ask you to sign an exclusive contract with me. I don't believe,' he added with a touch of pride, 'there is any other agent in London who would be prepared or in a position to offer you this kind of work.' I asked him if I could have time to reflect and he agreed, but said: 'An offer like this is only given once in a lifetime to an artist, so don't be too long.'

Jean said we shouldn't be hurried into deciding; work seemed to be coming in from all quarters and I must be careful not to over-reach myself, otherwise my standard, which she had helped guard so carefully, would drop. However, on consideration we both confessed we had a passion for travelling and loved seeing the world, quite apart from the money that tours might bring in. So we decided we would sign an exclusive contract with Wilfrid van Wyck.

In the meanwhile, we met Walter Todds who gave us a rundown on the proposed music quiz. He said it was to be called *Call the Tune* and there would be a panel of three well-known people. Walter had already got the names of Anona Winn, Joyce Grenfell, Michael Ayrton, Gerard Hoffnung and Stephen Potter; also Paul Dehn, Paul Jennings, Peter Scott and Wynford Vaughan Thomas.

We did a 'pilot', which is the name given to a kind of trial, for the BBC, which could be used, if successful, as the first broadcast. The panel for the first occasion consisted of Anona Winn, Michael Ayrton and Gerard Hoffnung. The guest musician was Harriet Cohen. The pilot was successful and it went out on the Home Service on 4 July 1955.

Already the peace and quiet of Trocks Mill Cottage was coming into its own. A BBC office was no place to dream up a radio quiz series, and as Walter and I were going to do all the questions together, there was no place like the music room on Barnes Common for absolute peace and quiet. Jean would answer the telephone and keep any unwelcome visitors away.

Call the Tune was an immediate success; the press were very kind to us and we were to run, off and on, for four years. Incidentally, the Hidden Melody was a feature of the very first programme. Thus it was that Joyce Grenfell (who, although not in at the start, soon became one of the favourite panellists), Walter Todds and I began an association – which I am happy to say is still going strong.

About the same time John Lade (then in BBC 'Gramophones', later to become head of the gramophone department) asked me to do some programmes introducing gramophone records. These programmes included not only broadcasts to this country, but broadcasts on the World Service, which I did from Bush House.

On the solo piano side the BBC had given me no less than six first performances of concertos to broadcast; the most interesting was the *Petite Symphonie Concertante* by Frank Martin, for solo harp, harpsichord and piano with double string orchestra; I played the piano part. Most significant of all, the conductor was the great Georges Enesco, Yehudi Menuhin's famous teacher, and a man I feel very honoured and privileged to have worked with.

In all the fields of work I've mentioned, I think I can honestly and fairly say without boasting, I did myself justice. My weakness was when it came to broadcasting solo piano 'live', especially at 9 o'clock in the morning. To reach Broadcasting House from Barnes by rehearsal time of 8 a.m., I had to set the alarm about 6.30 a.m., and I am never at my most musical at that time in the morning. I did give some very poor performances over the air. Many of them were recitals shared with a singer and accompanist. I must just mention Josephine Lee; she was on the accompanying staff of the BBC at the time and was on hand to accompany the singer. Quite apart from her great expertise as an accompanist, her soothing manner and kindness to nervous people like myself was something I will never forget.

When I had done so many things already that required courage and self-control, I felt puzzled and angry with myself that I was so disturbed by these solo broadcasts. Remembering that Claudio Arrau had promised to give me some more help, and seeing that he was coming to London, I left a note for him at the Savoy. He telephoned and we fetched him and took him down to Trocks Mill Cottage. Claudio was overjoyed with the place. He asked if he might come and practise there, because he so loved the music room; I was very happy for him to do this, especially as I had an upright piano in another room, well away from him, so we shouldn't disturb each other when I was practising. Between whiles Claudio would give me all sorts of advice, go through works with me and help me to solve many technical problems.

After Claudio Arrau felt that I had sufficiently acquired his methods of playing and practising, he suggested that I might take some of his pupils in his absence, to give me practice; he said there was nothing like teaching if you want to learn. The plan was that I would prepare the pupils, who came separately for lessons; then when Claudio came to London, he would give a few master classes to all the pupils assembled together. I think it was during those master classes that I learnt more than I even learnt when I was with him alone; with a copy and a pencil in hand, I wrote down every remark he made to each pupil. From that I gleaned so much, not only of Arrau's profound musical thoughts, but about the composer's intentions. All these things that Claudio taught me have become very much part of me; and I shall always be grateful to him for making me realize the importance of studying a composer's life, the time the composer lived in, and his own particular style.

I once confided in Claudio my terror of playing in a studio alone for the BBC. He sympathized with me and said everybody has an area of nervousness; he reminded me to count my blessings that I had so much going for me in other directions. He also added with a smile that he was no stranger to nervousness, but it took different forms. I was to realize this on one very funny occasion.

Claudio was recording the Beethoven Piano Concerto No. 4 at the EMI Studios and he had to record the cadenzas separately. I took him up and waited while he recorded them and listened to them; then EMI suggested he chose a piano for a forthcoming solo recital he was going to record in a smaller studio. Claudio asked me to go with him and he was shown a piano; he sat down at the piano in complete silence, looked at it and then beckoned me to come over. He whispered: 'I do not know what to play.' I said: 'Play anything.' 'I can't think of anything; you try the piano for me.'

So I sat down and played a few chords. Claudio said he thought it sounded very good and it would be fine. Afterwards he said, 'Now you see my kind of nervousness.' 'But, Claudio, I don't understand,' I replied. 'You know by heart every piece that every composer has ever written, and yet at that moment you couldn't play a single bar?' 'No, and what's more,' he admitted, 'I cannot improvise – so you do realize that everybody has their weaknesses. I was, as you might say, musically tongue-tied.'

35 A *Face the Music* team: (*left to right*) Robin Ray, Joe, Joyce Grenfell, Walter Todds (the producer) and David Attenborough.

36 Party given by the BBC for the hundredth programme of *Face the Music*: Joe with Bernard Levin.

37 Dame Eva Turner, Richard Baker and Joyce Grenfell.

38 Sir David Willcocks and Sir Keith Falkner, present and past Directors of the Royal College of Music.

39 Andrew Lloyd Webber telling Joe all about *Evita*.

40 The host of the party, Ian Trethowan (*centre*), talks to Valerie Solti and Humphrey Burton.

41 Greek meets Greek: Lina Lalandi and Arianna Stassinopoulos.

42 Valerie Solti, John Julius Norwich, Joe and Robin Scott.

43 At Trocks Mill Cottage.

44 Carol and Joe enjoying a drink with Moura Lympany and Malcolm Williamson, Master of the Queen's Music, at the opening of Broadwood's new showroom.

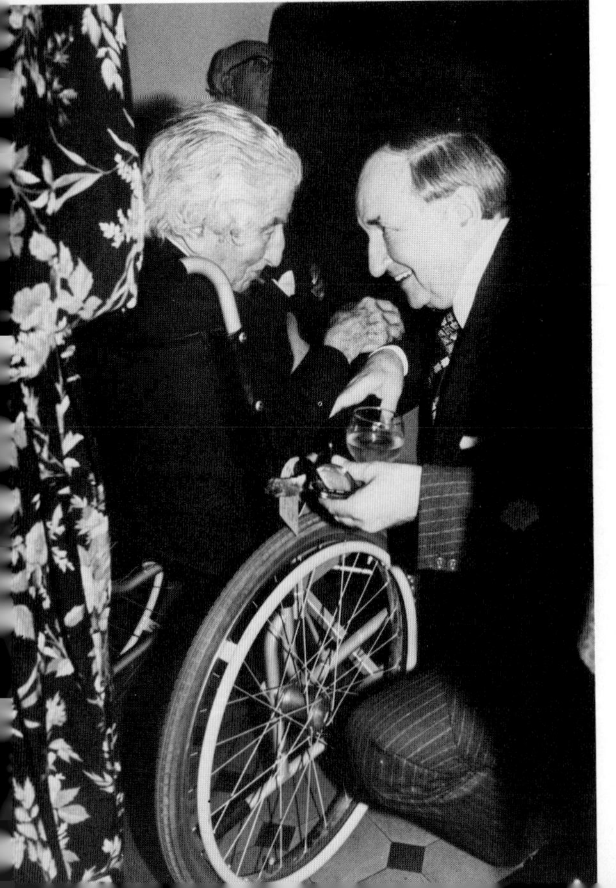

45 Old friends, Edward Heath and Joe, making faces at each other at the Boult birthday concert, Royal Albert Hall, 8 April 1979.

46 Talking to Sir Robert Mayer a few weeks before his hundredth birthday.

47 Aunt Beg (Beryl Colbeck) and Uncle Dunk – both in their nineties – still keen croquet players.

48 *Face the Music* producer Walter Todds still laughing with Joe after twenty-five years' partnership on BBC programmes, at the theatre, Shepherd's Bush, London, May 1979.

49, 50 Carol and Joe, partners in everything: in the music room at Trocks Mill Cottage, and entertaining a packed Royal Albert Hall.

Eventually the pressure of outside work became so enormous that I reluctantly had to give up the idea of forming a school and ask the pupils not to come any more. I missed them very much, because I had learnt so much, but I also realized that they were taking up precious energy which should have been going into my own practising time and there was always the fear of my own standards deteriorating.

The next big excitement came when Wilfrid van Wyck rang and said Bulawayo were inaugurating a new concert grand piano in 1956 and they wanted a celebrity to go and open the occasion. He had put my name forward and it had been accepted: he hoped that I would go.

It seemed rather strange to travel 6,000 miles and give an inaugural concert and come home again, but we said 'yes'. All was fixed and arranged and Wilfrid warned that probably I would be required to do some broadcasting and might have to give some talks in Bulawayo, all of which I was very happy to do. He thought that a white tuxedo would be the right dress, because it was very hot out there and they obviously wouldn't wear tails in Southern Rhodesia. So taking his advice, I left my tails behind.

On the aeroplane I suddenly spotted an old friend from Harlyn Bay. He was one of a delightful family called Hopcraft who had a farm near Lake Naivasha in Kenya, and who loved Harlyn so much that they came all that way for their yearly summer holiday. Bobs Hopcraft, the youngest, was terribly thrilled to see me and meet Jean. During the flight he made us promise that on our way home we would come back via Kenya and stay with him for a few days. This was actually the time of the Mau Mau rising and I think we were a little apprehensive about the idea, but anyway we said we would.

Flights were very slow in those days and we were quite exhausted when we finally landed. As we had a day in hand I was very anxious to visit the Victoria Falls, so we booked in at the Livingstone Hotel. As I lay on the bed I put my hand out to turn on the radio and you'll never believe it – I heard my own voice talking about Rachmaninoff on the World Service!

From Livingstone to Bulawayo by air was only a short hop. I

remember approaching Bulawayo airport, looking down and seeing a large crowd. On the tarmac was what looked like the mayor and his whole corporation, complete with brass band. I remarked to Jean there must be some VIP expected. When we landed it turned out I was the VIP!

Bulawayo had really gone to town in its reception for us: flowers, speeches, drinks – it was the full treatment. Unwisely, considering the great heat, I accepted more gin than I should have done and rather quickly I felt a little tipsy; however, I didn't suppose that would matter. Unfortunately the organizer then came up to me and said: 'Now, Mr Cooper, if you're ready, I'll drive you to the hall, where the orchestra is waiting for you to rehearse.' What with all the travelling, excitement and the gin, I was in no state whatever to play, and when I unsteadily mounted the platform, amid applause from the orchestra, I sat down and realized that my fingers had great difficulty in making contact with the keys. I thought the only thing to do was to make a clean breast of it; so I made a little speech and explained to the gentlemen of the orchestra what had happened. I asked if it would be possible to postpone the rehearsal until some time the next day.

My confession was greeted with roars of applause and laughter and I arranged with the conductor to have a rehearsal the next morning, by which time I had recovered. The concerto was, after all, the Tchaikovsky No. 1 in B flat minor, which is not one to be trifled with or undertaken light-headedly!

The next crisis came over clothes. The organizer said: 'You've got your tails, of course?' 'No, I was told to bring a tuxedo,' I said. 'I expect you thought we were a lot of people in grass skirts, living up trees. We are civilized here,' he said, rather scornfully. I said very quickly: 'It wasn't that at all, but the agent thought it would be too hot for tails.' 'We are quite used to the heat; you can't possibly wear a tuxedo here. But we do have a firm which hires out evening dress and we'll get you fitted up.'

The next shock came when I'd been practising happily in the hall after the rehearsal. Two Africans were cleaning up the stage and obviously enjoying my little bits of practising. I spoke to them and said I hoped to see them that night and they said: 'We're sorry, but we will not be there.' When I asked why, they said there was a colour bar.

A further surprise came when I went across to the Bulawayo Club. I had taken my tie off because I was so terribly hot and had forgotten to put it on again. I was immediately told I was not allowed to enter the Bulawayo Club without a tie. I put it on again, without comment.

The biggest shock of all lay in store and I didn't hear too much about it until after the concert. But I was asked by the organizer if I knew Thomas Fielden. Remembering him to have been the soloist who played the Grieg Concerto all those years ago at Keble College, Oxford, under my so-called conductorship, I said I had met Dr Fielden. Iwas told he was the Director of the Rhodesia Academy of Music. The organizer continued: 'I'm sorry to tell you, but he has taken against you. His objection to your coming is that you may be a very good pianist, but you are not a celebrity; unfortunately he has lobbied quite a lot of people and there have been some nasty exchanges in the press. To cut a long story short, he has really tried to sabotage your audience.'

'Well, all that matters is, has he?' I asked. 'No, we've got an almost sold-out house,' the organizer replied. 'There are just about five or six seats in the front row where a few of the grandees on his staff have purposely stayed away. But he certainly doesn't want to meet you during your visit.'

I didn't say anything much; I thought the least said, soonest mended. I certainly didn't make any statement publicly, but I thought to myself, obviously Thomas Fielden was still resenting my bad conducting in the Grieg Concerto and hadn't forgiven me – otherwise I could think of no reason why he could have so taken against me; unless of course it was that he felt himself that he should have been invited to inaugurate the new piano. In fact when I was finally shown the whole correspondence in the Bulawayo press, a point of view that his 'side' expressed was that surely somebody local of equal eminence could have been found to play at the opening concert (or words to that effect).

It was a storm in a teacup really, but the fact was that Thomas Fielden at the time was the big fish in a little pond in musical Bulawayo and they had to listen to what he said, even though they politely disagreed.

Fortunately for me the press were not in the least influenced by Thomas Fielden's strictures and were prepared to take an absolutely independent view of my playing and found it favourable; I got good notices.

But we weren't happy in Bulawayo, and having done a broadcast interview and an official lunch we made our excuses and booked an aeroplane for Nairobi, where we had cabled Bobs Hopcraft to tell him what flight we were on. He met us full of joy – he was one of those people who made you feel it was good to be alive. We got into the car and, as we were driving along, Bobs said in his usual cheerful way: 'If we are stopped or anything, just sit in the car and I will deal with it; but I'm not expecting anything.' Nothing happened and we arrived at his farm at Lake Naivasha, which was 6,300 feet up.

Bobs said, 'Now I'll make you a cup of coffee.' We sat back and relaxed and felt happy to be with Bobs and to be away from Bulawayo. As Jean took her first sip of coffee she exclaimed: 'Oh, to taste coffee where the beans are actually grown!' 'That's only half true,' Bobs said, 'you're drinking Nescafé. But the beans were grown here, and by a process of recycling the coffee came out of a tin! So much simpler.'

'When it comes to bedtime,' Bobs said, 'I must warn you that if you hear a dog barking, knock on my door, which is that one,' and he pointed to the door, 'because it means that the Mau Mau are around and we've got to be careful.' We said goodnight and went to bed. To my horror, in the middle of the night I awoke to the sound of a dog barking. I whispered to Jean: 'Are you awake?' and she said she was; she had been lying there in frozen horror, because quite apart from the fact she could hear the dog barking, she was dying to pee, and the loo was seventy-five yards away in an outside hut in the garden. She was wondering what to do. I bravely said I would put on her big sun-hat and stride down the garden singing 'Rule Britannia', which would keep away all the wicked spirits. It had the desired effect, so Jean repeated the process and we never disturbed Bobs at all.

At breakfast the next morning we told Bobs that unfortunately we would have to get an aeroplane that day to get back to England, as I had a whole series of concerts and we were already late. But we said how much we had enjoyed it and what a pity it was that we couldn't stay and see some of the lovely sights Kenya had to offer – we particularly wanted to see the game reserve, but time was against us. So Bobs drove us down to Nairobi, saw us off and I haven't seen him since – more's the pity, because there aren't many people that I liked more than Bobs Hopcraft.

Apart from a round of concerto dates that lay ahead of me, including Manchester, Edinburgh, Glasgow, Birmingham, Belfast and Bournemouth, I had a new series which I was to record for the BBC Overseas Service; a very intriguing series in which I had to interview all the best-known British composers. 'Interview' is perhaps not quite the right word, because in fact the whole idea was to let the composer do the talking; so often in an interview the interviewer does as much talking as the interviewee. So the producer deliberately called the programme *The Composer Speaks* and he gave me my brief, which was to keep my own speech to an absolute minimum, yet at the same time try and draw from the composer intimate aspects of his life and what he really thought of his compositions. Any special points were illustrated with recorded music. Alas! the series was never used in England – it was kept for 'the people living up trees in grass skirts' (to quote the man at Bulawayo).

We had most of the composers lined up, including Sir Arthur Bliss, Michael Tippett, John Ireland and Lennox Berkeley. One composer the producer was rather afraid to write to was Benjamin Britten; recalling our old acquaintanceship at Blackheath, I volunteered to write to Ben Britten myself. I got a favourable reply; he thought that he wouldn't be up to much as a broadcaster, but he was prepared to have a go – in any case it would be nice to see me again.

Britten was not entirely at ease when he was talking and at one point he dried up altogether with, 'Oh dear, I can't remember what I was going to say next.' I reminded him it was actually being recorded and we could rub it out and start again and perhaps we might stop for a cup of tea. We did, and after that Britten went ahead quite smoothly.

One interesting point is that he prophesied the building of the Snape concert hall; he said that it was a little dream that he had in the back of his mind, but he didn't really want to talk too much about it. Britten also recalled the value to him of the days in the GPO Film Unit. Having had to turn out descriptive music to order, and use small 'forces', partly due to lack of space and money, was an exercise in discipline and resourcefulness.

Going back to his days at the Royal College of Music, Benjamin Britten said of Arthur Benjamin (his piano professor) and John Ireland (his composition professor) and I quote: 'They were both very kind to me and really nursed me very gently through a very, very difficult musical adolescence, which I was going through at that time.' Strange, because at Blackheath I was the one with the stumbling blocks, and he seemed so confident and brilliant.

One composer whom I very much wanted to interview was Dr John Ireland. The BBC recording crew and the producer met Jean and me at John Ireland's home in the Sussex Downs – the house was a converted windmill. As soon as I met John Ireland I became nervous, because he was not at all welcoming. Eyeing us all suspiciously, he started to ask what other composers I had interviewed and then, recalling an old rival (Ralph Vaughan Williams), he asked: 'Have you got that man Williams in this series?' I was able truthfully to say we hadn't (by then Vaughan Williams was rather old and deaf). He relaxed perceptibly. He seemed jealous (or 'chipsville' as we call it) of other composers.

I myself was slightly on edge, because that very evening I was due to be playing Brahms and Beethoven violin and piano sonatas with Yfrah Neaman in Birmingham, so I had half-an-eye on the clock during the interview. I was slightly alarmed that Dr Ireland was in no mood to hurry, and he started to play the piano as though he had forgotten the purpose of our visit. 'Perhaps you'd like to play a few bars during the interview, to illustrate a few points?' I suggested. 'Yes, if you pay me an extra fee,' he retorted!

Anyway, eventually we sat facing each other across a large table, with the microphone between us. Everything was going tolerably well, until I mentioned a work of his called *Mai Dun* and he looked across at me sardonically and said: 'Mai not be Dun is what I always call it – it's never performed,' and then the interview took on a rather lugubrious, pessimistic tone, John Ireland always suggesting that he had not been given a square deal.

I asked about his songs and confessed that I had a great passion for 'Sea Fever': he said he had a record of that and he put it on. The singer was Robert Irwin and I was so overcome with the music, the singing and the pathos generated by the composer, that with the words 'And a grey mist on the sea's face' I started to weep. Ireland, who up to this time had been entirely taken up with himself and his own problems and defeats and frustrations, lifted his spectacles above his eyebrows and stared incredulously at me. When the music was over he seemed a changed man. 'I think it's time for a glass of sherry,' he said. So we drank sherry and he then became cheerful, answered any question I liked to ask, and the interview changed to a note of great optimism.

I started talking about the piano concerto and the muted trumpets in the finale. John Ireland said he went to listen to Jack Payne's dance band. Payne demonstrated several mutes, one – the fibre mute – which Ireland thought infinitely superior to the one that was being used by symphony orchestras. He added: 'I think I was the first composer of serious music to specify that particular mute, which is now in universal use.' He also said he was hauled over the coals afterwards by some critics, who thought it was a bad thing for a serious composer to be hob-nobbing with a dance-band leader.

By now John Ireland was in full spate. He had warmed to me and his subject, and if only I hadn't had to leave for Birmingham, I would have secured a fabulous interview from an under-rated composer. Dr Ireland's devoted housekeeper and friend, Mrs Norah Kirby, wrote afterwards to say how much good the interview had done the composer, and would we please go again.

After we had left the Sussex Downs and were speeding towards Birmingham, I was thankful that Jean always liked to do the driving. This gave me an opportunity not only of relaxing after an exhausting recording, but also of spending some time limbering up my fingers on a small dummy keyboard which sat neatly on my lap. We only made one stop, for sandwiches and coffee; otherwise we kept trundling on, because it was a long cross-country journey and I wanted to get to Birmingham in time to have at least a word with Yfrah Neaman, if not even a quick rehearsal.

As it turned out, we arrived about half-an-hour before the concert, leaving just enough time to change. Fortunately Yfrah and I had quite often played together before and the particular works for that programme we knew very well. The recital took place in Birmingham Museum and Art Gallery and, as Yfrah and Jean and I proceeded to the recital room, we passed the massive statue of Epstein's Lucifer; since we were plunging into the vigorous, manly Brahms D minor Violin and Piano Sonata, Epstein's statue couldn't have set the scene better for us.

This might be a moment to remind the reader that I never took Jean for granted. She was the most perfect wife it was possible for anyone to imagine; having learnt to become a musician, she was prepared to drive hundreds of miles, always remained cheerful, and what was more, for recitals like the one I was about to give with Yfrah Neaman, she became a one-hundred-per-cent reliable turner of the pages. Most music I played by heart, but chamber music or BBC studio broadcasts, never.

It had become an amusing bet between us many years before that as soon as Jean had learnt to turn the pages of the music in public, I would learn to ride a horse. Jean's chosen 'arena' was the BBC Maida Vale Studio No. 1. The work she chose for her 'turning-over' début was the concertino by Christian Darnton. I was the piano soloist in the first broadcast, with Sir Adrian Boult conducting the strings of the BBC Symphony Orchestra.

For my side of the bargain I chose a less frightening venue, the Greigs' Scottish home on the Moray Firth, not far from Inverness. The horse, fortunately, was a sleepy and rather ancient lady called Camilla. There was no question of her running away – the only difficulty was that sometimes she just stopped and quietly went to sleep. I never told Jean, but I felt very uncomfortable on a horse and didn't refer to riding again – and I hoped she wouldn't!

But I was aware that not only did we take far too few holidays, but that Jean herself was not given sufficient outlet to indulge in either of her great passions, riding and sailing. I had done enough sailing and heard enough squabbling on board (also in Scotland) to be very wary of it, but at least I was a good sailor, in the sense that I was never seasick. I thought that as soon as we could take a break, we would hire a boat and Jean could teach me the rudiments of sailing. But in the meantime, she understood as well as I did that we were living entirely on what I was making; my fees were still not enough for me to be able to afford to turn down work. So we were hopping about all over the place, getting a little tired, but tremendously happy, and feeling that we were gradually making a success.

The enterprising Wilfrid van Wyck had recently sent us on tours of Holland and Czechoslovakia, playing solo recitals and concertos. He rang up one day saying he thought a change of musical diet would do me good; I'd been very serious to date in my concert career and he'd always known that I had a big streak of humour running through me, which he now wanted to exploit. I wondered what on earth was coming. Then he spelt it out.

Anna Russell, who was advertised as 'the funniest woman in the world', was coming to the Edinburgh Festival in August 1957, to be followed by a London concert at the Royal Albert Hall. Wilfrid suggested that I act as her piano accompanist, both at Edinburgh and at the Albert Hall. I was at first delighted, but on reflection Jean and I wondered if this engagement might seriously affect my hard-won reputation as a serious musician. However, having heard Anna Russell analysing Wagner's great operatic masterpiece *The Ring* on a record, I couldn't resist it; we went to Edinburgh and we never regretted it.

We found Anna Russell as a person quite hilarious and I enjoyed playing for her. However, I was glad to have had the Edinburgh Festival performances first, because the Albert Hall could have been an ordeal for me, if I hadn't been thoroughly conversant with Anna Russell's tricks. Fortunately they were entirely predictable; she had her act and all her movements, gestures and routines timed and worked out down to the last detail. That didn't mean that they were easy for me to learn; on the contrary, there were so many of them, and so often I was taken up with fits of laughter, that I hardly knew how to go on playing. But having thoroughly digested her programme, when it came to the Albert Hall, which was packed to the roof, I was as cool as anyone could have been in the circumstances. *The Times* and *Telegraph* gave Anna rave notives the next day – and were also very nice about me.

Although I only worked with Anna Russell that one season, her fun was something I shall never forget. I also learnt much that was later to prove useful. Thinking back on Edinburgh, I was delighted that two people I had always associated very much with the serious world of music, Sir Robert and Lady Mayer, were the first to come round and congratulate Anna after her performance at Freemasons' Hall. Sir Robert, in an aside to me, said: 'I'm so glad that you can laugh too, as well as cry, over music; both are very important.'

It was almost impossible to be in London musical circles and not meet Austrian-born Lotte Nicholls (in private life Mrs Charlotte Nicholls, married to a distinguished Wimpole Street doctor). Deeply musical, Lotte became a sort of unofficial artists' manager to a small group of soloists. Her persuasive advocacy helped more than one artist to reach the top of the musical tree. She was friendly with Wilfrid van Wyck, who found her a useful and helpful colleague. Lotte was to be seen at concerts and musical parties; she also made a way of life her Wimpole Street luncheon parties, inviting distinguished as well as up-and-coming musicians to drop in. There was always a nice lunch. (I remember seeing a young boy there in shorts – his name was Daniel Barenboim.) Lotte had offered to help me. The fact that I had been so busy for the last two years had been partly due to Lotte's splendid publicity and her readiness to seize an opportunity, if she saw one, to help an artist friend. Naturally generous by nature, she so enjoyed doing things for people that their appreciation was her reward.

In 1958 I had recorded three Beethoven sonatas for World Record Club (the 'Moonlight', 'Pathétique' and 'Appassionata') and rather felt I'd done enough recording for a bit, because as usual I had *Call the Tune* on my hands, as well as many other broadcasts and concerts. But in early June the telephone rang and Lotte said: 'Have you seen the papers? Poor Richard Farrell has been killed in a motor accident, isn't it sad.' 'How dreadful, but how did it happen?' I asked. 'This is no time to ask now,' Lotte replied. 'Do you play the Tchaikovsky Piano Concerto No. 3? You do play, of course, the Litolff Scherzo and the Saint-Saens *Wedding Cake Caprice* and the Weber *Konzertstück*?' I told her I played all except the Tchaikovsky and with that Lotte said she would ring me back in a few hours. I reported this to Jean, as I wondered what Lotte was up to; Jean decided that perhaps she was trying to secure an engagement for me that Richard Farrell was to have done.

By lunch-time Lotte had telephoned again and said: 'Joe, it is all done. I have spoken to Pye, with whom poor Richard Farrell was going to record all these works in three weeks' time. They were wondering what they were going to do, but I have persuaded them that you are prepared to take on the recording. It is now just a question of discussing it all with the recording manager and signing the contract.'

I was absolutely flabbergasted. How was I going to get all these works ready for recording in just three weeks, especially as I'd never heard of the Tchaikovsky Piano Concerto No. 3 (and I felt I'd had enough battles with the first and second concertos)!

There was no copy of the third concerto in England, as far as I could gather, except one at the BBC; they very kindly lent it to me. Then Jean and I set about a campaign of really working night and day. We felt this was a moment in our lives where we must take another gamble, because if I could make a great success for Pye, I was in with a big recording firm, which would notch up many more marks for me in the profession.

The recording was made at Walthamstow town hall on 26 and 27 June 1958, with Charles Mackerras conducting the Pro Arte Orchestra. Charles Mackerras was a marvellous help to me, and he was especially pleased with the performance of the Tchaikovsky No. 3. It contained a very long solo piano cadenza; the custom was, and still is, not to waste the orchestra's time while the pianist records a long unaccompanied passage. Instead, the solo artist usually comes back to an empty studio a few days later and records the cadenza.

In this case the cadenza was not recorded until six months later – why Pye arranged it like this, I have no idea. But I had to return the score to the BBC when I'd finished recording in June, and by the time I borrowed the score again in December, I had almost forgotten how the concerto went. However, I mugged up the cadenza, but arrived at Walthamstow with a very heavy heart, because there was no atmosphere, no orchestra, no Charles Mackerras – just a piano in a bare hall, and a fiendishly difficult cadenza in front of me. I don't think it is the best part of the record. Anyway, it was slipped into the recording and probably nobody would have known that it was made six months after the rest of the record.

Unfortunately, after all that sweat this turned out not to be my big break into recording. Although much of the performance is good, there are various faults and naturally these were noticed by the critics. But I have no complaint with the critics; I have been extremely lucky all my career and I've had very few bad notices. In fact I have often had much better notices than I've deserved. I was just unhappy on this occasion, because working into the night for the three weeks leading up to the June recording had drained the last ounce of energy from both Jean and myself; we were completely and utterly exhausted. Unfortunately we simply couldn't afford to be.

There was a tremendous amount of work on hand. I had a new Schools Music series to present for Associated Rediffusion – the first ever on television – in which we gave schools an introduction to the instruments of the orchestra, in conjunction with the Hallé. The series, extending over many weeks, finished up with my playing part of a concerto with the Hallé Orchestra and Sir John Barbirolli, an encounter which I thoroughly enjoyed. At the same time I was doing for BBC a schools series on sound, and on BBC Television I was presenting a series of three programmes called *Confessions of a Pianist*.

So we were working as it were, on reserve, Jean helping me all she could. We went for quiet drives into the country whenever possible, just to get away from the terrible pressures. On 23 August I played at the Proms the Grieg Piano Concerto. I didn't play well, but fortunately it was in the second half of the programme, which wasn't broadcast, so the world didn't hear the inadequacy of my performance; but I, and everybody else connected with it, knew it to be erratic and lacklustre.

The last straw came in October when I was asked by Scottish ITV to play 'live' the Tchaikovsky Piano Concerto No. 2. I had just come across from playing in Londonderry and Belfast a series of different concertos, including the 'Emperor', a Mozart and the Philip Cannon Concertino. So I was already tired. When I got to the studio I found the piano had been placed to suit the cameras, but it was in such an awkward position that I couldn't possibly see the conductor. Although I knew the Tchaikovsky No. 2 inside out by this time, there was a horrible moment in the finale where the conductor and I missed each other and we were out for at least half a dozen bars. Fortunately very few people noticed. As Hans Swarovsky, the conductor, couldn't find it in him to address a word to me either before or after the performance, I have no idea what he felt.

Jean and I knew very well how we felt: a change of direction was due. I simply couldn't carry on with the strain of the piano profession, combining it with all the talks and features, without killing myself. It was quite obvious. Although I was still only in my mid-forties, it was no good pretending I was twenty.

8
Sea Fever

After much discussion and thought in 1958, we decided that the following year we would accept less dates and try to coast along and make our plans for a change of course. I thought it would be a splendid idea if we had a holiday on water; this would give Jean a chance to go back to one of her great skills. She was a beautiful helmswoman; she had been sailing in small boats since she was four. To watch Jean sailing was a joy: she knew the wind, she knew the sails, she knew exactly the feel of a boat in all conditions, and I thought it would be wonderful to do some sailing with her.

Jean decided the Norfolk Broads would be the safest and best place for my initiation into sailing. So we investigated, and finally arranged to hire a sailing motor-boat on the Norfolk Broads for June 1959.

The holiday was so successful that Jean and I resolved to buy a boat. I stressed that the very special appeal of the Broads was the sense of security these stretches of inland waters gave me. Diplomatically, Jean agreed that the open sea didn't appeal to her. There were so many estuaries on the east coast to explore and we both loved East Anglia, so our holiday situation seemed solved for years to come. Now to buy a boat.

We started to explore various east coast harbours by car. Sitting comfortably in the office of a yachting agency at Woodbridge, Suffolk (on the River Deben), we started looking through bookfuls of boats for sale, comparing prices, shapes and sizes. Strange words like draught, clinker, beam, as well as Gaff, Gunter and Bermuda Rigs, kept cropping up as Jean and the young male assistant (clearly a boat fanatic) discussed all that was on offer. After a discourse on the advantages of bilge keels as ideal for estuary sailing (none of which I understood), we were directed to go to Melton, a mile or two up-river, where a Mr Debbage would already be alerted to receive us.

Mr Debbage, who owned a small boat-yard at Melton, was, luckily, uncomplicated, friendly, trusting and trustworthy. He said we could look around and clamber aboard any boat marked 'For Sale'. They all looked a bunch of old crocks to me, but Jean was immediately intrigued by one called *Cormorant*. I noticed the boat was pointed at both ends, like a lifeboat: Jean whispered to me, 'You call that a double-ender.' Mr Debbage told us that *Cormorant* had been custom-built by Kenneth Gibbs at Shepperton (on the Thames) for a man who loved estuary sailing. She was basically sound, but needed a refit. Jean, using the same 'hunch-mechanism' that secured us Trocks Mill Cottage, asked Mr Debbage the price: £600 was the answer. I, having noticed prices around £2,000 and more in the Woodbridge office, nodded approval – and *Cormorant* was ours. The official description of our boat was that she was a Gunter Rig Sloop with auxiliary engine.

Mr Debbage undertook to have her ready to sail by the summer of 1960. Whenever we had a day to spare we went over to Melton – not to spy, but because we couldn't keep away. Our interest and appreciation of all Mr Debbage's efforts spurred him on. It was worth braving the traffic of the A12, which in those days was an eighty-mile crawl, to ensure that some other customer hadn't demanded priority.

When we proudly launched *Cormorant* and set off, I found that I had absorbed more from the sailing holiday on the Broads the year before than I had realized. I felt completely at home in *Cormorant* and although I couldn't remember the names of many of the technical terms used to describe quite ordinary things – I called everything a 'thingummyjig' – the general principles that Jean had taught me were firmly in my mind.

So much so, that when we reached quite quickly the mouth of the River Deben and Jean said: 'Would you like just to put *Cormorant*'s nose out into the sea?' without thinking I said: 'Of course; it looks a lovely day, let's have a sail.' I quite forgot that my whole intention was never ever to go to sea.

So we went left, or turned to port as one would say, up the coast; we then turned in to a little river which took us up to Aldeburgh. The boat was going so beautifully; she was newly painted and to us seemed terribly smart. We longed to show her off to somebody. Jean had an aunt and uncle living at Sternfield, not very far from the river, so I went ashore and telephoned Mr and Mrs Humphrey Scrimgeour – known as Uncle Dunk and Aunt Tootie – and asked if there were any volunteers who would like to come for a sail. Aunt Tootie, an intrepid little lady, was the only one who seemed willing to risk her life on *Cormorant*. We agreed to pick her up at Iken.

Aunt Tootie admired *Cormorant* and climbed aboard enthusiastically. She was extremely sensible, determined to enjoy every minute of the sail, and said: 'Just tell me what I must do, and what I must not do, and I will follow instructions.' So Jean advised: 'When we are getting the sail up, you should sit still; likewise keep still when we're pulling the sail down. Otherwise there are no particular things you need know. Oh, you might like to see the heads.' 'Heads,' said Aunt Tootie, 'what on earth are they?' 'Sorry; that's the technical word for the loo,' Jean told her. Aunt Tootie was shown the heads, which were right up in the front of the boat. She remarked on the astonishing double bed, or double bunk I should call it, which took up the entire cabin. Jean was determined that our boat was going to be as comfortable as possible; she had no intention of making it a racing boat. This, of course, delighted me. The double bunk was about as comfortable as anything you could imagine. It had been cleverly made so that it could be turned into two single bunks if necessary; it wasn't necessary in our case.

We got the sails up and had a lovely sail; there was just enough breeze to make it safe but satisfactory. Then we decided to take the sail down again and have our picnic lunch. Aunt Tootie knew her drill – this was the time for her to sit absolutely still. Jean went up to the mast and let down the upper part of the sail. In fact she could only let a certain amount of the top part of the sail go before she had to hand over control of it to me, because she ran out of rope. I then had to catch it and make sure that not only the sail, but the heavy beam, or spar, to which it was attached came safely and slowly down. Unfortunately, on this occasion I didn't catch it. The top part of the sail, plus the wooden beam, came down with an enormous crash, the sail covering everything – including Aunt Tootie. She was invisible and from underneath the sail there was an ominous silence.

Jean came down quickly from the mast and whispered: 'What

had we better do? Why isn't she saying anything? Did she get hit by the beam?' I carefully picked up bits of sail, until I saw a small figure, sitting quite happily; Aunt Tootie was undamaged and apparently unfrightened. 'Well,' she said, 'you told me to sit still, so I sat still. I did wonder if everything was going according to plan, but I thought it would be unseamanlike to make a fuss.' She was marvellous, but I think inside she must have been a bit shaken.

After lunch Aunt Tootie said she had done enough sailing for one day, so we returned to Iken. She said bravely she would like to come on board again some time, if the opportunity presented itself, but added she didn't think Uncle Dunk would enjoy it very much; he preferred the dry land.

We had some wonderful trips during that holiday; we sailed up to Lowestoft and even right up to Norwich. East Anglia is really the novice yachtsman's paradise, because quite apart from the Broads, there are so many harbours up and down the coast that you need never be in the open sea for long.

I think Jean had started this holiday without any preconceived ideas about where we would terminate it – I think a lot depended on the performance of the boat and the reaction of the crew (me). *Cormorant*'s new engine, a Stuart Turner eight-horsepower, went spendidly; the sails and rigging were excellent, too, so Jean thought it would be a good idea to take the boat up the Thames to Shepperton and winter her there, at Dunton's Boat-Yard.

On our way south, we called in on the River Orwell, which took us up to Ipswich; then we nosed in on the River Stour towards Manningtree. Next we went up the Crouch and had a look at Burnham, before finally making the rather nasty turn into the River Thames; it is very shallow and you have to go out a mile or two before you can turn the corner. But I had carefully made a note of all the buoys; I knew that when we reached a certain buoy we were safely round the Maplin Spit and could turn into the River Thames.

When we arrived at Shepperton I suggested to Jean that we visit Kenneth Gibbs, the man who originally designed *Cormorant*. I thought he might be interested, so we called; at first he didn't understand what I was talking about when I referred to *Cormorant*, but like most boating people he was friendly and came down and looked at the boat. He said: 'Oh, that was *West Wind*. She's been changed to *Cormorant*, has she? She was originally a ketch – in other words she had another sail, aft of the mainsail.' Kenneth Gibbs gave me a picture of her as she was in his original design. Anyhow, he thought she looked lovely and was pleased to see us. He told us he was happy when he designed *West Wind*, because it was a piece of really creative work on his part. That was in 1950. Now he was on fibre-glass jobs, turning them out by the hundred and all exactly alike. 'But one's got to live,' he added philosophically.

We continued up-river to Dunton's Boat-Yard, where *Cormorant* was slipped out of the water. Dunton's was a sort of do-it-yourself place, where for a small rent you bought standing-room for the boat. This was excellent, because Shepperton is near enough to Barnes for us to go and tinker about with *Cormorant*, re-paint her and gradually formulate new ideas for her comfort and seaworthiness.

I had a shock coming to me: one day Jean announced she thought that next holiday we would sail across the Channel. I said it was ridiculous; the boat was designed for estuary sailing and the idea of crossing the Channel was absolutely preposterous. But Jean, who was not to be over-ridden in these matters, thought it wasn't at all a ridiculous idea. Before I could say anything further, the decision was taken.

Come summer 1961 we were sailing to Dover, *en route* for Calais. Needless to say, I listened to every weather forecast on the radio. When we were in at Dover, a force eight gale was forecast; we pulled right in to an inner harbour. I had been across the Channel enough times in big steamers to notice how they were tossed about in such weather; I knew it would be quite impossible for the two of us in *Cormorant* with our little experience to cross in these conditions. I said so firmly and clearly to Jean. On matters of sailing Jean was the captain and she didn't greatly like suggestions from me, but I knew this was a matter of common sense.

Suddenly I had a brainwave: if we made for the Dover Yacht Club, we would be sure to find some congenial people and we could ask their advice. We did just that. Sitting at the bar was a charming Scotsman called John Hendrie; he was an experienced seaman and said he was going to take some enthusiastic amateurs across to Calais, just as soon as weather conditions improved; he would be delighted if we went, as it were, in convoy. Greatly comforted by this, we retired to bed in our little harbour. The storm raged for two days and the sea was quite white outside – even the Channel boats had difficulty getting into harbour. Jean was still raring to go; but I said: 'When John Hendrie says go, we'll go – but not before, or you go without me!'

Finally the gale slackened; the only unpleasant thing left was a rolling, but not dangerous, sea. John Hendrie asked me how much I knew about currents in the Channel and the fact that there were tides – it was no good just pointing towards Calais, otherwise I'd find myself somewhere in Holland. I confessed I was no expert. John said he would give me the right compass bearing: 'Stick to that and although you won't be pointing at Calais, you will in fact arrive at Calais.' Jean made a careful note of the bearing, but didn't seem at all worried. Her great thing was that we were going to cross the Channel; she had this marvellous new boat and she was absolutely up in the clouds with delight.

Curiously, although Jean and I started at the same time as John Hendrie, our boat was quite a lot faster. After four-and-a-half hours' sailing we found ourselves in Calais, so we slowed down and dawdled, until we saw the other boat coming. I noted, by the way, how meticulously Jean kept *Cormorant* on course.

We were across the Channel and we were still alive. We each had a swig of rum from the bottle I kept in my oilskin pocket. Over a meal in Calais John Hendrie gave me a tide-table and showed me exactly how to work out the compass bearings, so that we could be safer and more independent when we came to make the return crossing.

So far we had been very lucky, while actually sailing, with wind and weather generally – no great dangers had come to us in *Cormorant*. But I realized that Jean's ambitions were almost limitless, so the first thing I needed was to have a full course in navigation. I persuaded Jean that we would spend the next year or two in English waters, starting with the Solent, and going right down to south Devon and Cornwall; during that time we were near enough a number of big boat-yards, in case we got into trouble. Above all, I could then put into practice all the navigation I was going to learn.

We had already become members of the Island Sailing Club at Cowes and we had quite a number of friends and relatives of Jean who were avid sailors.

I had another reason for not wanting to be too far away: my

mother had been in poor health for the last two or three years and she had moved from Harlyn Bay to London. In 1963, when we were actually sailing off the Cornish coast, we had news that she had died. We sailed the boat into Plymouth harbour and took the train back to London for her funeral. We still had a few days of holiday to run, so we returned to Plymouth, picked up the boat and started slowly on the journey back towards the Solent.

My mother had been suffering from progressive hardening of the arteries and this resulted in her never feeling well and getting bouts of appalling depression. I think that she was not sorry to leave this world. I'm always happy to feel that before she left it, she did come to the Royal Albert Hall and hear me play one of her favourite concertos, the Rachmaninoff No. 2. She dressed up for the occasion and no one would have believed there was anything wrong with her; but the next day she lapsed again into this state of near melancholia. My mother had done much for me, especially in my early life. I was only sorry that Jean had never had the opportunity of seeing her when she was in her prime, the life and soul of every party.

Incidentally, I heard recently from my friend Mr Long, an ironmonger in Westbury-on-Trym, that my mother's jaunty manner and her long chats on the telephone to the various shopkeepers in the village earned her the affectionate nickname of 'Mrs Feather'.

My mother had always made her age a matter of the greatest secrecy and I think I, for one, was very surprised to hear she had finally clocked up eighty-four years.

Cormorant had become a sort of holiday home for us – a home that we, like a snail, took around on our back. Now that I had got used to sailing and understood the niceties of navigation, I think I loved *Cormorant* just as much as Jean did. In 1965 we decided the moment had come to do a marathon journey.

We had a trailer built to fit *Cormorant* and bought a Land-Rover. Then we planned to drive the boat across Europe and put her in the water at Rijeka, in the northern part of Yugoslavia; we would then sail down to Dubrovnik. We planned our route so that we could make the maximum use of the magnificent German autobahns, because while towing *Cormorant* we were anxious to avoid narrow, twisting or bumpy roads. Although she appeared a fairly small boat when in the water, once on land and loaded on the trailer we did seem to have an awful lot of boat behind us – after all, *Cormorant* was 24 foot long, 8 foot wide at her widest point, and weighed 3½ tons, without allowing for all our stores and equipment.

After crossing to Ostend and driving through the outskirts of Brussels, we reached the German frontier at Aachen and noticed immediately a tremendous improvement in the road surface. Once on the autobahn Jean remarked what a treat it was to drive on something smooth at last; she put her foot on the accelerator and we went up from our accustomed 30 mph to between 40 and 50 mph. What we hadn't allowed for was a sudden strong side wind. The first symptom we had was that the boat and trailer started swinging violently, lurching into us; without our being able to do anything about it, the Land-Rover started swerving from side to side in a terrifying way. Suddenly with an enormous bump we crashed into the barrier of the central reservation and shuddered to a halt. The silence that followed the crash was appalling, neither of us knew what to say.

Jean's first words were: 'We must send for the AA.' My first reaction was thank God for that splendid barrier – it had stopped us careering into the traffic coming in the other direction. We clambered out and managed to thumb a lift back to the German frontier, where I explained our predicament in my rather bad German. The official was extremely obliging and telephoned a garage at Aachen who said they would send a recovery vehicle as soon as they could. In the meanwhile we went back to the wreck – on close inspection it really did look rather a mess; the front of the Land-Rover on the passenger side had taken the main impact and it was quite obvious we couldn't drive it as it was. I was determined not to take too pessimistic a view; after all, we were not hurt. Whereas so often in our professional life Jean had to be calming me down, I found that now I had to calm her down; of course, being the driver and finding yourself in such a situation must have been terrifying.

However, once the recovery van arrived, the battered bodywork of the Land-Rover was soon wrenched away from the wheel, so that the wheels were free to go round. A tow-rope was attached and we made a slow procession to the Aachen garage: the van, Jean and I in the Land-Rover, and *Cormorant* still behind.

Mr Niessen, the garage owner, thoroughly inspected all the

damage. He was extremely friendly, but spoke no English. In German, he did his best to explain to me patiently and slowly, and I grasped the dismal fact, that a number of spare parts required renewal on the Land-Rover; being a British vehicle they hadn't got them in Germany and it would take quite a long time for them to come from England.

Jean didn't speak or understand a word of German, but I told her the situation. Mr Niessen kindly said we could sleep on *Cormorant* overnight in the garage while we decided what to do next. One of my bad habits when I'm worried is to lie awake and try and think out solutions; suddenly I had a brainwave! A neighbour of ours in Barnes was born in Germany and although he was now completely English he could still speak fluent German; what was more, he was a professional mechanic, and a fellow boat-enthusiast – as indeed was Lois, his wife.

First thing the next morning I told Mr Niessen I intended contacting my friend, Henry Meyer, to see if he could help. I got Henry on the telephone and, losing no time at all, put him on to Mr Niessen. When the two experts had finished their German conversation, I had a word with Henry and he said, 'Don't worry, Joe, I've fixed it all up; I'm going to look for the parts and I will ring you later in the day and tell you how I've fared.'

It's amazing, because it was a Saturday and everything was closed, but when Henry Meyer rang back some hours later, he told me that he himself had put all the spare parts on an aeroplane to Cologne and we could collect them late that evening. If that wasn't marvellous neighbourly goodness and kindness, I don't know what is. I've never ceased to be grateful to Henry Meyer for his help to me and I consider him a true friend – so many people look the other way when help is required.

Mr Niessen drove us personally to Cologne airport; we got special clearance for the box of Land-Rover parts and next day at the garage Mr Niessen's staff got busy with true German thoroughness. By Monday all the work had been completed; the Land-Rover was tested and found to be going perfectly.

We had been so concerned with the Land-Rover repairs that we hadn't examined the boat in great detail and in any case we thought it would be best to wait until we reached the Yugoslav coast and could arrange for a boat expert to examine her. So we set off down the autobahn again, but from this time on, Jean never went more than 28 mph.

The journey seemed never-ending, but eventually we reached the north of Italy and finally our destination, Yugoslavia. There we made for Rijeka, where, on Jean's very wise advice, we contacted the Lloyd's representative, Mr Somerville, who helped us in every way possible; I think we would have been lost without Mr Somerville, because he spoke fluent Yugoslavian and in no time at all the boat damage was examined. Fortunately it wasn't serious, but Mr Somerville took charge of operations, supervised the workmen, and helped us to fill up various forms for Lloyd's. He also took us to meet his charming wife and daughter at his house, which was wonderfully cool – the temperature outside was about 90° Fahrenheit. On top of all the wear and tear of the journey, Jean and I found it difficult to stand the heat.

In a few days Mr Somerville declared *Cormorant* was ready and she was duly launched; so saying *au revoir* to Mr Somerville, we set sail down the coast of Yugoslavia in the direction of Dubrovnik.

If you look at the map of the coast of Yugoslavia you will see numerous tiny islands dotted along the coast, and you will appreciate how glad I was that I had undergone all that training in navigation, because it proved highly necessary. I had a good light over my chart-table. The other hazard of which we had been warned was a fierce wind that blows from the mountains down to the Yugoslavian coast; it is called the Bora and can blow up suddenly to gale force, with hardly any warning at all.

The weather seemed fairly settled for the first few days, but one day I was at the tiller while Jean was preparing some lunch. It all seemed smooth, the wind perfect, but suddenly there was a terrific flutter on the mainsail and I called to Jean in the galley inside: 'Come quickly, the wind's changed.' She shouted: 'Take the mainsail down at once.' We hauled the sail down and by this time the sea was very rough. The situation looked rather nasty, but providentially there was a little harbour to our left and we managed to put in there. The Bora lasted for two days, but finally cleared as quickly as it had come, and happily we were able to continue on our way.

The greatest possible help to me had been a book on the Yugoslav coast by Henry Denham; it gave details of every harbour, any pitfalls in navigation, and also information on restaurants, as well as places of historical interest. Generally speaking, I relied on this book. When, after reaching our first target, Dubrovnik, and wanting to proceed south, we found Henry Denham gave a very high recommendation to a place called Budva; we decided to call in there. As we were going into Budva harbour we noticed a boat carrying a Blue Ensign, which meant the captain must have had something to do with the Royal Navy.

As we tied up, we could hear English voices and soon made friends with the captain and crew of the other boat. The captain described to me a harbour which they intended to call on next, and about which he was rather doubtful – he wasn't absolutely sure if there was enough water for him to get in. I said: 'I'll tell you what, if you'll wait, I've got an excellent book on the whole subject by Henry Denham.' He looked at me and said quietly: 'I am Henry Denham.' After recovering from the initial shock, I fetched my book and asked him to autograph it.

Despite the autobahn accident, we enjoyed a blissful holiday and when it was due to come to an end we were so in love with that part of the world that we decided to leave *Cormorant* in Dubrovnik, come back the next summer and proceed down the coast. In fact we were to leave our boat in Mediterranean harbours for five whole years. Gradually, each summer holiday, we made our way down to Piraeus in Greece, where we left her in Tourkolimano harbour for two winters, carefully tended by a boatman. For me the climax of the holiday there was visiting Epidauros and watching a comedy by Aristophanes, *The Knights*, in the gigantic amphitheatre, under the stars.

I have one very happy memory of our final journey back to England. We had arranged for the Land-Rover and trailer to catch us up, by land and sea, and once more *Cormorant* was on her trailer. We were driving through France and looking for somewhere to stop for the night; we found a great space right outside Evreux Cathedral in Normandy. In some countries we would have been banned from the streets; but certainly in Normandy life was, and still is, fairly free and easy.

Nobody worried about the sight of this fairly bulky boat on a trailer, behind a Land-Rover, just outside a majestic cathedral. In fact the next morning, as we were eating bacon and eggs on board *Cormorant*, the prelate, who had been celebrating mass, came out of the cathedral and, passing very near us, called out '*Bon appétit*!' and returned to his lodgings.

As soon as I started this chapter I realized that I had enough material practically for a whole book on *Cormorant* in the Mediterranean alone, but I have spared you many minor misfortunes such as stoppings of engine and rows with customs officials.

However, there are many places where I would have liked to have lingered and taken you on a tour through the town; specially when we got down to Corfu, which we loved and, incidentally, found at Paleokastritsa the best lobsters anywhere!

On the other hand, the Yugoslavian coastal towns are now visited by millions, as package tours have become big business; Greece and its many islands have also been 'opened up', and now guide books abound. Speaking entirely selfishly, I am glad Jean and I did it the hard way and had most of the gigantic coast almost to ourselves.

No one was more relieved than Phyllis Greig, Jean's mother, when we finally brought the boat back onto a safe mooring on the River Thames. She had done enough sailing in Scotland to know the dangers of the open sea. Incidentally, I always left Jean to tell the stories, which were so heavily edited we might have spent five summers on a mill pond!

Phyllis had long since left Richmond Park and had taken a large flat in Gloucester Square, W2. We used to have (concerts allowing) a Sunday date with Phyllis – supper, plus Scrabble and/or television. *Dr Finlay's Casebook* was a must.

Lady Greig was a close friend of Lady Rachel Stuart. At Findhorn they were often rivals in sailing races – inside Findhorn Bay, not out in the dangerous Moray Firth! Rachel Stuart's younger son, John, was devoted to Phyllis Greig and a frequent visitor to 26 Gloucester Square, either with Jean and me to make up a foursome for Scrabble, or *à deux* during weekdays, when apparently the battles over the Scrabble board were keen, to put it mildly. If Jean's mother won she would ring us next morning and say triumphantly: 'Well, I beat him.'

Lady Greig's younger sister, Mrs Beryl Colebeck, lived in the flat above. They had bedside intercom and used to enjoy late night and early morning chats. Aunt Beryl's daughter, Pen, had married

Charles Chilton of *Oh What a Lovely War* fame, whose work for the BBC had earned him an OBE.

Over the years I have taken part in a number of Charles Chilton's Victorian programmes on the radio – I was very glad that I did not throw away my mother's Victoriana from her music cupboard; the pieces have all come in handy and have provided nostalgic memories for many listeners of 'Victorian Top of the Pops'.

9
Television, Triumph and Tragedy

In the last chapter I purposely bunched all the *Cormorant* holidays together in one – an indulgence I simply couldn't resist. Of course, it wasn't really like that, as each winter we had to return and earn our living.

In 1959 I had been approached by a recently opened ITV company – TWW (Television West and Wales) – who invited me down to Pontcanna Studios at Cardiff to do a short piano spot in a lunch-time series called *Friday Special*. They liked it, and offered me five more. The moving spirit behind the programme, and behind getting me there in the first place, was Michael Frostick, a musician, motoring expert, journalist and also one-time personal representative in England of Sol Hurok, the American impresario.

Michael, who had joined TWW almost at its birth, had seen my recent BBC Television solo programmes and he had already instigated some concerts for me at the Royal Festival Hall. He very much liked what he called my television 'bedside manner' and told Bryan Michie (ex-BBC), then programme controller of TWW, that I was a potential winner. Bryan replied that he gave me my first BBC sound broadcast in 1936 in a series called *My Piano and I*. He welcomed the idea of my coming down to TWW.

Michael Frostick, encouraged by this, not only arranged some more, rather extended programmes for me, but when TWW's new early evening magazine programme started in February 1960, I was made chairman. In this, in addition to playing the piano, I was required to do interviews on a wide range of subjects. For example, in 1961, soon after his autobiography in verse, *Summoned by Bells*, was published, I had the privilege of interviewing John Betjeman.

When a lion-tamer brought a full-grown lion into the studio, I did that interview too. That could have been dangerous, especially when I stood up to say goodnight to the viewers. The lion suddenly got up too and, with its huge paw, knocked me to the ground. This was seen, live, by a million-and-a-half viewers, and the switchboard was jammed with anxious callers. The item made national headlines. Fortunately I am a great cat-lover; to me this was a huge lovable cat having fun. Therefore I was not in the least afraid; if I had been, the lion might have detected the smell of fear and would probably have mauled me. The lion-tamer told me afterwards that my love of cats probably saved a nasty situation. But he added, 'Both I and my assistant are armed against emergencies.'

The programme was called *Here Today*, but some cynics used to add 'and gone tomorrow'. The programme director himself only gave it six weeks. But after a year we were still going strong; in fact in 1961 the Royal Television Society awarded me the Ambrose Fleming Award for the personality of the year. By 1963 we were constantly getting into the local 'top ten'. We ran until 1965.

Soon after the programme first started I was joined by various other interviewers; one was J. Douglas Henry (at that time married to novelist Elizabeth Jane Howard). Brian Vesey-Fitzgerald did a weekly animal spot (after the lion episode, a professional was thought necessary). Another interviewer was Gordon Wilkins, the well-known motoring correspondent, who gave us a weekly motoring spot, as well as sharing some of the other interviews.

One day in May, Michael Frostick announced that he had in mind a motoring marathon for the coming June. We'd see if by leaving the Cardiff studio on Friday evening after the programme (about eight of us including Jean and me with a mini-bus and a Snipe estate car), driving straight to Monte Carlo and spending the weekend there, we could be back in time for the live programme on the Monday evening. Well, of course, had we had the advantage of the Severn Bridge and the better roads of today, it wouldn't have seemed so much of an adventure. From Cardiff we drove immediately to Lydd, from where we flew to Le Touquet; and then we did twenty hours' solid motoring to Monte Carlo. Gordon Wilkins drove one car and Michael Frostick the other. They are both marvellous drivers, but I found the drift turns round those precipitous corners in the Alps terrifying. We had stops, of course, for a meal and nature's necessities, but we didn't sleep. When we arrived at Monte Carlo the next morning, there was a hotel reserved and we had some breakfast.

The famous dance-band leader and impresario, Jack Hylton, who was also one of the directors of TWW, had a luxurious yacht in Monte Carlo harbour. He was on board, so after asking permission, we took our cameras, microphones and other equipment and I interviewed him. We also filmed the mounting of the guard outside Monaco Palace. After a quick lunch we left for the return journey.

We had from Sunday afternoon until Monday at 6 p.m. to get back; so again we had to drive right through the night, stopping for a stupendous French dinner at Le Pic, Valence. Reaching Paris at about five in the morning, we sped right through the city, as there was no traffic at all – an extraordinary sensation, with dawn just breaking.

Everything was going absolutely splendidly and we had time in hand, until we got to the dreaded Aust Ferry, long since replaced by the Severn Bridge. We had taken very special precautions and paid an extra £7 for the ferry authorities to give us priority, when we displayed a card which they gave us. But when we got to the Aust Ferry they said they hadn't heard anything about the priority, and we'd have to take our place in the queue. We started arguing furiously, but it was no good. We missed one boat and had to take the next. Then we got stuck in the Newport traffic; but somehow we got through and finally arrived at the Pontcanna Studios at Cardiff, just as the programme was going on the air. I tore into the studio, sat in my seat and remember being so out of breath that I couldn't speak; I signed to a colleague to take over for the first two minutes.

Anyway, we had achieved our object and enjoyed the adventure.

After all the steep hills and hairpin bends of the French Alps, I had hills rather on the brain. When we moved over to the Bristol studios, which opened soon after the Cardiff ones, I was walking around some roads behind the studios one day and happened to find an incredibly steep hill; there was a corner which must have been about 1 in 2. I said to Gordon Wilkins, who was the great motoring expert; 'Gordon, I'll bet you a dinner that there's a hill within a mile of here that you won't get up.' He roared with laughter and asked where it was. I took him to it, made him stop his car at the bottom of the 1 in 2 bend and told him to start from scratch and go up it. He started, but his engine stalled. He said it was about the steepest bit of hill he had ever seen. So I got my free dinner!

When *Here Today* eventually came off the air in 1965, I don't think any living soul dreamt that in a short time TWW itself would lose its licence. We were very shocked to read this. The company just disappeared and Harlech Television took its place. Fortunately many of the best people on the production side of TWW were absorbed into the new company, which has become one of the most thriving in the country.

Looking back over those five, very happy, years in Cardiff and Bristol and thinking of all the visitors who came to the studios to be interviewed, one stands out in my memory as the kindest and pleasantest person of them all: George Thomas, MP for Cardiff West, who in 1976 became the Speaker in the House of Commons. Towards the end of 1978 I was in the Visitors' Gallery of the House of Commons. Raphael Tuck, my very charming host, told George Thomas that I was there; he looked up, caught my eye right across the chamber, and waved heartily at me, as though to say, 'Nice to see you Here Today!'

Throughout the five years of *Here Today* I had continued to undertake concert engagements all over England, and when the programme ended a great deal of work awaited me ahead. I had found I increasingly enjoyed giving informal recitals, where I talked about the music in addition to playing it. Such concerts proved popular with audiences, too, so I decided to concentrate on this type of programme and I did less and less concerto engagements – to me concertos were far more of a worry and far less enjoyable.

When I had made this change of direction I had asked Wilfred van Wyck to release me from my exclusive contract. I became a freelance artist, with my name appearing on the lists of several concert agents.

My name was also on Foyles Lecture Agency list; they had been trying to get hold of me for some time, but found it almost impossible while I was in the West Country. But now I was free, I was importuned by ladies' lunch clubs; I used to go round, especially in the North Country where such clubs are very prolific, giving a talk called 'Confessions of a Pianist', illustrated either by a piano or by tapes of my piano playing. Later I gave short illustrated talks about composers.

In addition to this, I started working regularly for John Lade's excellent Saturday morning programme *Record Review* on BBC

Radio 3. At this time also I was undertaking quite an amount of adjudicating at musical festivals and my adjudicating work included a marathon coast-to-coast tour of Canada, lasting nearly six months. As usual, Jean travelled with me and we especially adored our journey through the Rockies.

The last series of the radio quiz *Call the Tune* had finished long ago. One of the reasons for its ending was that Walter Todds, its creator and producer, had left BBC Radio and gone over to BBC Television, with the express idea of transferring the programme to the small screen. But first he realized he knew nothing about television. He didn't even own a television set at this stage. However, he said he would get in touch with me when he had been on various courses and was ready; and also when the BBC was willing to have a pilot programme.

In the autumn of 1966 Walter Todds rang me up and told me the BBC were full of plans for putting the music quiz on television: we were going to record one programme and put it out on Boxing Day. I was to be in the chair and the panel members were two old friends, Joyce Grenfell and Paul Jennings, with one newcomer, the news reader Richard Baker. The guest musician was Denis Matthews. We changed the name of the quiz from *Call the Tune* to *Face the Music*. That was just one solitary programme; we enjoyed it, but I don't suppose it attracted much attention.

Then a short series was requested for the following August, which is about the worst month possible, because most people are holidaying in August. So I don't suppose we collected very many viewers and certainly we weren't at all well known at that stage. After a year or two we were asked to do another short series, but it wasn't until 1971 that we became, as it were, airborne.

Our venue changed from London to Manchester; the studio was an old disused church on the outskirts of Manchester. We had an excellent new director, Denis Moriarty, who was enormously helpful; his optimism and diplomatic way of handling crises was of tremendous assistance to Walter and myself, and the programme as a whole.

From 1971 we never looked back; it became obvious to everybody in television that we had a major success on our hands. I personally think this was due partly to the individual brilliance of panel members such as Robin Ray, Richard Baker and Bernard Levin, and the intense magnetism on the screen of Joyce Grenfell, who won for herself millions more fans. As well as that, I think we welded ourselves into a team, under Walter and Denis, and the teamwork shows very well on the screen; we worked with a sense of great enjoyment and dedication, because we believed in the programme so much – as indeed, we are told, did the people you don't see, the expert technicians who put the programme on the screen.

The fact that we had to go to Manchester when most of us lived in London didn't seem in any way a handicap. At the start it seemed to add to the fun; it was a sort of safari atmosphere. Also, we were given twelve programmes, which was a great boost and gave us a chance to establish the programme. The public and the press warmed to a music quiz which had no kind of scoring, where the panel were seen openly to cheat and whisper to each other, where there was no kind of priming of the panel beforehand.

I would like to single out a few individual talents of our regular panel members, which may not be obvious to the viewer. One is Joyce Grenfell's extraordinary ear for music: for example, if I were to say to Joyce, 'Sing the first note of Debussy's *La fille aux cheveux de lin*', Joyce would sing the note and it wouldn't be just any note, it would be actually D flat, the very note that the piece starts on. If you go to the piano and check, you will find she is right a hundred times out of a hundred. This is what I call having a marvellous ear. And that same ear of hers makes her very receptive to the trade marks of various composers. Joyce is an inveterate visitor to the Aldeburgh Festival and knows Benjamin Britten's music very well. There are certain trade marks of Britten's style and even if Joyce doesn't know the actual piece she will say instantly, 'That's Benjamin Britten.' She also excels at the 'Reading Music Backwards' question. Again I think her sense of pitch helps.

Robin Ray and Bernard Levin, apart from having excellent musical memories, also have an extraordinary knowledge of Shakespeare. At one of our suppers after a performance Robin and Bernard had a friendly competition to see how much Shakespeare they could recite. Pages and pages of Shakespeare were recited by heart and they really couldn't have done it better if they'd been reading from the copy. The rest of us sat in blank amazement.

Richard Baker also has a retentive memory for music and words, and he can memorize words in an astonishingly short space of time.

On one occasion Richard and I were presenting a concert together, each introducing a young artist. Before the performance I heard Richard talking to a singer about the songs he was going to sing; Richard made some quick notes as the singer described quite elaborately the meanings of the words of his songs. Then Richard and I sat at a table and each made our notes. Richard started writing pages and pages of notes. When he had finished he put his pen in his pocket and said, 'That's it,' and proceeded to tear up all he had written. He didn't need the notes any more; by writing the information out, he had committed it to memory, and when it came to the concert he recited everything, completely and perfectly memorized.

David Attenborough is always a great pleasure to have on the programme, partly because of his boyish enthusiasm for *Face the Music* and partly for his obvious love of music. If you watch David's face you can see he is very often quite moved by a passage of music that is being played. He also has a formidable overall knowledge of music.

In addition to the panel, we have had as guests some of the greatest artists in the world. If asked to pick my favourite guest artist on *Face the Music* I should be very hard put to it, but I think that Isobel Baillie talking about *Messiah* and half-miming in close-up to her own original singing of 'I know that my Redeemer liveth' was perhaps for me the most intensely moving moment I've experienced in the programme.

The viewing figures were going up rapidly and the night that Dame Eva Turner appeared we clocked six million viewers.

I also remember Sir William Walton in peak form – not only as star guest, but for guessing the 'Hidden Melody' ('Easter Parade') before the panel! Our signature tune, as most people know, is the 'Popular Song' from Sir William Walton's *Façade*.

Not only as an accompanist, but for quick repartee, Gerald Moore is in a class by himself. When I made him judge the panels' so-called conducting spot the lady panellist happened to be a pretty young actress. I asked Gerald: 'As a pianist would you let her conduct you?' Snap answer: 'Wherever she likes!'

Walter and I had to think up as many visual ideas as we could, because this is very important on television – you don't just want to be watching the panellists all the time. One of Walter's best ideas,

I thought, was the 'Funny Opera', where you see one opera and listen to another – and have to name both; this creates some very comical situations.

I claim sole credit for the 'Dummy Keyboard': we were searching for visuals one day, working in my accustomed studio at Trocks Mill Cottage, when I suddenly walked over to the dummy keyboard and started rattling off a piece of music. Jean came in, wondering what we were doing, and I asked her what piece I was playing. Walter wasn't sure, but Jean said, 'Chopin's B flat minor Scherzo', so I suggested perhaps we had the seeds of a question – we could give the panel a similar question and by a little ingenuity we could probably arrange for only the viewers to hear the music, after a bit. And so it came about. In the end this question became so popular that I don't think *Face the Music* would be *Face the Music* without the dummy keyboard. Quite often when people can't remember my name they say, 'There goes Mr Dummy Keyboard.'

Another factor that contributed enormously to the success of *Face the Music* in Manchester was the studio audience. People in the North tend to be very musical, I find, but especially in Manchester where the Hallé Orchestra and the Mid-day Concerts have regular, built-in audiences, which provided the nucleus of our studio audience. Quite often they knew the answers before the panel, and although they were never actually seen, their presence was very much felt and appreciated by us in the studio. There was one lady, Hilda, who I think attended every programme and always got the autograph of the guest. She was our most faithful follower.

We had a large number of letters from viewers ranging in age from about nine to ninety, all expressing their appreciation of some part of *Face the Music* – some would go for the 'Dummy Keyboard', others would fancy 'Funny Operas'. The 'Hidden Melodies' intrigued people and some people would ask specific questions about a particular piece of music we had played. As the programmes progressed our fan mail increased until we were getting upwards of a hundred letters a week.

I can remember vividly a few critical moments. One was when we suddenly heard, only a few hours before the programme, that the visiting guest artist was ill and couldn't come. We had the idea of telephoning Martin Milner, the leader of the Hallé Orchestra, and asking him if he would come along. Very bravely he said 'Yes' and he did one of the best interviews we've ever had. It was particularly good because, coming from a leader of a famous orchestra, he was able to tell many amusing stories that a great conductor would never admit to. We had many letters of appreciation about Martin Milner and very few people knew that he had been called in at the last minute. We are very much indebted to him.

Another crisis which was not so easily solved was when we had been recording for about twenty minutes. The guest musician was George Malcolm, and Walter Todds came into the studio in the middle of the recording, with a very red face. He whispered something in my ear which nobody else heard, 'Nothing has recorded; we shall have to do the whole thing over again.' I whispered back, 'And how do you expect us to do that?' Walter said he would have a word with the panel first.

What we decided to do, when once the machines got into action again, was to do the whole thing from the start as though the panel didn't know the answers; that included George Malcolm, because it was just after his interview that the equipment broke down. After that there was no more trouble. Looking back at the recorded result later when the programme was transmitted, everybody played their parts so well that it was impossible to tell that we'd had to fake the first half. I think that was the only breakdown we ever had.

There was an occasion when we had to make about five false starts; in the end, having arranged my *Face the Music* smile carefully for the viewers, I impatiently called out, 'For goodness' sake, will we never get started?' It transpired there was an unfortunate whistle and the experts thought it was some fault in the works somewhere. But it turned out to be a lady with a hearing-aid who was sitting in the front row of the audience; she was hastily and politely removed to the back and we started without further trouble.

Jean, I may say, never missed a visit to Manchester and behind the scenes she played a very important role in helping me in my work. She often used to nip off to the library and settle some point that I wanted to clarify, and she also joined in the rehearsals. We always had a run of the programme with everybody present, except the actual panel and the guest, so we needed people to stand in for our artists. Jean used to love to be the lady – Joyce Grenfell or whoever else. Apart from that, her ease of manner and extraordinary knack of getting on with all and sundry endeared her to everybody.

After each programme everybody (the artists and the production team) used to go off and have a hilarious supper in the town, and that was one of the most enjoyable parts of our visit to Manchester. I think these parties were very important to the programme itself, because they established firmly the friendship between all the participants.

In the earlier stages of our marriage Jean and I were quite social – we used to go away for weekends and we used to have people to stay; during the week we were guests at numbers of London dinner parties. We also used to enjoy entertaining a large circle of friends in our own house. But as the various professional engagements started to pour in, we cut down the social side of our life and tried to avoid late nights (I for one need a lot of sleep).

In fact, musicians excepted, almost the only people we made much contact with through the years were Richard and Virginia Sykes at Sledmere in Yorkshire. Virginia used to keep in touch by telephone and implore us to go up there and stay, either for a weekend or for Christmas. We found her company so delightful, and indeed her whole family, that we did go there quite often.

Richard and Virginia both adored jokes, charades, leg-pulls and imitations; and so did the children. They always expected me to dress up, in order to deceive the fellow guests. For instance, I might be in the guise either of the local parson or some dignitary who wanted money for the parish. I think of all the various antics I got up to, perhaps the funniest was when they were having their yearly Christmas party, with all their friends and relatives present.

Richard was a very good organist and in the hall at Sledmere was an organ; the pipes were hidden high up in a gallery. Before the party started I agreed secretly with Richard that I would dress up as the organ tuner, 'as Joseph Cooper was coming to give an organ recital'. I put on very old clothes and as the guests arrived I was somewhere among the pipes, high up in the house. One of the boys, I think it was Tatton, sat at the organ below, calling 'A flat' and I would call back from the top of the house 'A flat', signalling I was ready for the note to be played. Tatton would then play A flat on the loudest stop on the organ. The procedure continued: the noise was indescribable.

Eventually the job was finished and I appeared in the drawing-room and was given a drink. I caused a loud stir by saying, 'Well, mud in your eye, Sir Richard.' Everybody stood back aghast at such language. Then I brought out what was in fact a bit of a child's toy, pointed to it and said, 'The trouble, Sir Richard, is that this part of your organ is worn out, it'll have to be replaced.' Richard, hardly able to contain himself for laughter, became scarlet in the face and, thanking me, showed me to the door.

Virginia had disappeared altogether; it was much too much for her and she could never hold out for more than about five minutes in these situations. Jean, on the other hand, was so used to my mickey-taking behaviour that she was able to circulate round the guests and explain convincingly that I would be arriving shortly to give a recital on the organ.

John and Liza Glendevon (formerly Hope) were great friends of the Sykeses and have remained friends of mine though we too seldom meet. Last time, we were recalling the Sledmere buffoonery, especially the occasion at a formal party when John had been called in 'to measure the room for a new carpet'. Dressed in overalls, he quietly went round the room with his tape-measure. Suddenly a piercing female shriek brought all conversation to a halt. John was seen measuring meticulously up a lady's leg.

It was at Sledmere that I first had the honour of playing to Her Majesty Queen Elizabeth the Queen Mother. I don't know whether it was by accident or design on Virginia's part, but one weekend we were staying when the Queen Mother was opening something in the North and she came to stay at Sledmere. After dinner the Queen Mother sat by the piano and I played for about two-and-a-half hours. I found she had a very wide range of tastes; she started by asking for something light, so I played 'Tea for Two'; Her Majesty asked if I could play it as a cha-cha. She sang it to me with the proper rhythm and I joined in with a suitable piano accompaniment. Then gradually we went to more classical music.

In 1970 we were very shocked to read in the paper that Virginia had died suddenly after quite a minor operation. She was one of those marvellous people who not only loved others, but made everybody feel equal; she had no snobbery or false grandeur, in spite of the exceptionally prestigious position in which she found herself.

There were many smarter houses in Yorkshire and there were many grander titles than Sir Richard's baronetcy; but Sledmere has always had a *cachet*, and something very special about it. I shall be forever grateful to Virginia for her friendship over the years and not least for presenting me to the Queen Mother.

Not many months after I had played to the Queen Mother at Sledmere I had a telephone call from Lady Fermoy, herself a brilliant pianist, and a lady-in-waiting to Queen Elizabeth. I had played for Lady Fermoy at King's Lynn, where she ran the festival and a regular concert series. Ruth Fermoy said the Queen Mother had asked for me to go and play at a dinner party that she, Lady Fermoy, was giving at her London house.

When the evening came and we went into the drawing-room, I saw to my slight horror that the piano was a long way from where the guests were to sit. The Queen Mother spotted this too, and said that she would like to be right by the piano. A chair was moved for her and suddenly we had the Sledmere situation all over again – the Queen Mother talked about various kinds of music and I played everything from Beethoven and Chopin to some of the favourite tunes of Jerome Kern and Nöel Coward. As a finale to the evening Ruth Fermoy and I played a little duet.

In March 1972 I was invited to give a charity performance in front of the Queen Mother at St James's Palace. I felt no nerves, but a feeling of eager anticipation at seeing Her Majesty again. But my enthusiasm for the concert had been somewhat tempered by my great anxiety about the health of Jean's mother. She had been failing rapidly in the last few days and her death was expected. As we were sitting with the Queen Mother at supper after the concert, a note was discreetly put in my hand and I read the sad news that Lady Greig had died. I decided not to say anything at all at that moment, especially as Jean had only just told the Queen Mother that her mother was very unwell, and Her Majesty had expressed concern and asked Jean to give her mother a special message of good wishes. I broke the news to Jean after the party had finished.

I loved and admired my mother-in-law. Through the whole of the twenty-five years of Jean's and my marriage she had been a whole-hearted and devoted supporter of my career; although not really musical, she watched all my television programmes, listened to all my radio broadcasts, came to all my London concerts and took the greatest interest in all I did. Going to Sunday evening supper with Phyllis was never a penance; it was always something to look forward to. Occasionally, in a moment of temper, she might kick the Scrabble board over, which gave the evening extra entertainment value. She shared my own hatred of snobbery and class distinction; when Jean and I used to throw the house and garden open at Barnes and ask all the neighbours, my mother-in-law made a special point of chatting to the ones who were considered by some of the people to be below their class.

I was due to give another charity concert at St James's Palace, this time in front of Her Majesty the Queen. The occasion was to celebrate the one hundredth anniversary of the Royal Choral Society. This time I was nervous and began to think I was going to be a flop; I tried hard not to look at the Queen during the performance, but hoped she was enjoying the evening.

I needn't have worried: next morning the telephone rang and when Jean answered a voice said, 'This is Buckingham Palace.' Jean was just about to say, 'And I'm the Queen of Sheba,' when something stopped her and she was serious, thank goodness, because it really was Buckingham Palace. The speaker was a lord-in-waiting to the Queen, who said Her Majesty was so entranced with the performance the previous evening that she would very much like me to entertain her guests at Windsor Castle one evening during Royal Ascot Week.

The date fixed for the Windsor Castle performance was 22 June 1972, a Thursday.* Excited as I was at the prospect of playing in front of the entire Royal Family and even being asked to dine with them, I couldn't help but notice a change in Jean; she was more nervous and on edge than usual and didn't seem herself. But as Jean hated talking about health I didn't say anything.

The evening at Windsor Castle was a glittering occasion and it went beautifully. I have kept the seating plan of the dining-table as a private souvenir.

After all the excitements of Thursday, we spent the next few days quietly recovering and going over and over again every detail, from the start of the evening to the finish. But on Monday

*The Queen had particularly admired the singing of Richard Lewis at St James's Palace, so I invited him to join me at Windsor.

26 June I was in for a terrific shock. Jean came into my music room and told me she had a lump in her left breast and said it was inflamed and discoloured. I went straight to the telephone and fixed an appointment for Jean to see our doctor at 6.30 that evening.

When we arrived at the doctor's I stayed in the room while he examined Jean. The doctor didn't say much, but he looked as white as a sheet. However, he said Jean was suffering from something with a long and unquotable Latin name, which helped to put Jean off the scent; but he said she would have to go into hospital and he would see what he could fix up. I mentioned that our next-door neighbour was a radiotherapist at the Royal Free Hospital; so a contact was made by letter between our local GP and David Skeggs.

Dr Skeggs moved very fast; he had to, because Jean's delaying tactics might cost her her life. She had lived with this secret lump and discoloration all through her mother's illness, solely because she thought the disclosure would only aggravate matters for her mother. Somehow she had concealed it from me – how I don't know.

On Wednesday I took Jean into the Royal Free Hospital and found myself a hotel in the district. The next morning, 29 June, Jean was operated on for the removal of her left breast. I waited in a nearby room, so that I should be with Jean when she came round. The building we were in was the old cottage hospital – since demolished and replaced by a new hospital, one of the largest in the country. The next day I moved into the Post House which was right opposite the hospital, so that I could pop in and out and see Jean constantly, because she desperately needed me and kept calling me her 'power point'. It was marvellous to see how under David Skeggs's attention and care, and the wonderful nurses at the Royal Free, the colour seemed to be coming back into Jean's cheeks and a smile into those marvellous blue eyes.

The only irritating symptom of post-surgery shock from both Jean's and my point of view was that she had developed a temporary pathological fear for my life; she was absolutely certain that I was going to get killed, either in the car – which she forbade me to drive – or walking across the road to the Post House; or some other way. As soon as I got to the hotel, which was only two minutes' away,

I used to telephone and say I was in my room. I did all I could to reassure her and tell her not to worry. When I crossed the road I used to look about a hundred times to left and right, because I thought it would be too awful if anything did happen.

I had a Sunday morning BBC Radio series going on and had to go down to Broadcasting House to record the programme. The first one was on the following Tuesday; as soon as I got to the BBC I rang Jean and she was happy. Before I left I rang again. But in the underground coming back we had a stop in a tunnel for about twenty minutes. I began to feel the sweat pouring off me with fear, because I would be late and Jean would be worrying. But my luck was in – she had been visited by the surgeon, who was in the mood for a chat. So I hadn't been missed.

Most of the hospital nurses were *Face the Music* fans anyway and they were quite happy for me to have lunch with Jean and didn't mind a bit if I brought in a few extra delicacies from the shops round the corner.

Within a fortnight Jean was back home and then had to have a course of deep-ray treatment, which can be so very debilitating for someone who's already had the appalling operation. Jean was most anxious that the whole matter should be kept a secret and that none of the neighbours, apart of course from the Skeggses, should be told anything about it. So I, of course, went along with that and said nothing to anybody.

By August Jean seemed completely well again and we set off from Dover to Calais and by train from Paris to Biarritz (with the car on board). The weather was marvellous. I had never been down to the Pyrenees before and was very anxious to see Ravel's birthplace at Ciboure, right down on the Spanish border. We stayed in a little hotel at a place called Hendaye. Jean was full of energy, and although I tried to persuade her to rest in the afternoon, she didn't want to; in fact she wanted to swim, which I told her was ridiculous because the water was very cold and the waves much too heavy.

One day we went right up into the Haute Pyrénées, to the Pic du Midi de Bigorre, which is 9,000 feet up. I personally am terrified of those twisty drives that go up and up. I was in the passenger seat, because Jean was happily driving again; I began to feel very giddy, but didn't say anything because Jean was so enjoying it. Anyhow we went up to the last 1,500 feet and from there you could either take a lift or walk. Jean chose to walk: her energy amazed me.

On the way home, when we got to Arcachon (a French harbour on the Bay of Biscay) we booked into a hotel, had some supper and went to bed. We were both dozing happily, when suddenly the windows started rattling, the furniture shook and the bed lifted itself off the ground. Jean said she thought there was a large dog under the bed trying to push it up. But it was no dog. It was an earthquake. A few minutes later we had a brief 'encore' and then peace was restored. The next morning the local paper carried a banner headline, '*Tremblement de Terre*', and photographs of damaged houses. (It was a slight anticlimax on our return home to find no report of it had reached England.)

We finished the holiday by crossing the Gironde Estuary into glorious Dordogne country; then up the map until we reached Nohant, the house of George Sand, Chopin's mistress, which is a favourite haunt of mine. Then back home via Le Havre to Southampton.

With the success of *Face the Music*, enquiries for my services, either at ladies' luncheon clubs or for music clubs, were coming in at such a rate that the diary from October to December 1972 had, on average, six concerts a week. Sometimes we accepted a lunch club and went on to do an evening concert on the same day. I had several kinds of programmes to offer, in addition to *Confessions of a Pianist* and informal talking-and-playing concerts.

One of the most popular was the result of a team effort – a series of composers' lives. For these I employed the services of a script writer, J.D. Henry (whom I had met in TWW days), also a recording expert, John Hassell. He and I thought up a way of having the orchestral parts of piano concertos put onto tape. So I took round with me all the necessary equipment, including an amplifier and two loud-speakers. The operator was Jean. She was strategically placed backstage: magically, as if from nowhere, she would bring in 'the orchestra', say, at the end of a cadenza – the way she did it never failed to startle and captivate the audience. Beethoven, Schumann and Tchaikovsky became the favourites.

Before Jean's illness we had had a few demands for these

composers' lives. Now they were wanted all over Great Britain. What is more, at ninety per cent of the concerts we were re-booked on the spot for the next season. 1973 and 1974 were already bulging at the seams. I can say, without a blush, that if *Face the Music* was our shop window, we paid back our debt in part by the public relations value of our efforts; especially as all concerts ended with a hidden melody!

Power cuts and pitch changes were occasional threats. Three different ladies – Carol Borg at Ibbs & Tillett, Terry Slasberg from Music International, and Kay Whalley from Foyles Lecture Agency – although in a sense rivals, worked as sensible human beings to co-ordinate the flood of dates.

One vital necessity was the health of the two performers – Jean and myself. In 1973 the BBC stepped up the number of *Face the Music* programmes to sixteen (all recorded in Manchester).

The inevitable crash was not long coming. By November 1972, Jean complained of back-aches, lack of energy and appetite. One night, driving from Redditch to the Post House at Thornbury, she said her right hand had packed up. I lay awake half the night, the truth slowly dawning on me: the monster – the foul, devil-sent eater of the human body – had not been exorcized by Jean's operation. It turned out, of course, that the GP and David Skeggs had known at once that her case was hopeless. Mercifully they had left us in ignorance.

By the middle of March 1973 Jean could no longer drive. So we bought a larger car (BMW 2500) whose vast boot took all the equipment. Jean lay along the back seat, and I acted as navigator while professional drivers, Reg Wheeler or Rosemary Martin, drove us expertly and helped move the equipment. By May, as Jean became weaker, mass cancellations started. The last concert ever was 10 June at Kenwood House on a glorious summer evening.

After that, with the sixteen *Face the Music* programmes safely in the bag, Jean spent the days lying under a tree in the garden. One great excitement was an invitation from Ted Heath, then Prime Minister, to a party at Chequers. Jean admired Ted Heath enormously (as indeed do I) and she 'came alive' for the occasion. This was 8 July 1973. What a wonderful place to take a final curtain call, surrounded by musicians who knew her and loved her. Jean died suddenly and peacefully on the morning of 18 August.

'J.G.' (Joyce Grenfell) wrote these moving words in *The Times*:

All who knew Jean Cooper realized what a large part she played in her husband's work. Theirs was a total and felicitous partnership. With her fair good-looks and spontaneous smile she was a pleasure on the eye. The smile came from her loving heart and positive approach to life. She was warm, friendly, helpful and very brave. A child-like trust coupled with a splendid zest made her rare, and dearly loved.

10
A New Beginning

For several weeks before Jean's death I had been in constant touch with her brother and sister-in-law, Carron and Monica Greig. Monica had been a great source of strength and practical help to me. When I told her that I was getting to the end of my tether as far as running the house was concerned, and trying to keep up with my practising, she said immediately that she knew a firm which supplied temporary housekeepers: to save me the trouble she would get in touch and see what was on offer. Monica telephoned again in about half-an-hour's time, saying there was somebody who was willing to come. The housekeeper arrived and she could not have been more helpful, right through the crisis, and after.

Ten days after Jean's death I was due to record for CRD. One side of the record was to contain popular classical pieces and the other was to consist of my hidden melodies. My first instinct was to cancel the recording sessions, but as the housekeeper took over the entire running of the house, which included answering the non-stop telephone calls, I resolved to practise seven or eight hours a day and go through with the recording. I felt this was what Jean would have wanted me to do. I made the gramophone record; it caught the Christmas market and I was very happy that one of *The Gramophone* critics picked it as among the six best records of the year.

Another very staunch ally and friend was an aunt of Jean's, Mrs Barbara Scrimgeour, who had always taken an enormous interest in my career. Aunt Barbara made one bald, flat statement, which helped me more than all the books, prayers and attempts to bring comfort that came from elsewhere. She said: 'It's quite simple, you either sink or you swim and it is better for all concerned if you swim.' She had lost her husband (Jean's uncle) some years before, so she was speaking from experience; she was certainly a living example of how to behave in bereavement.

Apart from that, Aunt Barbara felt that good as these temporary housekeepers had been, it would be splendid if she could help me find a permanent housekeeper, because the continual changes were naturally very unsettling. So we put an advertisement in a magazine, which brought forth all sorts of strange people. But there was one who seemed to have a lot going for her and so we asked her to come and stay for a night or two. She was a very kind, sweet person, but I was a little worried because she seemed to have a memory problem. In particular she could never remember her way around the cottage.

Anyway, I invited Aunt Barbara to a specimen lunch and we chose a simple dish, shepherd's pie; this was to be a test case. In the middle of lunch when I had taken a mouthful of pie, I felt something very hard in my mouth; I thought it must be a bone, but I picked it out and found it was one of the small cogs from the meat mincer. This was too much for Aunt Barbara, who blew her nose violently to disguise a sudden fit of laughter. It was clear the lady was unsuitable.

My sister Mollie was, as she had been throughout my life, a tower of strength and encouragement. In the middle 1950s Mollie had married an old friend of Louis Greig's, Foster Cox. Foster is quite a lot older than Mollie in years, but very young in heart and brimful of energy. They live almost opposite Charterhouse School, above Godalming. They have a son, Simon, who was then just leaving Eton and had caused great excitement in the family by winning an open scholarship in law to Trinity College, Oxford, his father's old college.

Mollie and Foster opened their house to me as a second home; it was a marvellous refuge and they were enormously kind to me. People's reactions to the death of a loved one vary tremendously: some like to tell all-and-sundry every gruesome detail, right up to the last moment; others don't want to speak about it at all. I was in that latter category. I dreaded so much that anyone would mention it that I kept myself very much to myself.

Another symptom of shock that many people go through in these circumstances is a desire to leave their house – to get right away and start life all over again in new surroundings. In my mind, I already had the house up for sale. But here, my local doctor (who prefers to remain anonymous) was a marvellous help to me; he advised me to stay where I was, do some work, go quietly about my life, and things would gradually right themselves. I took his advice and never regretted it.

Another piece of advice was from an old friend, Sophie Lyell, whose husband had been killed in the war. She used to pop down and see me and on one occasion, seeing my distress and dilapidated appearance, said: 'You must just allow in your timetable that for two years you won't be yourself. But one day you'll wake up and will be able to meet the world again.'

Apart from the recordings of *Face the Music* I felt that I must cancel all my concerts; I simply couldn't face the platform and the public. Carol Borg, of Ibbs & Tillett, kindly undertook to mastermind 'operation cancel'. Keeping in close touch with the other two agents, Terry Slasberg and Kay Whalley, between them they sorted out all the dates and cancelled them. It was a mammoth job.

Carol Borg also very kindly offered to come to the house and straighten out my diary and sort out the mail, in her spare time. Finding me dispirited and inert, Carol then suggested looking round for somebody else to operate the tapes for my concerts of composers' lives, which had been such a fantastic success. Carol was anxious that I should be in action again by the following season. I think she felt that if I didn't make a fresh start by then, I might never do so. In the meantime, we had plenty of time to look around for someone to operate the machines that produced my 'invisible orchestra'. After various trials I did find somebody. Without further ado, Carol quietly went ahead and booked a light winter's work for me for the 1974/75 season.

I had never handled any accounts, either to do with concerts or with our private life; of such things as rates demands coming in, telephone and electricity bills, I knew nothing. Jean had them all in the room she used as an office and dealt with them methodically. So after months of life with housekeepers, a lot of bills remained unpaid. I was starting to get threatening letters that various services would be cut off if I didn't pay up. I asked Carol if she would come down and help me go through my accounts. We sat on the sofa together and she suddenly said: 'You have got yourself in a mess, haven't you.'

That remark, I don't know why, made me feel so absolutely helpless and useless, that I lowered my guard completely and found myself on the verge of tears. It always seemed permissible to cry over music, but never over personal things – that I took to be the height of unmanliness – so I did my best to restrain myself. Carol (agent-trained to deal with temperamental artists) simply said: 'Well anyway, let's get on and do the accounts,' and she put a friendly arm on my shoulder, as if to reassure me that all would be well. That was the first time I had allowed anyone to come near me, let alone touch me, and the tears came more copiously; but suddenly they were followed by a feeling of excitement, physical excitement. I didn't let Carol know this; I kept it to myself, but I slept that night for the first time without doping myself heavily. I had broken through the emotional barrier. I wondered if I had found another life partner.

I asked Carol if she would come down again as soon as possible to carry on with the accounts. But although we had many sessions on the sofa, the accounts were left undone. In the end Carol got me to sign some cheques and she took the bills away and just coped with them all.

Meanwhile, I'd had a letter from my uncle-in-law in Suffolk, Uncle Dunk (Humphrey Scrimgeour), whom you remember my mentioning earlier as the man who liked to stay on land while his wife, Aunt Tootie, braved the dangers of *Cormorant*. Uncle Dunk asked me to come and stay. It so happened that Carol had a concert to attend at Aldeburgh in connection with her work, so I wrote to Uncle Dunk and said my agent would be accompanying me and would it be in order if I brought her to lunch. The Scrimgeours said they would be delighted for Carol Borg to come for a meal, but – they told us later – they did not in fact ask her to stay because their picture of a London musical agent was of someone in their late fifties, forbidding, and talking of nothing but Bach and Britten (especially as Aldeburgh was her official 'port of call'). Imagine their surprise when a pretty, fair-haired outdoor type in her mid-thirties arrived and seemed happier talking about sheep and farms than sharps and flats.

The first night Carol slept in the hotel in Saxmundham, but the second night she slept in a dear old Romany caravan in the garden of Uncle Dunk's farmhouse. Every morning, during our stay, I used to take Carol a cup of tea – watched I think quietly, with amusement, by the occupants of the house, whom one could see peeping from behind the curtains.

The joy for me was that Uncle Dunk took to Carol immediately. There was an extraordinary rapport between the two. This was so noticeable that other people remarked on it, and ever since then Carol and Uncle Dunk have kept up a regular correspondence (Uncle Dunk is now in his ninety-first year). Unfortunately he was deaf and it was difficult to have private conversations with him. There are some things, of course, that you don't need conversations about. Uncle Dunk for all his years was not slow in the uptake; he knew very well what was going on, and he approved with all his heart.

But one thing I did know. I couldn't be hurried; however much Carol and I suited each other, and however much everybody felt what a perfect match it was, the thought of marrying her seemed a little premature. A lot more time had to elapse before I could be ready. Looking back it seems stupid, but Sophie Lyell's forecast of two years was not far wrong. So poor Carol was rather kept hanging about; just occasionally she registered impatience. I countered this with my secret weapon, which was to say: 'You were the one who got me working again. Here I am, doing six or seven hours' practice a day and giving concerts, and you want to rush me to the altar.' Which, of course, was a pretence argument to cover the feelings that I couldn't disclose to anybody – the haunting memories that I still had of Jean.

I was very lucky about this time to be asked by Decca to make a record for them; it was to be called 'The World of Joseph Cooper' and they wanted some popular classics. Fortunately the record got very good reviews.

The record sleeve showed me practising the dummy keyboard in the garden, with autumn leaves strewn carelessly (?) on my shoulder. It also showed a very important member of the household – my half-Siamese cat, Miss Suti-Mia – enjoying a meal. Some of my friends thought the photograph 'contrived', but thousands of cat-lovers all over Great Britain thought otherwise, and the record quickly became a best-seller.

Miss Mia has listened to my piano day in, day out, since she walked in from nowhere in 1970 and decided to make this her home. Letters poured in via the BBC from people wanting to know Miss

Mia's age, sex and favourite foods, as well as giving me long descriptions of their own cats. Quite a number of the letters also remarked on the nice selection of piano music on the record. So congratulations to sleeve-designer Alain Judd who, alas! has left Decca to take up singing. The back of the record sleeve contained expertly written notes by my friend and colleague Richard Baker about the fourteen piano pieces. Dickie writes informally and steers clear of technical terms. His descriptions of the music added great selling value to the record.

Nothing could have been a bigger boost to my morale than the success of my first venture with Decca. When in the spring of 1975 Decca suggested my making another record, I asked if it could be postponed until 1976, as I had important domestic matters to attend to of a highly confidential nature; I stressed that I felt sure the record would be much better for the delay. My prediction proved correct.

Carol Borg left Ibbs & Tillett in late June; on 4 July 1975 we were secretly married. The delayed record for Decca was duly made in July 1976 and won an award. Incidentally, on 3 July 1976 another Borg (Björn) had just won his first Wimbledon.

But back to the wedding and 1975. I had only mentioned the possibility of my marriage to a handful of trusted and discreet friends. One was Evelyn Barbirolli, when she was guest on *Face the Music* in Manchester; the other was Valerie Pitts, alias Lady Solti, who was on the same programme. When we finally told Sir Georg and Lady Solti we had got married, they gave us the most marvellous wedding present it is possible to imagine – the loan of their beautiful house on the west coast of Italy. There were staff to look after us, and delicious food. All we had to do was to swim, sunbathe and enjoy ourselves. Our visit happily overlapped with that of Lord and Lady Grantley and their two sons.

Incidentally, we had one rather traumatic occasion. We had just come out of the sea, having had a blissful swim in the warm, clear water. Walking up the beach we saw to the right a huge cloud of black smoke in the distance, but coming in our direction. The Soltis' house was actually in a clearing of a pine forest and the appalling thought suddenly dawned on us that the forest itself was on fire. We ran to the house and warned Clara, the housekeeper. She immediately rushed for the hose and watered everything in sight, repeating some incantation which we discovered afterwards meant: 'We must take to the ships, we must take to the ships.' Seeing that the fire was coming nearer and nearer we, too, were very seriously alarmed.

Then a miracle happened: there was a sudden change of wind and, instead of coming in the direction of the house, the fire spread away towards some barren fields a little way inland, where it spent itself. Nobody was hurt, no serious damage was done, except that hundreds of beautiful trees were lost. I thought back that night and many nights on that holiday; if the wind hadn't changed, about ten minutes later the whole house would have been engulfed in the flames.

A diary was always kept in the Soltis' house, either by guests or by Valerie herself when she was there. In this particular diary the forest fire was very much played down; we didn't want to frighten the Soltis into thinking there might have been a disaster. But we hadn't counted on Clara's ability to tell the story with her own trimmings, which almost suggested that the whole of Italy had been on fire.

After our superb holiday in Italy we wondered how we could possibly repay the Soltis for their generosity. Their knowledge and love of art extends far beyond music, so we wanted to think of an original kind of present. We consulted Carol's younger brother, Dr Alan Borg, Keeper of the Sainsbury Centre for the Visual Arts, in Norwich, who at that time was working at the Tower of London as Keeper of the Blades. Alan kindly agreed to help us and he scoured London for something suitable; eventually he located a beautiful ancient Egyptian Shabti figure. The inscription, in hieroglyphics, revealed that the lady was a singer, although her name is tantalizingly unreadable. The figure dates from about 2000 BC. Georg and Valerie Solti were delighted with it.

During our wonderful Italian holiday we had plenty of time quietly to consider our plans on the concert front. One of the difficulties we had discovered, was that the composers' lives, with the new tape-recorder operator were not working as they should. From an expert's point of view, it couldn't have been better. But of course the vital chemistry of Jean's and my married life, which had spilled over into our slightly eccentric concert platform duet, was now missing: the operator was just doing a paid job. Also, I felt it was time for a change of presentation for my concerts.

One idea Carol had was for me to abandon the use of tapes. For some concerts, in addition to solo piano pieces, a few songs were included, with the excellent baritone Brian Rayner Cook; I enjoyed working with him and the concerts were very successful. One performance was in aid of the Yehudi Menuhin School; it was arranged by the beautiful and tireless charity organizer, Keturah Hain, one of many people for whom I had had to cancel concerts during Jean's illness.

Carol then thought it would be an excellent idea for me to give informal recitals, with the first half entirely serious, but the second half becoming progressively lighter; so there was really something to suit all tastes.

We are rapidly coming up to the present and I am anxious to avoid the temptation of reeling off strings of dates and engagements which would read rather like *Mrs Dale's Diary*. So for the remainder of my story I am going to pick a few of the most significant events.

At the beginning of Jubilee Year, 1977, the BBC gave a party at the Television Centre, in honour of the 100th performance of *Face the Music*. The Director General of the BBC, Ian Trethowan, invited all the guests and panels who had taken part in *Face the Music*. Not everybody could be there, of course, but we had a splendid representation as you will see from some of the photographs taken at the party. One much missed absentee was laughter-loving Moura Lympany, away either on a concert tour or tending her French vineyard.

On 7 June practically everybody in this country must have had their eyes glued to their television set, because it was the day of the Queen's Silver Jubilee. On that day I was doing my musical stint for a local organization, the Richmond Concert Society, run by the enterprising Howard Greenwood, who has built up Richmond Concert Society into one of the leading music clubs in the country.

Carol and I thought this might be a good chance to try out the idea of the play and talk programme she had suggested. I started with serious talk and classical pieces and progressively made the programme lighter. I finished by playing hidden melodies – the melodies were often tunes from musicals or the Twenties and

Thirties, which the audience sang lustily. I asked Howard Greenwood what he felt about the mixture; he said the audience had thoroughly enjoyed themselves and loved the opportunity of being able to give tongue. I might add we had started the whole proceedings by singing 'God Save the Queen' and that evening it seemed to have a special meaning.

Emboldened by Howard's encouragement, I played a similar programme to a packed Queen Elizabeth Hall, London, on Bank Holiday Monday, 16 April 1979. I don't remember a more appreciative audience. Someone remarked that the Green Room afterwards was like a wedding reception. So it was in a way – a reception following the wedding of classical and popular music.

Back to 1977: a plan that I had been mulling over for several years was beginning to take shape in my mind. It started when I heard Sir Thomas Armstrong broadcasting an appeal on behalf of the Musicians' Benevolent Fund, of which he is chairman; this must have been in early 1974. I was so deeply touched by Sir Thomas's words that I immediately sent off a cheque, but said that I intended to do something on a rather bigger scale when I could see the chance.

I was now beginning to see an opportunity for an unusual evening for which I would be a kind of impresario. My plan was for a concert to take place in 1977, Sir Thomas Armstrong's eightieth year, at St James's Palace, where Sir Thomas himself had been a boy chorister in the Chapel Royal. I thought also it would be a good opportunity to ask Joan Drogheda (in other words the pianist Joan Moore) to play.

Apart from my admiration of her playing, I owed a debt to Joan and Garrett Drogheda: they had been so kind over the years, first of all to Jean and me, allowing us the hospitality of their box at the Royal Opera House, Covent Garden. Also, Joan and Garrett had been especially welcoming to Carol; we are both devoted to them. We have spent three very happy Christmases with the Droghedas and have had a great many laughs and much fun. We have also been privileged, as their guests, to attend the beautiful Christmas morning service at St George's Chapel, Windsor; the exquisite singing of the choir under Christopher Robinson is some of the most beautiful I have ever heard.

My next thought for the St James's Palace concert was how lovely it would be if Her Majesty Queen Elizabeth the Queen Mother could be present. And, since the Queen Mother is President of the Royal College of Music, what a good idea it would be to invite its Director, Sir David Willcocks, to conduct the concert and for the orchestra to consist of college students. David Willcocks was delighted to co-operate. We had known each other since those early carefree days at Harlyn Bay; he is now a very distinguished and senior man in the music profession and I treat him with respect – at least in public!

Garrett Drogheda kindly agreed to put forward my idea to Her Majesty Queen Elizabeth. The Queen Mother expressed the greatest pleasure and to my intense delight suggested the date of which I had been dreaming – 15 November; Jean and I had been married on 15 November 1947. I had longed to commemorate all that Jean had done for my life in music.

Fortunately, on many happy occasions at St James's Palace I had become friends with Sergeant-Major C.H. Phillips, Superintendent of the State Apartments; I knew he would give Carol and me every assistance with the complicated arrangements for 15 November. During the course of trying to think of everything from all angles, I realized that we needed a member of the aristocracy to act as hostess. I invited an old acquaintance and great lover of music, the Marchioness of Zetland.

Although the main object of the exercise was to make some money for the Musicians' Benevolent Fund, we wanted to do it in a pleasurable way. We arranged the evening as a musical party, with a sit-down supper following an hour's music making. In spite of the fact that all the artists generously gave their services, the over-all costs were high, so in order to leave a reasonable profit for the fund we had to make the tickets very expensive. But we had an extraordinarily generous response from the many people to whom we sent invitations: I am happy to say the hall was sold out and when the final reckoning was made we were able to hand over £3,000 to the Musicians' Benevolent Fund.

As to the programme itself, apart from the Mozart Piano Concerto in A, K.414, which Joan Moore played most beautifully, we had up our sleeve a surprise finale, which I introduced. It was a Toy Symphony by Joseph Horovitz, which he had composed earlier that year for the ninety-eighth birthday of Sir Robert Mayer. It is an excellent little work. I had played and was very taken with the nightingale part and I was allowed to have that again. We had such a distinguished list of toy instrumentalists, in addition to the Royal College of Music Orchestra conducted by Sir David Willcocks, that I append them here. Joseph Horovitz himself played the piano part.

John Oaksey (minus horse)	Jill Balcon
Evelyn Barbirolli	Richard Baker
Iris Loveridge	Humphrey Burton
James Blades	Phyllis Sellick
Marisa Robles	Terence Beckles
Christopher Hyde-Smith	Howard Shelley
Alan Fluck	Hilary Macnamara

But in the event there was another surprise finale awaiting us. Princess Anne's child was due to be born at any moment and luck was on our side – the birth took place that very day. The Toy Symphony was so arranged that 'Happy Birthday' was already included in the score; but a simple adjustment of the words and a little priming beforehand of the orchestra and friends in the audience, we were able to sing 'Happy Birthday, great-grandson, happy birthday to you'.

It brought the concert to an unexpectedly riotous conclusion. The Queen Mother herself was delighted; after dinner she mingled with the guests and stayed right to the end of the party. Afterwards I had a charming letter from Major John Griffin, Her Majesty's Press Secretary, saying how much Queen Elizabeth the Queen Mother had enjoyed the evening, especially Lady Drogheda's lovely playing and the surprise finale.

One of the most exciting developments in the music world during the last twenty-five years has been the increase in the encouragement and opportunities for young talent. There are numerous schemes to assist and encourage musical training – from an early age through to arrival on the professional concert platform. One of the best-known organizations is Youth and Music, led by the indefatigable Sir Robert Mayer.

In 1975 I was asked to become a trustee of the Countess of Munster Musical Trust. Under the chairmanship of Leopold de

Rothschild, the trustees (who include Dame Janet Baker, Jacqueline du Pré, Sir Charles Groves, Raymond Leppard, Sir Anthony Lewis and Sir David Willcocks) audition a large number of advanced students; those who prove themselves worthy are awarded generous grants for further study, either in this country or abroad. Many well-known concert artists before the public today have been helped there by the generosity of the Munster Trust and similar organizations.

Good training at a young age is essential, and in 1963 Yehudi Menuhin started his now famous Menuhin School at Stoke d'Abernon in Surrey. This boarding school is for young musical talent from the age of six. To me Yehudi Menuhin represents all that is fine, both as a musician and as a man; his personal involvement in the training of the next generation of musicians is an inspiration to us all.

Competitions play an ever-increasing role. Back in the 1960s the way was paved by the National Piano Playing Competition, organized by Mary Baxter of the Society for the Piano. I remember joining a jury that included Sidney Harrison, Cyril Smith and Solomon, with Sir Malcolm Sargent as chairman. But after several successful years I had a letter from Mary Baxter saying the competition had to be closed down owing to lack of funds.

For pianists, the pinnacle of all competitions is the Leeds International Pianoforte Competition, the brainchild of Fanny Waterman, who remains its driving force and who has done so much to raise the standard of piano playing in this country.

But not all young hopefuls should start by jumping in at the deep end with a major competition. It is essential first to get experience playing in public under somewhat stressful conditions. This is where competitive festivals and local competitions are invaluable.

In my own area, Surrey's Young Pianist of the Year Award is giving a splendid lead in this direction. As guest judge I have heard some excellent young talent at this competition, run enthusiastically by Mark Joseph and his family. Local resident and music-lover, Sir Robert Mark, takes an enormous interest in SYPYA; you might think by virtue of the great office he held in the police force that Sir Robert would be a frightening man – on the contrary, he is friendly and charming. He communicates easily with people of all ages, and made an amusing off-the-cuff speech at the competition finals.

Another competition I have much enjoyed as a guest judge is the Rediffusion Choristers' Awards, run in conjunction with the Royal School of Church Music, to select Britain's top parish church choirboy.

The greatest debt young musicians owe is to the BBC. Not only did the BBC rescue the Proms and, more recently, the Saturday morning Robert Mayer Concerts for Children, but they have organized many competitions of various types. The one that has created the biggest wave of interest is the BBC Young Musician of the Year, which via television has created in homes throughout Britain a state of excitement akin to the finals at Wimbledon (I was one of the judges of the piano finals).

We have also the BBC to thank for *Face the Music*. In fact, I must stop writing now, as I am off to the BBC Television Theatre, Shepherd's Bush, to start recording a new series to test your wits and, I hope, to give you pleasure.

Index